Praise for **HEIDI** Acr

"In the tradition of *Wild* and *Eat, Pray,* takes us on a courageous, unflinching journey of the road and spirit. Written with the kind of searing honesty so deeply needed in today's Facebook and TikTok world, this book is a feast, an inspiration and an invitation to look within and find out what really matters."

—**Sara Connell,** bestselling author of *Thought Leader Academy* and *The Science of Getting Rich for Women*

"Heidi Beierle lets us sit side-saddle as she rides from coast to coast, facing heat and headwinds, finding new friends and old demons, searching for this place called America and her place within it. At once propulsive and poetic, epic and intimate, *Heidi Across America* will make you want to drop everything, take to the road, and see where you end up."

—**Brian Benson,** author of *Going Somewhere* and co-author with Richard Brown of *This Is Not for You*

"Heidi Beierle's memoir, *Heidi Across America,* is what we all need to read in our current climate of cultural and political division. Beierle brings her open-hearted curiosity to every roadway, every diner, and every person (or animal) she encounters, offering the reader a glimpse into what it really means to be a true citizen of a homeland as vast and diverse as the United States. On a bicycle and depending upon the kindness of strangers, this author takes us on a journey that is more than a grueling ride through the heartland. It is a guide for all of us to slow down and really look at what is right in front of us. If you need a shot of optimism and hope, *Heidi Across America* will put it right into your veins."

—**Cami Ostman,** founder of The Narrative Project and author of *Second Wind*

"A journey of discovery from the Pacific to the Atlantic, Heidi Beierle's solo bicycle adventure reveals an America writ small but full of generous, kind-hearted people. It is a vivid tale of a soul stretched across a continent, a story of strength and pain and resilience. It's like seeing old friends in the people and places of America through new eyes."

—**David Goodrich,** author of *A Hole in the Wind*
and *A Voyage Across an Ancient Ocean*

"*Heidi Across America* is a thrilling ride and glide through both landscape and story space. In these times where travel has turned into a complex labrynth of stress, I found a home inside the journey, and heart enough for all of us. A triumph for those of us who care about moving through the world with care, compassion, and consciousness."

—**Lidia Yuknavitch,** author of *The Chronology of Water* and *Thrust*

"Beierle's honest account of her cross-country adventure scrapes off the veneer of bike touring and exposes the truth of pedaling away from the past. Readers will discover the grace and power that come from being vulnerable on a bike and on the page. I was rooting for Beierle to the very last page."

—**Sara Dykman,** author of *Bicycling with Butterflies*

"*Heidi Across America* is a glorious celebration of adventure, the unwavering spirit, and the boundless potential that resides within each of us. As she pedals her way across the heartland, Heidi discovers magnificent and challenging landscapes, captivating characters, and what it means to be a woman on her own in contemporary America. An unforgettable adventure that transcends miles, this beautiful book reveals the transformative power of the open road and the profound joy of self-discovery."

—**Karen Karbo,** author of *In Praise of Difficult Women*

HEIDI
ACROSS AMERICA

HEIDI
ACROSS AMERICA

One Woman's Journey on a Bicycle Through the Heartland

Heidi Beierle

Health Communications, Inc.
Boca Raton, Florida

Disclaimer: While this is a true story of real events and people I encountered, some of the names and characteristics of people in this story have been changed to protect their anonymity.

"Carnage" was originally published in *VoiceCatcher Journal*.
"Blood" was originally published in *High Desert Journal*.

Library of Congress Cataloging-in-Publication Data
is available through the Library of Congress

Publisher: Health Communications, Inc.
301 Crawford Blvd., Suite 200
Boca Raton, FL 33432-3762

Cover, illustration, interior design, and formatting by Larissa Hise Henoch

To my parents,
BA and Lenny, for your love and
for giving me the space to find my way

CONTENTS

PROLOGUE

Ten bike lengths ahead, a brown lump rested on the fog line of the shoulder-less highway. If the lump was scat, I'd put money on bear.

Scat wasn't one of those things that typically prompted me to stop, although I would if there was something compelling about the shape, volume, or contents.

As I neared, the lump looked as if it could be a work glove or knit hat.

Its edge wavered.

Roadkill. I was excited, as if this dead animal were a longed-for birthday present. I stopped and looked down at tidy, chocolate-colored feathers. Long black eyelashes were set against a white face blaze. The bird was belly down, head turned to the side, feathers spread like a blanket, gray beak curved to the road. A slight breeze raised some feathers, and they flapped noiselessly back into place.

I took a picture and continued on.

Did the spirit stay connected? When a car drove over the physical trace, was the spirit brutalized, did it feel crush and tread mark again and again? Feathers on roadkill don't stick to the road—they lift when cars pass.

I returned to the owl and laid my bike on the embankment.

Three male cyclists loaded with touring gear stopped on the other side of the road.

"Do you need help?" one of them asked.

We talked across the road. They were from Oklahoma.

"There's this little owl," I said. "It doesn't seem right to let it get squashed. I'm going to move it."

They traveled onward, west down the highway.

I picked up the owl, folded its wings around its body, light and tiny in my cycling-gloved palms. The owl's head hung forward, weighted by its skull. In my left hand, I turned the owl over, tracing the bones along its left wing and then the right. The wing bent between elbow and wrist; the bone crushed like eggshell. I slid my fingers down the owl's beak, touching the tawny feathers on its breast and then its feet. The tiny talons, black daggers. The toes that held them, yellow, dainty, and gecko-like, their undersides minutely dimpled, sticking out from sandy bloomers. Between my thumb and index finger, I held a toe, the talon, smooth and warm with a sharp point, like a cat's claw.

Away from the road embankment, I laid the owl on dead leaves at a plant's base.

I hefted my bike onto the road and journeyed on.

Every day, every moment, the owl's fate could be my own. I lived and pedaled in acknowledgment of this, hoping that when death arrived for me, a radiant heart would free my feathers from the road.

Part 1
CLIMBING

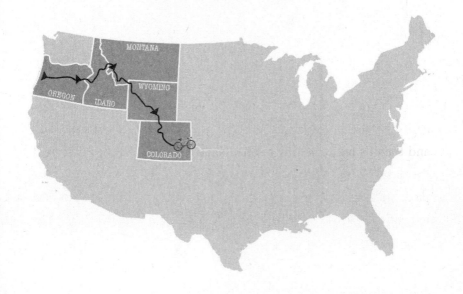

1.

On the Road

Harsh blue light from the Prineville, Oregon, ranger station entrance shone on the twiggy shrubs above me. Below the glare, I lay on the ground, hidden in my sleeping bag, having just been startled awake. I held my breath and listened, afraid someone had found me or was stealing my bike. The only sound came from sprinklers on the other side of the building. No intruders. I peeked through the bushes. My bike was still there. I exhaled. 12:03 AM. All was well. I drifted back to sleep.

Two hours later, I was yanked out of sleep again, this time by noise like a jet of water spraying a taut sheet of nylon. I fumbled for my glasses. My watch read 2:01 AM.

Beneath my ground cloth, an active sprinkler head blasted water that collected on top of the cloth and wet the bottom of my sleeping pad. As I considered where I might move, the noise underneath stopped. The sprinklers next to me came to life, and water droplets pattered the nylon of my down bag. I scrambled to my feet, grabbed my sleeping bag and pad, and darted over to the building where the water didn't reach. I ran back to the bushes to rescue my panniers, the waterproof bags that attached to my bike and held the gear for

3

my cross-country trip. My left hip sparked with electricity, a familiar pain that dissipated quickly.

Next to the building under an eave, light reflected from the wet lava rocks, but there was a dry space wide enough for my sleeping gear if I snuggled the building. I wormed my way back into my sleeping bag and took long, slow breaths to calm my body.

I slept maybe another hour when the sun woke me.

I packed my gear in grumbly half sleep and took pictures of the bushes and eave. The adventure didn't seem worth the sleeplessness, but I milked the experience for a Facebook post before leaving for the sagebrush-studded high desert.

```
Prineville rodeo weekend, no motels.
The town is flat and dry. The sprinkler
systems, which get ample use in this arid
climate, have down-home charm and show
great delight in hosting guests, with
new areas of hospitality activating every
hour on the hour starting at midnight.
The light at the ranger station is on all
night. Welcome!
```

I was on summer break following my first year of a master's program in community and regional planning at the University of Oregon in Eugene. At the end of my first term in December 2009, all I wanted for my summer was to ride my bike. I had returned to school at the age of thirty-four and was shocked by how all-consuming and fast-paced the coursework was. I hardly saw friends. I sat in class. I sat and read. I sat and wrote. I slept long enough to keep going. My years of physical adventuring were nothing compared to the arduous sitting that came with full-time studies.

My body grew soft. I cried often.

By my birthday in late January 2010, the winter term was already punishing, but I was moving on a research project that would put me on my bike all summer.

I planned to pedal from Eugene to Washington, DC, for a historic roads conference and to study the economic effects of bicycle tourism during my journey. To make this happen, I would need to secure acceptance to present my research results at the conference, fundraise, and plan my biking route. The promise of being on my bike all summer carried me through the agony of running deadlines.

The November before, I started having hip pain when I walked or fully straightened my leg. The pain was a momentary zap of electricity from my left hip joint down the inside of my leg that blinded me for a second or two. Neither massage nor chiropractic had any effect on these periodic jolts of pain, and the trip felt even more urgent. If my mobility continued to decline, I might not have the chance again. I could pedal short distances without issue, but I had no idea how my hip would respond to pedaling every day for ten hours a day.

Since January six months before, I'd done fewer than ten rides longer than ten miles. I crammed training rides into the hour before I went to class. I took the steps to my tenth-floor apartment.

Late morning on June 23 in my building's entry plaza, I loaded two panniers on the rack on the front of my orange creamsicle Trek 2.1 road bike and rolled onto the street.

The Trek 2.1 was my first road bike, and I bought it new in 2008 for $1,000 after a month of comparison shopping and test rides. The bike's color and the service I received at the shop decided it for me even though the bike cost more than I wanted to spend. Since I no longer had a car, I wanted a faster bike than my 1991 mountain bike to reach my friends' houses.

When I left home that June morning in 2010, I'd never ridden my bike with loaded panniers before, and the change in balance and lower center of gravity made the bike feel as if it had no rigidity. I'd worked around my road bike's lack of rack attachment points with a cargo rack that fastened to my handlebars and fit into the front axle. For the first several blocks, I feared I had broken my bike frame. By the time I was on the rural highway east of town, I'd adjusted to the handling.

That first day, I spent the night at Paradise Campground—sixty-three miles from home at the base of the Cascade Mountain Range. The terrain seemed flat, and I wasn't in a hurry. The forested surroundings filled me with calm and delight. Large yellow and black western tiger swallowtail butterflies played in the dappled sunlight. The hardest part had been leaving; Day One was a triumph!

When I departed Paradise the next morning, I pedaled uphill for twenty-eight miles and gained four thousand feet of elevation. My body whimpered. The muscles in my lower back squealed. My quads burned. I didn't expect how much my arms would work to balance the load I carried on the front of my bike. When I stopped at a coffee shop in Sisters, Oregon, after finishing the climb, I could barely hold my cup of tea.

From Sisters, I raced across the plains to reach Prineville before dark. I rolled into town in falling light, planning to treat myself to a motel stay. The front desk person at the Motel 6 informed me that all the motels in town were full. The Crooked River Roundup-Rodeo was celebrating its fifty-fifth year.

I left the motel feeling defeated and followed signs for camping at a recreation area as night bled into the clear sky. I had bike lights, but I didn't want to ride in the dark. People wouldn't expect a touring cyclist on the road in the dark. No matter what I did, I would be invisible. Plus, riding in the dark with big trucks driven by drunk people seemed like a good way to get myself killed. The panniers made my bike wide. What if a vehicle nicked them or a mirror hit me?

About three miles from the motel, a sign indicated the camping area was thirteen miles ahead. There was barely enough light to read the sign. In a car, thirteen miles was nothing, but on a bike, it would take at least an hour to get there. I crumpled over my handlebars and wished I had known how far the campground was before I went out of my way following the signs. I turned back to the main road.

Prineville was eighty-five miles from Paradise. I added six miles to account for this damn detour. Ninety-one miles was the farthest distance I'd biked in one day in my life.

Somehow my legs kept pedaling.

Night flooded the road and adjacent fields.

I would have to improvise a place to sleep. I didn't need much. I'd be up early in the morning and pedaling again. I had snacks and enough water to reach the next town with services.

At the east end of Prineville, I stopped and snooped about the Prineville ranger station.

No outdoor restroom.

No picnic table.

No matter.

The sixth day and approximately 330 miles into my trip, I was saddle sore as I approached Baker City, Oregon. I couldn't bear the pinpricks in the skin over my sit bones. The only fix was to get off my saddle regularly, but I knew the pain was inevitable, like breaking in a pair of boots. The only way to get my body used to pedaling for ten hours a day, day after day, was to do it.

I experimented with my body position to offer my sitting parts relief, but my few attempts to stand on the pedals and turn the cranks felt wobbly, and I feared crashing. On downhills, I could lift off the saddle and coast without concern. Occasionally on flats or gentle climbs, I would stand on my pedals and coast for a few seconds. To rest longer than those few seconds would mean stopping, but my ambition wouldn't allow it. I permitted myself breaks for food and bathroom needs, photos, interactions with other cyclists, or reading interpretive signs. It was a point of pride for me to make it to the top of a climb without stopping.

On my first bike tour to San Francisco the previous year, I had similarly sore sitting parts after nearly a week riding. I was in Arcata, California, and stopped at a bike shop desperate for any tips that would stop my thoughts from looping "poor pussy." A woman who staffed the shop suggested I check that my saddle was level and encouraged me to use chamois cream to prevent chafing. When I returned to my hotel room that night, my saddle appeared level, so I didn't mess with it. The directions on my new tube of Chamois Butt'r read, "Apply to skin to soothe and soften" and "may be applied to any skin areas that rub together." The lube had restored my squashed and neglected parts in multiple ways. I applied it liberally in the morning before departing and in the evening after showering. My ride turned dreamy—cruising down Highway 1, the fog had lifted, and the sun sparkled on the Pacific Ocean. The newfound relief and positive focus on my girl parts made me amorous.

Now, in eastern Oregon, I hadn't arrived at the point of loving what I was doing. I had more than three thousand miles and the Rocky Mountains ahead of me, and I hadn't had an orgasm since leaving Eugene. Butt'r simply couldn't soothe the tenderness that felt so close to the bone.

My original plan had been to leave two days after the spring term ended, but those days stretched. I'd started a thing with Daniel, my cute upstairs neighbor and friend with benefits. Our occasional film watching and casual sex had offered needed relief from my demanding schedule. With my departure imminent, our off-and-on interactions turned into every night. While I loved the idea of riding my bike four thousand miles for the summer, I didn't want to give up the sex. Sex felt like the reward for months on overdrive.

I rolled into Baker City in eighty-degree temperatures under a clear blue sky. Focused on washing and easing the pain in my ass, I strode into the shiny lobby of the Geiser Grand Hotel, the pedal cleats on the soles of my shoes clicking on the floor. The hotel had a room available the following day, which I reserved for my first rest day. For lodging that night, staff at the hotel found me a room at a nearby motel.

In the first-floor room, I leaned my bike against the wall next to a dresser that held a Hello Kitty phone. I peeled off my salt-crusted cycling clothes and left them in a moist, rank lump on the floor while I stood in the hot shower for thirty minutes.

Clean and dry, I lay naked on the firm bed and used the lube. My breath constricted in a pre-cry for the tenderness of my parts and for my longing to connect with Daniel. When I'd left Eugene, Daniel had asked for the link to my blog but otherwise didn't indicate he wanted to stay in touch.

After a failed orgasm in full view of Hello Kitty and breathy crying that didn't produce tears, I put on my black cotton tank dress, black yoga pants, and a light long-sleeved zip neck shirt and carried my six-days-of-sweat cycling clothes to the motel washing machine. From there, I walked to a Chinese restaurant, hungry for vegetables, and was rewarded with a plate heaping with vibrant colors.

The next afternoon, I checked into the Geiser Grand. Huge room, bed, and west-facing windows. Gold wallpaper and bedspread. I watched a storm billow in the west as the sun went down in electrified oranges and pinks and lit up the pendulous underside of the purple-green storm cloud. It seemed unfortunate to be alone instead of sharing the romance of this room and its view with someone.

I pedaled out of Baker City on a hot Tuesday morning across a sagebrush-knotted rumple of land on my way to Halfway. My sitting parts were still sore, but a day off the saddle had reduced the tenderness. Heat reflected from the pavement, and the parts of my head exposed by my helmet's vents baked.

Few vehicles passed on Highway 86. No bicyclists. The road through this sere emptiness was mine. The landscape was quiet and expansive.

I pedaled and sweated, scanning the hillsides for visual relief from the sun's glare. None. I hoped for shade farther ahead. None.

The road east of Richland climbed at a 7 percent grade. It was midday. My head sizzled as I inched up the treeless hillside. My quads burned.

After what seemed like two or three miles of climbing, the road bent to the left for another mile. The grade steepened as I crawled to the road crest.

Short evergreens marked the ridge. I strained past a gravel pullout, wanting to stop but determined to keep going. I could rest on the way down.

Over the crest, the landscape changed to deep greens, tall grass, coniferous trees, and yellow, lavender, and white wildflowers.

Following the squiggling road down, my head cooled in the rush of air. A broad smile etched my face.

The colorful structures of Halfway stood amid hayfields and woods.

I stopped at the library for Wi-Fi and sat at a picnic table in the courtyard because the building was closed.

"Oh, hi, didn't mean to disturb you," a woman's voice said.

I turned to find a gray-haired woman in shorts and a T-shirt pulling on a garden hose. "You're not disturbing me. Is it okay that I'm here?" I said.

"Yes. It's a great spot."

"I agree. The garden is really pretty."

"Oh, thank you. I volunteer twice a week to take care of it. If you want some water, help yourself." She indicated the spigot on the wall. "It's nice and cold."

I thanked her and turned to my computer.

After twenty minutes, the woman returned to the table. "Do you know where you're staying tonight?"

"I haven't sorted it out yet. I wanted to get my blog post written while I have a connection."

"You're welcome to stay with me and my husband. We often host cyclists. It's nice to have company. We're about three miles from here."

I accepted. I wanted to talk to people who could tell me about life in towns like Halfway and what kind of economic impact touring cyclists, such as myself, were perceived to bring, especially since homestays didn't immediately bring economic benefit to rural communities. Did touring cyclists get something out of it beyond a free place to stay? How were the people offering homestays served? What was the longer-term economic benefit of hosting cyclists? In Baker

City, I'd interviewed a couple who moved to town because they were artists and cyclists and liked what living in a place with a lower cost of living enabled. The risk of being entrepreneurial was also low. They missed their city cycling community but organized bicycle races, which brought people and money to town. Everyone benefited.

Linda offered dinner around 6:00 PM in addition to lodging. Were people really that nice?

Around 4:30 PM, I stopped at the gravel drive leading to Linda and Tom's house. A lake of grass swooshed and rose in the breeze. Dark blue mountains crowned the view.

We began with cocktail hour in chairs on the back patio, watching the weather move across the ridges and valleys. As the thunderstorm and rain curtain consumed the higher ridges to the east, Linda used a large, pagoda-style house on the ridge as a reference point for the storm's movement. In that house lived the first *Sports Illustrated* swimsuit cover model from 1964. "She's an artist," Linda said. The artist in me stirred.

The storm came rushing over us, and we scrambled inside for a bounteous salad made from vegetables grown in their garden.

Linda and Tom told me stories about different biking tours they'd been on, retirement, irrigation, the difficulty of keeping young people in Halfway, and the challenges of finding a doctor who would live in such an isolated place. I didn't know that someone like me could address what they saw as needs in their community. Cycle Oregon, the organization that produced weeklong event rides in rural parts of the state every year, had a giving program to support communities that the rides visited. There was also the new Oregon Scenic

Bikeway program and the established state and national Scenic Byway program. Even if Halfway had annual events around scenic tours, I doubted young people would stay unless they loved farming, ranching, or had the vision and savvy to make conservation or outdoor adventure experiences into their livelihood.

Linda excused herself to turn on the heat lamp for her adolescent chicks while Tom told me about the forest. Linda returned, wide-eyed: "You should see the light out there."

The three of us returned to the back patio. In the evening's low light, the clouds had an unearthly glow to them, ominous and playful.

2.

Be Safe out There

Day ten. When I arrived in the outskirts of White Bird, Idaho, my fuel tank was empty.

Between breakfast and dinner, I usually ate only a Clif Builders Bar and some jerky and dried fruit, maybe a packet of GU. Dinner was my principal meal of the day, usually eaten when I was near my overnight accommodation. Experience taught me that eateries along rural byways and in small towns could be closed by 6:00 PM. Limited hours of operation aside, most towns, no matter how small, usually had one place to eat, even if it was a convenience store.

The Adventure Cycling Association maps I was traveling with identified restaurants, groceries, and convenience stores. The maps also showed elevation profiles, distances between towns, lodging options, water stops, restrooms, libraries, post offices, and bike shops. Most important, the route followed quiet, low-traffic roads as much as possible.

From west to east, Adventure Cycling Association's TransAmerica Trail traversed the country from the Oregon coast to the Virginia shore. At the eastern end of Oregon, the route cut northeast across the Idaho panhandle to Missoula, Montana, the northernmost point

on the route and Adventure Cycling Association's headquarters.
From Missoula, the TransAm angled southeast to Yellowstone and
diagonally across Wyoming where it crossed the Continental Divide
numerous times into Colorado for the eleventh and final crossing
at Hoosier Pass, the route's highest point of elevation at 11,542 feet.
From there, the TransAm dove into Pueblo, Colorado, before beginning a trek across the Great Plains through eastern Colorado and
Kansas. The terrain crinkled again in Missouri, crossed the southern
portion of Illinois, covered the length of Kentucky, and crossed the
Appalachian Mountains in Virginia.

I was early in that northeastward passage through Idaho when I
arrived in White Bird and encountered a white-haired man wearing
a pastel-plaid short-sleeved collared shirt on an ATV. We exchanged
hellos.

"Go to the Silver Dollar and get yourself some dinner," he said,
"then come back this way and stay at my RV Park. It's nice camping
along the river."

"Do you have Wi-Fi?"

"Yep. There's a shower room also."

The Silver Dollar was one of two commercial buildings in the
town center. It had a weathered wood façade with SILVER DOLLAR
spelled out in pieces of bark-covered limbs. Several pickups were
parked in front.

Through my sunglasses, the dim interior hid the details of people
and furniture but not the smell of beer and cigarettes.

"Can I help you with something?" The gravelly voice matched
the facial movements of a bearded bartender. I imagined he wanted
to ask me, *Are you lost?* Why else would a lone woman wander into
a small-town bar in tall striped socks, a pink and lavender bicycle
jersey, dark sunglasses, and a lavender bike helmet?

"Do you serve food?"

"You can go in the back there if you're just looking to eat," the bartender said flatly. He pointed to a short hallway that split the building in half.

In the back were six empty tables with menus held between the salt and pepper shakers, bottles of Heinz ketchup, and A-1 Steak Sauce. 4:30 PM. I sat at a four-top, removed my cycling gloves and helmet, traded sunglasses for regular glasses, and scanned the menu.

The bartender appeared and asked me what I wanted.

"Burger and tots please. Do you have any salads?"

"We don't have salad. I could give you some extra burger toppings. You know, the lettuce and tomato."

"That sounds excellent. And an iced tea and a big water."

I moved my helmet. I liked that it was purple and matched my U.S. Bicycle Route System cycling jersey. The jersey had a subtle map of the United States across the chest and back. I coordinated the rest of my pedaling attire to match. No red, white, and blue. No Stars-and-Bars. By design. I was embarrassed by American arrogance and pained by how we treated our own people. As much as I could hide my Americanness, I did.

After I finished dinner, I paused at the end of the hallway on the bar side. A woman's voice called out to me from a table of five, two of whom were in bright yellow reflective wear, "Hey! Did you ride in on Highway 95 about an hour ago?" The table was cluttered with tumbler glasses and beer cans.

I nodded and scanned the sunburned faces around the table.

A skinny person wearing sunglasses and smoking a cigarette was the questioner. She had shoulder-length, wavy brown hair. "We saw you on the bridge."

I crossed at least four big bridges that day. Two or three were under construction. "What bridge?"

"The one right down there," she tipped her head.

"The one with no guard rail and logging trucks and a big river below?" I offered, trying to sound upbeat about a situation that had been freaky.

"Yeah! That one."

"Yeah. I made it."

"Sit down. We'll buy you a beer."

Beer and cigarettes could not compete with the lure of a shower and Wi-Fi. I declined beer but not conversation. The road crew looked different without their hardhats and sunglasses.

"How far did you go today?" the woman asked.

"It felt far. I don't know. Ninety miles?"

"Where did you leave from this morning?"

"Council."

"Wow. That is far. A hundred miles."

"Really?" I didn't have a cycle computer and relied on my maps for mileage. If what she said were true, my day's ride included two milestones—the longest one of my ride so far and my first one-hundred-mile day.

An older woman in pink shorts and an oversized souvenir T-shirt at an adjacent table joined the conversation with "Where are you headed?" She held a can of beer in one hand and a cigarette in the other.

"Tonight, just here. But I'm riding to Washington, DC." I stepped closer to the woman in the pink shorts, so I wouldn't be yelling across the road crew table.

"That's so amazing," the woman in pink shorts said. "Where'd you start?"

"I left from home in Eugene, Oregon, about a week and a half ago."

"By yourself?"

"Yep."

"You go, girl. That's amazing."

"Thanks. It isn't an easy way to go, but I'm meeting nice folks, such as yourselves, and seeing beautiful country."

"I hear ya," the woman in sunglasses said. "Our crew has been working on that bridge for three months. I've been here since the start. Others have been here three weeks. It's seven days a week, ten hours a day."

Did they feel as vulnerable out there as I did? All I had for protection from fast-moving vehicles was a white line painted on the road and a bubble I imagined around myself. Nothing protected me from vehicle exhaust or falling hay, wood chips, or gravel. The fright of an unanticipated noise, such as honking, someone yelling a compliment or insult, or—the worst—a dog barking from a passing vehicle, would cause me to flinch, and I feared crashing or swerving into the travel lane.

"Do you ever get tired of it or get a day off?" I asked.

"It's good money," she said and drank from her can.

I felt uncomfortable about being perceived as someone with money and leisure. I had busted ass to raise money to support my ride and knew I could look forward to more student loan debt when I returned. This was not a trip of luxury. Maybe the woman in sunglasses could see that. Maybe she'd checked her own idea of luxury at the door when she signed on to live in White Bird for as long as the money flowed. Or maybe living in White Bird was her idea of the high life.

"Good on ya," I said. "Was it difficult to uproot from where you were to do it?"

She lifted her beer slightly in my direction and gave a little nod.

I shifted my weight toward the door, and she said, "Be safe out there."

It was a common refrain. I hadn't been but two days in Idaho and had already experienced what felt like callous disregard of my vulnerability by the log truck drivers. Someone had told me that log truck drivers got paid per load, so they drove fast to maximize loads per day. I stayed as far to the edge of the road as possible and was cognizant of the draft that could suck me under the wheels.

"So far, so good," I said. "Thanks for your concern."

On my way to the RV park, I heard a vehicle coming from behind me, moved to the far-right side of the road, and glanced over my left shoulder. It was a pickup. I kept pedaling and glanced again. To my horror, it approached fast and instead of crossing the double yellow line and giving me a wide berth, it veered toward me and the edge of the road. I was trapped with a drop-off at the pavement edge and a road bank that sloped down to the river. The truck overtook me with a rush of air and only inches between me and its hulk.

My heart pounded. Why would someone do that? Were they drunk? Were they fucking insane? Was it funny to threaten to kill someone?

No other vehicles passed me as I jittered my way to the RV park. I found the man in the pastel-plaid, Alfred.

"You made it!" he exclaimed.

"I did make it, but I almost didn't. Someone swerved into me on the open road."

His features fell. "Are you okay?"

"I am. Shaken up. But still here. The jitters will go away."

"You're sure?"

I nodded.

Alfred oriented me to the RV park and its facilities and gave me laundry detergent so I could wash my clothes. He asked me what I was doing on the ride and about my background. I told him I grew up in Wyoming and hopped around the country getting educated. At my mention of Colgate University, his eyebrows lifted under the brim of his ball cap, and he shared his own educational background and how intellectual conversation was hard to come by in White Bird. Then, he told me about his wife and family. I related how my mom forwarded me the call for papers for the Preserving the Historic Road conference, which prompted this crazy idea to ride across the country.

Mom had not encouraged me to go solo. In fact, I had to tell her while I was planning the ride that she could not follow me the entire way in her car, which she had proposed. She was understandably worried I might get hit, break down, encounter a human or animal that might harm me, or find myself in a tornado. To ease her concern, I gave her the job of home-base support, which she took to expertly, having done the recon for the church hostel I stayed in the night after the sprinkler adventure.

I erected my tarp shelter on the RV park lawn, arranged my sleeping gear, and headed to the community house. After showering, I sat at a table in the common room in my tank dress, feeling immodest. My riding clothes and other off-bike clothes agitated in the washer. The west-facing side of the building had picture windows and provided me with a sunny view while I responded to e-mails and worked on a blog post.

Alfred mentioned that some of the road crew were staying at the RV park. As I worked, the woman in sunglasses came in and out a couple times, but we didn't talk. She was cleaned up from her day and going about the business of her life.

One of the road crew I hadn't seen at the Silver Dollar came in to use the pay phone. He and I talked before he called his wife in Coeur d'Alene. Even with my back to him, I felt awkward sitting in on his conversation. His exchange was short, and then he left.

I moved my clothes into the dryer and kept working on my blog post. When the dryer completed its cycle, I ducked into the bathroom and put on my yoga pants and a sports bra. Back out in the common room, I covered up with my long-sleeved shirt and returned to my laptop. The sun went down in a glow of orange and pink.

The same guy who used the pay phone returned. He grumbled, "You're still here?" and went straight to the phone. I looked at my computer, wanting to create as much privacy as possible in the space between us. I heard him pick up the receiver and dial. He fidgeted.

"Hey, baby," he said almost chipper. In my mind's eye, I saw him standing at the pay phone with an arm resting over the top of it.

"Not a whole lot," he said, his voice mellowed. "I was just hanging out thinking about you. I miss you."

I paged through my past. No guy had ever called me and said that before.

"No," he said with a touch of defensiveness.

I was all ears.

"Well, I've had one or two."

How long had it been between when he first called his wife and the current call? An hour? It seemed strange to me that "Baby" would respond to his call of "missing you" by asking him if he'd been drinking.

"I'm suffering here without you." His voice was sharp, loud.

I held my breath, uneasy with the change of tone and glad that the room was lit with fluorescent lights and visible from the grounds.

"That's why I'm here," his voice sounded exasperated, "making money to support you."

He held the "m" in his words longer than normal, and I realized he was intoxicated. "Baby" had known immediately.

"You don't appreciate me. You don't understand." His voice was loud, his words slurred.

My hands hadn't moved on the keyboard since he'd come in. My computer still didn't have a full charge.

"You don't understand how hard this job is!" His retort startled me, and I flinched. "How hard it is to be away from you and have no day off!"

Was this a special occasion fight? Had my being here prompted it? Would it have happened regardless?

"Yes, she's still here!"

He made no attempt to lower his voice, yet I had the sense that his anger and exasperation were directed at the phone and "Baby." I turned off the Wi-Fi on my laptop and closed the lid.

As I pulled on the charger cord, he yelled at the phone again. "I don't even know what you're talking about! I love you!"

I froze, bent forward in my chair, the cord limp in my hand and disconnected from the outlet.

The receiver slammed in its metal cradle. "Bitch!"

He stepped past me and flung the door shut. When he was gone, I gathered my clothes and computer and returned to my shelter.

In the dark, under a thin wing of nylon at an isolated RV park in the middle of the Idaho panhandle, I lay awake, afraid the lonely, intoxicated pay phone abuser would come for me. I'd basically been naked when the man and I talked, and there was no mystery about where I was on the property. With my hip, I couldn't run. Would I have the presence of mind to scream? If I did, would anyone hear? Was I strong enough to fight him off? Would he come to his senses? None of my support system at home knew where I was. With no cell service, I couldn't call anyone.

Under the cover of my sleeping bag, I felt cold and vulnerable. I'd worked so hard to get to this RV park, and I hated the feeling that someone could take all the effort away, just like that. This ride was supposed to be the remedy for the slow-moving train wreck that was my life. My bicycle was a lifeline, a gift I needed to pull myself from that wreck. How could it land me in a place I couldn't survive?

For the four years before returning to school, I'd been scraping by doing odd jobs for friends despite having undergraduate and graduate degrees in English. I didn't need my education to paint walls, pull weeds, prune trees, house-sit, water gardens, trim pot, or sell earth-friendly household products. I wanted a reliable paycheck and intellectually engaging work that would stretch me.

When the economy tanked in 2008, I was already considering applying to a four-year program at Naropa Institute in Boulder, Colorado, for art therapy. As the unemployment rate rose in Oregon and my friends lost jobs, went bankrupt, and struggled to stay afloat, Naropa seemed impractical to the point of foolish and Boulder an expensive city to be financially marooned in. Meanwhile, I had seen appealing job postings for bicycle and pedestrian planners. The qualifications required a relevant degree, such as landscape architecture or planning. Both degree programs were offered in Eugene. Landscape architecture was a four-year program, and planning was two. I chose planning—shorter commitment, less debt. I could hide out in school while the economy righted itself and emerge in two years with my pass to a well-compensated professional position as an active transportation planner.

I had never considered riding across the country until Mom e-mailed me about the historic road conference in DC. Once I had the idea, it seemed natural that I would undertake this journey. I wasn't just going to a conference. I'd be pedaling toward relevance, a career, financial security, a leaner body, a mate. I needed the freedom to find my way and embrace what the universe offered along with the associated challenges and discomfort.

I fell into an uneasy sleep.

Awake at 4:00 AM, I opened my laptop to finish and publish my blog post.

I wasn't sure what it meant to "be safe out there." As far as I could tell, I made it through yesterday. I clicked "publish." With that action, my family and friends would know I made it through yesterday, too.

Now, there was the matter of today.

3.

Lolo Pass

With my sights set on Missoula, Montana, I pedaled onward. On a map, Missoula lay on the middle of the fringed part of Montana near the Idaho border. Adventure Cycling's headquarters. My next rest day.

The fifty-two-mile climb to Lolo Pass and the Montana state line followed a road with a narrow shoulder that clung to the forested mountainside. There were few vehicles. South of the road flowed the Lochsa River. The traditional Nez Perce route traversed the high ridge to the north. The sky was overcast, the air misty, the temperature pleasant—between 65 and 71 degrees, I guessed. I never checked weather forecasts and didn't have a way to gauge temperature apart from my observations while being outside.

On the road, I met John, an east-to-west rider of the Trans-America Trail. We talked, our bikes front wheel to front wheel at the far edge of the downhill lane. He told me that I could camp anywhere on National Forest land and enjoy free hot chocolate and Wi-Fi at the visitor center at the top of Lolo Pass. Later, when I reached Missouri, there was a great place for pie.

I pedaled up the pass. The river slithered along my right, sometimes close, other times hidden below conifers.

Around 4:00 PM, I arrived at Lochsa Lodge, a resort in the middle
of the forest. My quiet day on the road intersected with clattering
activity—cars, a mini gas station, a timber-framed lodge, people
milling, and kids squealing. The crush of humanity made me uncomfortable. I leaned my bike against a tree and went inside. People
crammed the lodge foyer, which also served as a souvenir shop, and
I dodged them and clothing racks on my way to the restroom. I soon
found an airy spot on the back deck where my stinky self was least
likely to offend other patrons.

Salad. Chicken parmesan on spaghetti. Double brownie sundae.
The quantity of food I ate seemed obscene, but my body welcomed it.

I kicked a leg over my bike and continued toward the pass.

A couple miles from the lodge, I found myself alone among the
DeVoto Cedar Grove's gray-barked trees in lengthening evening
light. I took a picture of my bike leaning against one of them, a portrait of myself dissolved in the landscape.

Back on my bike and following John's guidance, I looked for a
place to camp. I had some worry about bears and cougars if I slept
in the forest. Roadside signs with DOS and DONT's signaled potential
encounters with these animals. My smell could attract them.

I turned onto a gravel lane. A few yards up, tall grasses and wildflowers grew on the other side of a locked Forest Service barrier gate.
I leaned my bike on the gate and bowed under the pipe arm, careful
not to twinge my hip.

Once my camp was set, I retrieved a hand-sized toy car from my
panniers. I bought the car, a 1955 Thunderbird, in eastern Oregon at

Austin Junction for $4.99. I considered the car my sag wagon and, for that reason, necessary gear. A sag wagon is the car that picks up cyclists, typically on an organized ride or tour when they have mechanical issues, injuries, or are too tired to keep pedaling. Since I was solo, the car symbolized what a solo sag would be. I was both the rider and the backup. If I had an issue on the road, I had to help myself. I drove the car along the top of the gate arm and took pictures of it parked over the Great Gravel Road.

As the sun sank, the warm, peaty, and vanilla-scented air turned cold. I put on all my non-biking clothes and buried myself in my sleeping bag. The temperature would drop, I knew, but I hadn't expected near freezing temperatures. My feet were ice, and I pumped my legs, trying to generate friction and warm them. It didn't work.

I woke with a start, certain someone was driving down the gravel road. I listened. No engine noise. No tires crushing gravel. No vehicle lights. Just a dream.

Then, a chipmunk ran over the top of me.

Later, an animal snuffling yanked me from a dead sleep. As I opened my eyes to the dark, all I heard was the pounding of my heart.

I cracked my eyelids open to overcast light and sat up in my sleeping bag. My breath made frosty clouds. My feet were frozen, immune to my attempts to warm them with my hands.

Inside my sleeping bag, I changed into my riding clothes and sat, afraid of the cold. John said there was hot chocolate at the pass. I got out of the sleeping bag and put on my wind jacket, the only piece of gear that didn't need to go into my panniers before I departed. Thirty seconds into disassembling my tarp shelter, my hands went numb with cold.

As I pedaled away, tears streamed from my eyes. The pass seemed a long way away. It was about eight miles from where I camped, and my hands and feet never warmed up.

From the visitor center, I wrote a Facebook post once my fingers were capable of typing.

> Imagine a sea of evergreen trees. Lolo
> Pass Visitor Center is in the middle of
> that sea. Imagine me sitting inside the
> Center in a comfy chair, hot chocolate
> in hand, enjoying an alpine meadow view.
> Imagine it taking 30 minutes and three hot
> drinks to thaw my hands and feet. Imagine
> there is also Wi-Fi. #americathebeautiful
> #whatiswilderness
>
> Happy Independence Day. I survived Idaho.

4.

Missoula and the Gandy Dancers

Under sunny skies, I rolled forty-seven miles in three hours down the mountain from Lolo Pass to Missoula. I hardly pedaled.

The hostel where I had a reservation was abuzz with backpackers and cyclists. One man who had recently arrived by bike and had a wad of gray and blue clothes in one hand asked me if I wanted to share a load of laundry.

The proprietor, Tim, appeared right then. "We're having a barbecue in the back," he said. "You're welcome to join us."

At the barbecue, I met three other touring cyclists: a graduate student on his way from Logan, Utah, to Glacier National Park, and two friends on an annual ride, one a criminal defense lawyer from Wisconsin and the other an easygoing architect from Minnesota.

None of these white men was riding across the country, but they typified my observations of the sort of person who undertakes a journey of this nature. Adventure Cycling Association estimates that about a thousand people each year ride across the United States on the TransAmerica Trail, which is one of three established coast-to-coast cycling routes. Generally speaking, people who ride across the country are older, college educated, and make more than $75,000 per year. About 8 percent of riders are international visitors. On the TransAm, early season starts are typically east-to-west travelers, and later season starts are west-to-east riders on account of snow-related road closures in the mountainous western states.

The day after the barbecue, I rode to the grocery store with the lawyer. He shared that freezing water in insulated bottles was the best way to keep water cold on the road.

After all the cyclists departed the hostel, I wandered downtown. I liked the historic architecture, Art Deco filling stations, and tree-lined streets. I went to a coffee shop to write. Two muscly men sat next to me. They were dressed in black leather chaps and jackets, wide bandanas over their foreheads, sunglasses. They both had reddish-brown bushy moustaches and shoulders and chests that seemed to burst the seams of their clothes.

I frequently saw motorcyclists on my route, and I supposed the same questions people asked me applied to bikers. The men were intimidating figures, but I made eye contact and took a deep breath. "Where are you traveling from?"

"Chicago," one of them replied.

"Where are you headed to?" I didn't want to bother them but was interested in their perspective.

"Las Vegas," the same man answered, "but via some places here in the north. We grew up in Missoula, so we're seeing friends."

They introduced themselves as Mike and Rick, firefighters.

"Are you writing a book?" Rick asked.

"I'm blogging. I'm riding my bike across the country and try to post an update every day."

"Wow, you're tough," Mike said.

"Me? You look tough."

People said I was tough a lot, such as my school friends who re-marked on my grit and intent to go alone. My parents said it, too, in a tone of admiration and concern when I called to update them. "Tough guy," Dad said. My friends outside of school said it when I shared my plan and invited them to follow my journey. I didn't know how to take it. It was easy to believe being called tough meant that I was a bulldozer. I struggled to accept or believe people meant I was physically and mentally strong, someone who persevered and over-came challenges. I did have moments by myself when I felt strong, but my confidence often crumbled in the presence of other people and was kept in check by my inner taskmaster.

Rick said, "For the Fourth, we had a great time with friends. We stayed up late listening to music and dancing in the living room. The girls went to bed around 5:00 AM, and we stayed up dancing until about 7:30 this morning."

I imagined these two strong men doing a slow dance together in a light-filled living room, the love between them clear.

"They call us gandy dancers," Mike said. "Do you know what that is?"

Given the context, it seemed to point to "burly biker guys who fancy each other." I shook my head.

"Rick and I used to work for the railroad laying ties and rail," Mike said. "It's incredibly hard work."

My eyes widened. And they called *me* tough?

"That's what gandy dancers are," Mike said, his chest seemed to puff up more.

"No way," I replied. I would look it up to ensure they weren't teasing me. I imagined these two men working as one, their movements choreographed, practiced, synchronous. They seemed a matched pair. "Are you two brothers?"

"Yeah, we're twins," Rick said.

The next morning, I stopped at Adventure Cycling's headquarters before leaving town. The staff gave me a tour and took my picture. Since I was also distributing Adventure Cycling Association TransAmerica Trail window decals to businesses on the route as part of my collaboration with the organization, they took special pictures of me holding the decals with dirty fingernails for the world to see. Even after two days off the bike, I had dirty fingernails from the accumulated grime of camping and being on the road. Embarrassing.

A line on the photo release form asked: "What are you carrying that's unusual?" I wrote:

> A 1955 Thunderbird toy car.
>
> A roll of black masking tape, a self-healing cutting mat, an
>
> X-Acto knife, and a pair of scissors. So I can make art.

I forgot to mention the glue stick.

5.

Big Hole, Wisdom

Along the road was a barbed wire fence, and beyond it, grassy open space dotted with pink, yellow, and lavender.

No cars, no people, no houses, no falling down structures, no scattered trash, no cattle, no water, no rest area, no billboards.

The wind swished the nothing and the something.

I floated. The flower-studded lake of grass was rimmed by snow-capped peaks.

The Big Hole was my reward for having climbed nearly 3,000 feet of elevation in twenty miles—first to Lost Trail Pass at 7,014 feet and then a short hop up to Chief Joseph Pass and the Continental Divide at 7,241 feet. The Big Hole was eight miles beyond the summits and 700 feet down.

At a roadside interpretive sign, I stopped to learn what the "big hole" was. I assumed it was a land scar from a meteorite or volcanic explosion, but I didn't see a crater anywhere.

The sign clarified. It was this expansive meadow, sixty miles long by twenty miles wide. Not a hole. I took a picture. Generally, I avoided taking pictures of broad landscapes since what romanced me about them didn't translate to photographs. Still, I hoped I could capture an impression. I wanted a souvenir of what felt like my heart expanding into the color, light, and space.

I pedaled past the Nez Perce National Battlefield Visitor Center. Later, I read that somewhere in this broad meadow approximately one hundred Nez Perce men, women, and children died in a U.S. Army attack in August 1877 that was launched to kill the entire encampment of eight hundred people. About thirty U.S. troops died in the battle. It was hard to stomach. The Big Hole was gorgeous and flat. I could see why a community would live in this abundance.

Ten miles farther, Big Hole ranchers moved cattle in my direction. The cattle walked and trotted in an arc between the roadside fences, a good portion of them on the road. I approached cautiously. Would the cattle trample me? Would they scatter?

The black beasts had shiny noses. The men on horseback moving the cattle weren't near enough to ask for direction. The cattle moved aside. I breathed shallowly, unnerved to be among so many large animals. Some of the cattle glanced at me, their long-lashed, dark eyes curious. Others showed me the whites of their eyes.

A mile farther, I encountered another herd. This time, I rode with confidence through them as if I were astride a horse, yelling as I imagined a cowgirl might, "C'mon cows. Gip. Ya! C'mon cows."

In the early afternoon, I arrived in Wisdom, Montana, a T intersection with a few buildings. I parked at the café and ran inside to escape the mosquitoes, ordered, and then studied my map. With no protection from mosquitoes under my tarp, I wanted indoor lodging. Jackson, Montana, eighteen miles ahead, had an inn.

"It's a hot one out there," the older woman who ran the café said as she refilled my water glass.

"You know, the mosquitoes are so thick I didn't even notice the heat."

"Oh. They flood the fields for haying. I drive between here and home. Being on bicycle I suppose you notice the mosquitoes."

"Yeah. There isn't much to keep them off. By the way," I thought of the other swarming creatures out there, "I rode through some cattle herds. I wasn't sure what to do when I came upon them. Do you know?"

"I don't know about being on a bicycle. Driving you want to be careful about splitting the herd."

"Good to know." Both times I rode through the cattle, it was like riding through a puddle. They made space for me to go through, and when I looked back, they were still one pool of ink. "How did Wisdom get its name?"

"Ah. The Big Hole River used to be called the Wisdom. Lewis and Clark named it that. The river got a new name, but the town didn't."

The flat road from Wisdom edged along foothills at one end of the Big Hole. Power poles stood on my left, and the plain of hayfields swished on my right. Here and there, hawks sat on the power poles.

My sights were set on a room that had a door and screens on its windows. I felt misled by the bear and cougar warnings. Mosquitoes were the real threat.

I passed a small electrical substation.

The road was empty and straight.

Something fell from the sky into the field on my right. Was it the play of late afternoon light on my sunglasses? Would a hawk, in humor or seriousness, play Icarus? I looked around. No birds on the ground. No flashes of light on my glasses.

A raptor that had been perched on one of the power poles jumped off and flew around making its bird call. A few years before, I had spent four hours every Sunday morning volunteering at the local raptor center picking entrails and owl pellets out of the enclosures' pea gravel and blasting water on long white guano spurts. Over time, I could discern the raptor voices that echoed from the center's hillside perch. The voice in question wasn't an osprey, which I'd seen on a nest at the substation.

A *whoosh* approached from behind me. A huge chocolate brown bird appeared at my head's height and climbed into the sky in front of me.

"Shit! Did I just get buzzed?" The sound of my fear surprised me. *Whoosh.*

"Again? What the fuck!" My heart pounded, legs and arms quivered as I pedaled.

One day when I'd been cleaning the goshawk enclosure at the raptor center, the goshawk, which was usually calm, swooped at me from behind and grabbed my head. I immediately retreated and felt for cuts. There weren't any.

Another time at the raptor center, I was training a new volunteer, an older man with calf muscles the size of pummelos. The first day I trained him, we cleaned the enclosures together. On a usual Sunday by myself, I often skipped the bald eagles or only cleaned part of their enclosure because they were nervous and vocal with people in their space. Since this man was interested in the baldies, I made sure we stopped in to say hello. The new volunteer went right to work picking up the moldy flesh bits, even going to the far end of the enclosure that I avoided. I cringed watching him turn his back to the eagles. The eagles shrieked from their perch but didn't move. Perhaps they were all voice and no action, and I'd been unnecessarily cautious. The next Sunday, the volunteer felt confident cleaning the enclosures by himself. I let him take the block with the eagles. I was inside the second enclosure of my cleaning round when I heard him call my name and say, "Something happened." I came out quickly. "One of them grabbed me," he said and turned a leg to show me several large punctures in his calf with blood streaming into his white sock.

I pedaled faster and saw flashing stills of the volunteer's bloody leg and then images of my head with dark pits that trickled red down my temple and forehead. I looked behind me. The hawk came straight for my head. I pedaled hard.

Whoosh.

I ducked.

Did it not like my helmet? I could take my helmet off. But if the bird made contact with my head, I'd want the helmet on. I preferred the talons grab my helmet than my scalp. But what if the hawk gripped the helmet and it was still attached to my head? I unclipped the chinstrap, willing to lose the helmet rather than be pulled from my bike.

Whoosh.

Maybe I was going too fast? Birds didn't like quick movements. I slowed.

Whoosh.

There was something about me the hawk didn't like. Going slow didn't help.

Whoosh.

I weaved on the road, sped up, slowed down, ducked, dodged.

Whoosh.

Two motorcyclists approached from behind me. I hoped they would save me. I pointed to the sky. They passed me in the other lane, didn't stop or even slow. Fear soured my mouth. I didn't know what to do.

Whoosh.

Feathers touched me. I watched the bird come in again and ducked right when I thought it would make contact.

Whoosh.

I yelled, "Noooooooooo!" Making noise was supposed to help deter a bear attack. Maybe it would work with this raptor.

Whoosh.

Again, I ducked.

Instead of wheeling around for another dive at my head, the hawk settled on a power pole. I glanced at it several times as I passed and left it behind, not certain it was done terrorizing me.

From the protection of my room in Jackson that night, I posted to Facebook.

> Here's the wisdom from Wisdom. Travel in
> a puncture-proof bubble. (I guess most
> people do that in cars.) Land of 10,000
> Haystacks is Land of 10,000,000,000
> Mosquitoes. Appreciate the Big Hole in
> motion (it's probably not what you think
> anyway), and pedal like hell when a raptor
> takes a dislike to your head.

6.

Flight

Day eighteen and three mornings after the raptor buzzed me, I rendezvoused with Bill, a local I met the previous evening, at a food truck in Twin Bridges, Montana, for our flight over the Ruby Valley. The day before, Bill had stopped at the town's bike camp where I had arranged my sleeping gear on the concrete floor of the screened-in dining area. He was friendly, fit, and white-haired, wearing a ball cap, jeans, and tucked-in T-shirt. Founding the bike camp was his idea. I explained why I had installed myself in the camp's common space, citing the mosquito bites on my backside from the Big Hole. Rather than ask me to move, Bill laughed. Just before he left, he invited me to join him on an airplane ride in the morning. I was up for the adventure.

Apart from a long-sleeved shirt, Bill appeared to be wearing the same clothes I'd seen him in before. We sat at the picnic table in the food truck's parking lot and discussed the bike camp while I ate my breakfast burrito.

"How did the bike camp get funded?" I asked.

"We had some grants lined up, and then they fell through at the last minute. After all the publicity we'd done, we couldn't not do it, and no one in town would contribute."

"So you paid for it? And the donations go toward maintenance and paying you back?"

"Yeah," he said flatly.

"How much do you still need to cover it?"

"Fifty-five hundred dollars."

I considered my own donation of five dollars, which was the going rate for a night at a hiker-biker camp. "How much do people contribute to stay there?"

Bill was matter-of-fact. "Last year the average donation to the number of campers was three dollars and twelve cents. This year we've had more people using it. Guess what the average donation is."

With more campers, I hoped it would be higher. Given what I'd heard from other touring cyclists, there were those who would stay somewhere for free if they could and those who would happily pay for amenities. With an honor system and a sliding-scale donation, I guessed many campers skipped the donation but still took a shower and stayed the night. I shrugged in response to Bill's question, my mouth full.

"Three dollars and twelve cents."

I swallowed hard.

"Someone donated one hundred dollars once, and that was amazing," Bill said, sitting up straighter on the bench.

Seeing him get excited convinced me to send him $100 when I returned to Oregon.

"It's a unique thing in the area," Bill continued. "We didn't know what we were doing when we started, but now we're trying to help other communities set them up." He looked at me as I put the end of the burrito in my mouth. "Are you ready?"

"Yep," I said, my cheek bulging.

Bill opened the hangar and pulled the two-seater plane out. I was surprised to see how simple it was to maneuver the plane. I took pictures while Bill rolled it to the boarding area.

"Maybe I shouldn't have had that breakfast burrito. I've never flown in such a little plane before. Does it bounce and bump a lot?"

"I'll make it smooth. Shouldn't be a problem. But let me know if you start feeling uncomfortable." Bill fastened me in. I felt like a kid in a car seat. The plane had vintage car smell—old vinyl, motor oil, and electrical parts. He closed the door, came around the other side of the plane, and handed me a headset. "Here, you need to wear this."

I put the headset on, and everything he said after that was muffled.

Bill climbed in, fastened his seatbelt, put his headset on, and away we went. He told me what he was doing through the headset's scratchy radio.

With the front propeller whirring, Bill steered the plane onto an open grassy area at one end of the runway. He ran through his checks, called the air traffic controller, scanned the cloudless sky for planes. "We don't want to trade paint with anyone," he said. Without leaving the end of the grassy runway, he steered the plane in a small loop. "I look to see if there's any oil on the ground before we take off. It's better to find out if something isn't working down here than up there."

His attention to detail was reassuring. I was going on an unexpected adventure, and I would be safe.

Bill pointed the plane down the runway. The propeller whirred faster until it appeared to rotate in the opposite direction, the noise intensified, and the plane vibrated. Bill punched some buttons, flipped some switches, and the plane went forward with increasing speed.

Bill eased the plane into the air as if driving up a ramp.

We made a wide sweep around Twin Bridges. Bill pointed out the different rivers. A silvery braid caught my attention. "The Ruby has incredible oxbows from changing course," Bill said. "They say that you can float the Ruby all day and never get more than a half mile from where you started." I wasn't sure how that could happen, but I supposed being on the river floating would seem like a maze with all the little islands. I didn't ask if the currents were circular. The headset quieted the noise from the plane and made me feel as though I couldn't speak. The ride was surprisingly smooth, and I loved the novelty of traveling unconstrained by road or topography.

"Let's fly over the route you're going to take today," Bill said. "You'll get a sense of what it's like." It felt intimate—Bill's voice in my ears, the small space of the cockpit, the seatbelt's secure hold.

After we flew over Sheridan, a tiny patchwork of tan-colored town within an expansive green quilt, he gave me the controls.

"It's all yours," he said, letting go of his steering column. "Most people think you have to use the controls hard. Just a light touch."

There was a steering column in front of my seat, too. I tried it out. A thrill ran up and down my spine. I steered us right, toward the silver braid of the Ruby and then left. Uuuuup. Up. "How do I get it going back up," I said, breaking my silence. "Feels like we're falling."

"See this bug spot on the windshield?" Bill pointed. "Keep that on the horizon and you should stay level."

I gave the old bug-spot-on-the-windshield technique a try but couldn't get over the feeling that we were losing altitude. I kept trying to get the plane to move up by squeezing my butt cheeks together and lifting my pelvis from my pubic bone. It didn't work. I started to sweat.

"If you want me to drive so you can look, that's fine," Bill said.

"Yeah. I'd like that." Bill took the steering column, and I let go. The falling sensation went away.

The plane hummed. Below us, the road made a sharp bend up a bright green bluff.

"We should get you back," Bill said.

I nodded. It looked like a simple bike ride, but I'd be getting a late start.

"We're going a hundred-sixty miles an hour," Bill said. "Doesn't seem like it, does it?"

I couldn't tell if his eyes twinkled when he said this, hidden as they were behind his aviator sunglasses. I suspected they were because the whole landscape below us sparkled.

7.

Tough Girls

The day after my flight with Bill, I arrived overtired and cranky at the hostel in West Yellowstone around 10:00 AM. I'd hardly slept. I'd improvised a campsite at dusk at a rest area thirty miles away under some oozing pines and on ground littered with thorny seeds. I hadn't used my sleeping pad because I didn't want to puncture it.

"We have a room on the second floor," the woman at the front desk said.

"Can I check in right now?"

"Yes. It's available."

After wedging my bike in a corner of the room and changing into my dress, I fell onto the bed with the whine of the vacuum in the hall and didn't move again until 1:00 PM.

My grouchiness was gone when I woke. I showered and went out for lunch. In a café, I reflected on what it had taken to arrive here, which made me think of my six-and-a-half-year-old niece, Sonora. We shared an interest in creepy things, being outside, and toughness borne of being the youngest. She was precocious, heading to third grade in the fall, and a chatterbox.

Sonora understood that she and I were similar in being little sisters to big brothers.

My brother, Kent, is a year and a half older than I am.

As the younger sibling, I suffered for being smaller, weaker, and slower. By the time Kent was a senior in high school and I was a sophomore, he treated me with more kindness and invited me to some of his parties. After college, he chose a traditional path and married and had kids. He and his wife had a boy first, Aidan, and then Sonora. After Sonora was born, he and I discussed if there would be a karmic payback for him in raising offspring with a birth order that mirrored our own. From afar, I didn't know if this was the case, but I felt an energetic tug with my niece.

I wanted to be there for her in relating to her older brother, to empathize with the hurts, recognize her talents and unique interests, and acknowledge the ways that she was strong. While I didn't know if riding my bike across the country was my own six-year-old self fighting back a physically dominating brother, I wanted Sonora to know what was possible. I wrote her a letter as a blog post.

> Dear Sonora,
>
> Remember when you and I were climbing up that steep slope on Spencer's Butte in Eugene talking about annoying older brothers and being the little sister and being tough? Well, little sisters are tough.
>
> I'm riding my bike across the country by myself and carrying all my stuff. Somehow I'm proving my toughness to myself even though I already think I'm tough. Isn't

that weird? When I'm out riding, sometimes all I can think about is how hard it is to keep pedaling.

I left one town early in the morning and thought I would ride to the next town for breakfast. As soon as I got out on the road, the sign said 48 miles to the next town! I had two mountains to climb over. Ugh.

At the top of the first mountain, there was a sign, "Cows Ahead." There were a bunch of mama and baby cows. I rode through them like a cowgirl.

I made it into the town at lunchtime and found a frilly coffee shop. Even though I was sweaty from climbing mountains, I went in. I felt like a badass.

I made it to Twin Bridges that evening and had a yummy dinner at a place called The Shack. I liked that their menu said, "We don't fry everything here."

I stayed at an awesome biker camp where I met a nice man named Bill. It was his idea to build the camp. He talked to cyclists who came through town and thought they were interesting people, and the community ought to do something nice for them. Now there's this great place to stay. I told Bill my whole butt is a giant mosquito

bite because the mosquitoes were eating
on me all day. No joke. Now I have Itchy
Butt but not in the usual place. Then,
he invited me to go for a ride in his
airplane. Talk about adventure!

I hope you're having an awesome summer.
Practice riding your bike so we can pedal
places together.

Love, Aunt Heidi

---

dear aunt heidi,

i thot that yor mesig was kool. i lik
knoing wot you er doing. i remebr woking
on the hil toking obout oldr brothrs
beeing onoying.

i lik beeing tof to. we went bakpaking
last week and we klimbed the hiast mountin
in new mexico (weeler peek). i felt
exhaustid. mommy said i kod wait bot i
klimbd with evreewon else. we saw big horn
sheep playing in the sno. im glad i klimd
so i kod see the top.

wen you takt about the cows it remindid me
about the big black bear we saw yesterday.

sorry you haf a itchy butt i hav a itchy
head wer the mosquitos bit me.

tok to you soon.

love Sonora

Dear Sonora,

How awesome that you got to see a black
bear!!

I'm impressed that you climbed Wheeler
Peak. After the story your dad told about
it, sounds like a steep, challenging
climb.

You are Super Tof Girl!

Love, Aunt Heidi

8.

Wyoming, July 10th

Early morning of July 10, I rolled out of West Yellowstone, Montana. Warm air. Clear sky. Low-traffic road in good repair. Pine trees. Cliffy rocks topped with prairie grass. A lone bighorn sheep. My stomach pinched around my breakfast. My chest and throat constricted. I tried to bring my shoulders down from their reach toward my ears. The skin on my arms, legs, and head tingled. Three miles to Wyoming.

Sensory memories flooded me, impressing on me the visceral imprint of Wyoming. The gray, weathered wood of a building. The rattle of dry grasses and ghost talk in the wind. The taste of a bloody nose in the back of my throat. The smell of prairie—airborne dust mixed with sage.

I grew up in Cheyenne, the biggest city in the state, with 50,000 people, a mere nine-hour drive southeast from Jackson, the Tetons, and Yellowstone. Unlike the northwest corner of the state with these famous destinations and forests, rivers, and lakes, most of Wyoming is austere, dry, and wind scoured. This rugged square of land is the nation's tenth-largest state, only five hundred square miles smaller than Oregon, and the least populous with fewer than 583,000 residents.

Even Rhode Island and the District of Columbia have greater populations. Six people per square mile ranks Wyoming next to last in population density. It's a desolate, harsh place that spawns self-sufficiency and a hard exterior.

Sagebrush defines most of the state's arid landscape. This shrub will drop its leaves in times of extreme dryness but otherwise keeps them year-round. Wyoming big sagebrush grows abundantly with only eight to twelve inches of annual precipitation. To survive the dryness, sagebrush has a taproot that at night brings moisture near the surface to hydrate its fine net of roots. This net holds the soil in place and grabs for any surface precipitation. Wyoming's opportunistic state flower, Indian paintbrush, lives as a parasite on sagebrush roots. Pronghorn antelope, North America's fastest land mammal and goatlike in its genetic lineage, subsists on sagebrush.

When my brother and I were young, this landscape served as our playground. Outside our house, we scampered about the fields to catch grasshoppers and garter snakes, dig in the drainage ditch we called the Canyon, and make caves in winter's snowdrifts. In summer, thunderstorms billowed up in the afternoons, alive with lightning and thunder, and dropped rain or hail for fifteen minutes and then moved on. If we were lucky, we would see a tornado, stepping outside during the wail of air strike sirens that warned of extreme weather. Once during one of these warnings, we had a clear view of a tornado at the end of our street. The curvy rattail of a funnel cloud waggled from a low, gray cloud and wasn't destructive, though many of them were.

Wind made any weather more extreme. It sandblasted everything in summer and made winters colder, driving needlelike ice into exposed flesh. One harsh winter decimated the antelope. We saw their corpses littering the barbed wire fence lines as we drove Interstate 80 near Rawlins.

If it wasn't extreme weather that challenged any being's will to survive, it was other threats. In Yellowstone and other places, boiling water bubbled from the ground. The earth around these hot springs was fragile. When I was four, Mom explained that if I stepped on the pretty parts of the hot springs or even stepped off the walking path, I might break through the ground and cook to death.

The desolate landscape, while beautiful, was also its own danger. During a hunting trip, Mom drove the car into a creek but couldn't get it out. In the time before cell phones, we were too far from anyone to get help. With the jack, a small shovel, and the rocks in the creek, we moved the car enough for the tires to gain traction and the four-wheel drive to get us out, but it took hours.

This environment taught me self-reliance. It also taught me to stuff down my feelings. I was five the first time I heard a rabbit scream. My rabbit. In a hutch out back. A neighborhood dog had visited our unfenced backyard at night and ripped into the hutch, mauling my pet.

My parents returned to Cheyenne in 1977 after my dad completed his pediatric dental residency in South Carolina. My brother was four, and I was two. My dad had been stationed at Warren Air Force Base in Cheyenne before his residency, and when my parents were considering where they wanted to live after South Carolina, they thought Cheyenne would be a good place to raise children. They bought a house on a hill at the north end of town.

My parents had also been eyeing a derelict building in downtown Cheyenne, an 1883 cattle baron's mansion. When Dad's father visited

Wyoming from New York in 1979, he told my parents that living in and rehabbing the historic mansion would kill their marriage. Heeding his advice, my parents built a passive solar house on the north end of town, which we moved into in 1980. The solar house was in the same neighborhood as the house on the hill. In 1981 when I was six, my parents bought the historic mansion with the intent to turn it into a fine-dining restaurant.

The restaurant had been open two months by the time I turned twelve. Because I was so young, there wasn't much I could do in the front of the house, such as busing tables, which my brother did. I spent my time in the kitchen. My first paid job at the restaurant was helping the pastry chef stretch strudel dough every Saturday morning for a month.

After the restaurant had been open for several months, Mom gave me a paid back-of-the-house job I did any time I was at the restaurant: wash, dry, and fold the tablecloths. During lulls in the laundry cycle and even when I wasn't working, I hung out in the kitchen. I stood next to the cold line and watched Lou prep lettuce, make salads, assemble appetizers, and plate desserts. My brain was sticky. I remembered the details of everything. When he got busy, I helped.

I loved being part of this activity. The restaurant staff were my friends and didn't judge me for my brains or lack of athleticism. I was smart, which was a social liability at school because it was cool to get bad grades. I wasn't good enough at volleyball to be on the varsity team or even enjoy practice, so I quit. The staff were adults and experienced in their different ways: Lou came from Florida with his wife who was in the military, Jeff was gay, Laurie was a recovering alcoholic, and Sonya was anorexic, but before she lost her muscle, she had ridden her bike up the Alps with guy friends.

I went through puberty at the restaurant. On my inaugural strudel dough Saturday, I had the first pimple of my life making a painful point on my forehead. Mom gave me *Period* when I was thirteen, and I read it at the restaurant. By the time I was fourteen and read about masturbation in eighth grade home ec class, I still hadn't started my period.

One sunny afternoon, I closed the restaurant's office door and climbed on one of the chairs and helped myself to a tampon. Mom kept a box each of pads and applicator tampons on a shelf over the door for staff and customers. The office was a glorified closet on the second floor in the back of the house. There was a west-facing window and enough room at the desk for two chairs. It was a good place to escape for privacy.

I crawled under the desk and inspected the tampon. The pink plastic tube had a plus-shaped cut on the fat end and a string hanging out the narrow end. I figured a person could masturbate with an applicator tampon. I unzipped my pants and pulled my underwear down in front. I positioned the tampon, but it didn't go very far. I was perplexed.

Period said it didn't hurt to use a tampon, and the drawings showed what one looked like when inserted. I probed places that didn't yield and then gave up. Maybe that was why people didn't talk about masturbating with applicator tampons—it didn't work.

I zipped my pants up and pushed the tampon through the applicator. In the women's restroom upstairs, I ran water on the tampon and watched it expand. I squeezed the water out and threw the applicator and tampon in the sanitary can.

One July night later that year, I stood on the restaurant's front porch, wearing my oldest cousin's ivory-colored lace prom dress. Her younger sister, Aimée, who was almost a year older than I, was on the porch with me in her shimmery black dress. Dad was in his tailcoat tux. The three of us had been out dancing during a black-tie formal as part of Wyoming's statehood centennial celebration. Mom took our picture. It was the summer I grew breasts. The summer I started my period (at the restaurant).

I looked slim and beautiful.

The restaurant attracted regulars but mostly served patrons celebrating birthdays, anniversaries, holidays, and other special occasions. Mom developed events, such as Lobster Fest and Murder Mystery Night, to fill some of the quieter times of year, but even with bursts of patronage, it was difficult to keep the restaurant afloat when many of the customers came from out of state.

My parents closed the restaurant after five years of operation on a high note: New Year's Eve. Fine dining was a tough sell.

When the restaurant closed, I was a junior in high school. I'd learned that my parents, who'd come from the East Coast, were outsiders in the community, a perception that persisted despite what they did and how long we lived in the state. Politics rarely came up. Mom explained that party affiliation wasn't private, so they insulated themselves from judgment by registering as Independents. Growing up, I didn't know how my parents voted, and I was well into my twenties before I cast my first vote for anything. Meanwhile, Dick Cheney served as Secretary of Defense during Operation Desert Storm, and I was proud. Someone from Wyoming was on national news. Bill Clinton came to Cheyenne the year the restaurant closed, and I went with a girlfriend to the airport hangar where he spoke. I wouldn't be old enough to vote, but his visit was as much celebrity as I ever experienced in Cheyenne.

I knew college would be my ticket out of Wyoming, and I started plotting my escape in ninth grade. Most of my college-bound peers were headed to the University of Wyoming, forty-five miles west of Cheyenne in Laramie. The East Coast lured me. I wanted to become a marine biologist and swim with whales, although the only ocean I lived near was the one of sagebrush all around me. Still, I used this interest, which would fizzle after my first year, as a filter and came up with a short list of schools.

Intellectual challenge was a high priority but not a requirement. Elite schools had geographic diversity targets, and being from Wyoming gave me a competitive advantage in admission. I searched for the most competitive schools and eliminated those that emphasized core curriculum.

I applied to Colgate University and Brown University and was accepted at Colgate, so upstate New York became home. I thought if I got far away from Wyoming and the bonds of its physical and cultural climates, I could escape the punishment of daring to survive. If I could have scissor snipped Wyoming from my life, I would have. I tried.

Who could I be if no one knew who I had been?

Even though college gave me an opportunity to re-create myself, I learned there were things about Wyoming that anchored me to who I was that couldn't be cut. It was as if my sense of who I was, as a place, was Wyoming. Nothing made the dry, abrading harshness go away, and the gentleness that came with moist, still air could not reach me.

Most of the year after I graduated from college I spent in Cheyenne with my parents. While I was there, my dad's office manager's seventeen-year-old son was fatally stabbed in the heart. Not long after, I had a chance encounter with a high school classmate who told me that John Candelaria, whom I remembered as the quiet and polite guy who sat behind me in high school chemistry class, had been shot in the face and killed during his freshman year at UW. Right around this time, news of the horrific death of Matthew Shepard shocked the nation. I was repulsed that a place that had marked me so fundamentally was the same place that gave rise to these savage crimes.

I did not want the hatred, cruelty, and intolerance that seemed to breed in Wyoming. How was it possible for me to grow from this desert and not also have venom in me?

On my bike, I felt this vibration of the past. Wyoming's mark in me was deep, and like the Indian paintbrush, its roots were entangled in my core self. I knew how to push through pain and adversity. This ability disturbed me, but I was proud of it, too.

And here I was about to cross the state line on July 10, Wyoming's Statehood Day and my brother's birthday. I pedaled across the unsigned state line in a landscape of grass, rocks, and trees. To mark the occasion, I mentally dashed off a birthday greeting to my brother. He hadn't been in Wyoming since 2001, the year my parents moved out of state.

Happy Birthday Brother.

I just crossed into Wyoming. It's weird to come "home" to this place where we grew up.

I've pedaled across three states and crossed the Continental Divide for this timely moment.

I feel like I'm tempting fate. After all the ways I survived growing up here and the extreme places it pushed me, I'm afraid it might kill me this time.

While I am solo, otherwise vulnerable in the middle of nowhere, and considering the likelihood of my demise, I want you to know:

- *I am wearing a helmet.*

- *I have a sag wagon tucked in my pannier.*

- *I have a cell phone. I keep it turned off between towns so it has battery life for when I might need it. There isn't a lot of cell service out here, so if something did happen, I'm not sure how much use it would be. But better to have one than not, eh?*

If Wyoming kills me before I have a chance to call you and wish you a happy birthday, I want you to know that I love you. My wounded girl self is pouty about me saying this, but she and I have many miles across the state to discuss her pain. Besides, it's not your concern. I know she wants you to fix it, but you can't.

Let's go with love. I hope you're having grand adventures this day.

Your Sister the Badass

9.

Yellowstone National Park

I paid my entrance fee to Yellowstone National Park. Even though Yellowstone was in my home state, I had only been to the park once, twenty-nine years prior. The ranger staffing the entrance booth handed me a park map and said, "Be careful out there with all the traffic."

"Do you mean the RVs and big vehicles because they're not accustomed to bikes?" I wasn't sure what her concern was—me or everyone else.

"Yes" was her colorless reply.

National Parks are the great American driving experience. Visiting the parks is like going to a museum, and because the museum is a landscape, people go from exhibit to exhibit in a car or SUV or RV. I wasn't any different in this regard except in my choice of vehicle.

A bicycle allows for a complete sensory experience of landscape while covering more distance than is possible on foot. Smells, sounds, textures, and sights enliven the body in motion.

Sudden differences in air temperature or velocity alerted me to landscape features or microclimates. I knew when I was near a dead animal, water, hot springs. A meadowlark called me back to my childhood with two pure whistled notes, then the burble of a water pipe. Columbines' star-shaped splats of yellow dotted the grassy road edges. Pink elephants stood tall in the bogs, and Indian paintbrush colored the drier areas in fat red strokes.

Ahead was a clot of stopped vehicles. Two bison grazed next to the roadway. People swarmed them, taking pictures. Cars were stopped in the travel lane; others were partway off the road.

Signs I had already passed cautioned people about wild animals in the park. On bike, I had no protection from an encounter with a 1,400-pound bison. In open range such as this, I planned to ride as fast as I could past the beasts or wait for them to clear the road. But more than the bison, I was concerned about my vulnerability around the cars and their people, as the ranger said when I entered the park. The potential of being doored by someone getting out of a vehicle was high.

I pulled into the oncoming travel lane, which was clear, and zoomed past the vehicles and bison. Not many vehicles passed me as I made my way deeper into the park. The road wound through forest that had burned and reseeded in 1988, the largest burn in Yellowstone's history when nearly 800,000 acres were destroyed. Charred trees stood in seas of twenty-year-old saplings.

Ahead, a two-paneled sign read, CAUTION WILDLIFE ON ROADWAY and BICYCLISTS AND PEDESTRIANS NEXT 16 MI. I was wildlife! Would people stop their cars to take pictures of me? If they did, I would welcome it. Daniel had e-mailed to suggest pictures of me would improve my blog. I hadn't considered that my readers would want to see *me* instead of just seeing what I saw. Getting pictures of myself wasn't easy. It was the time before selfie cameras. I had Photobooth on my laptop, but I only got my computer out when I planned to stay somewhere for a while.

I stopped on the side of the road to photograph a cluster of columbine. Straddling my bike, I bent forward and twisted to frame the shot. Just then, another cyclist passed me with a ring of his bell and a "Hello." I was embarrassed. He must have had an eyeful of my ass. At the next parking area, I saw his bike, identifiable with its BOB trailer. I didn't stop.

At Old Faithful Lodge, I bought a cup of tea and sat on the sunny upper patio.

"Hey, I'm not following you," the guy's voice came from my left.

I turned and recognized the cyclist who'd passed me earlier by his blue plaid shirt. He wore bug-eyed orange sunglasses, had thick, dark brown hair, and showed his long upper teeth with his smile.

"Hi!" I said and felt my cheeks warm.

"Are you going to Craig or West Thumb?"

Neither place sounded familiar. I pulled my map out. "Where?"

"Craig, the first big pass."

I still didn't know where he was talking about and searched my map. "Where?" I looked up at him.

He sat down on the bench next to me.

The cyclist took my map. He pointed to Craig Pass, the second crossing of the Continental Divide on my route and the first one in Wyoming. "Here." He traced the road up to Yellowstone Lake. "And here's West Thumb."

"Oh. I'm going that way but will likely stay outside the park tonight. I don't need to be around so many people. Are you going to watch Old Faithful?"

"I'm not sure. I stopped to get some water and saw your bike out front. Thought it would be nice to say hi since we passed each other a few times already this morning."

"Ah, so you are following me." I gave him a sideways look. He looked young and fit. "Old Faithful should erupt in about ten minutes. I'm going to wait for it."

"So where are you headed?" His body had ease, like he wasn't weighed down by worry.

"Washington, DC, for a historic roads conference."

"That's aggressive." He looked straight at me.

"It doesn't leave me a lot of time to sightsee." I looked back toward the mound of Old Faithful.

"I suppose. But you're seeing stuff all day wherever you are."

"True." I glanced at him. He was looking toward Old Faithful. "I like being surprised by what catches my attention." My cheeks tingled.

"People develop false expectations of the wild," he said. "Undeveloped places are perceived as Edens where animals and humans live abundantly and peacefully together. There are no predators, and nothing ever dies or is destroyed."

"You know, most of the wildlife I've seen is dead on the road. The carnage is awful, but I still find beauty in it. And I learn about the local fauna."

"You're sick."

I couldn't tell if he was repulsed or being playful. "Come on. Tell me you don't look."

"No, seriously. It bothers me that people kill things with vehicles. It's so violent."

His concern surprised me. "I'm not condoning killing things, especially using blunt force," I said. "If the only way I can get a good look at an animal is to see it dead, I will take that opportunity."

"How many of the people down there"—he gave a nod toward the crowd on the boardwalk— "would want their money back if they didn't see any wildlife?" He looked at me. "And I mean alive."

I smiled. "Yes. They would want their money back if the only animals they saw were dead." I considered the WILDLIFE ON ROADWAY sign and figured he wasn't referring to us as valid wildlife sightings. "They do the darndest things, like try to pet the bison."

"They have no sense of how dangerous that is. They see people playing with seemingly wild animals on TV or YouTube and think that's the norm rather than the exception. They don't even consider that those animals might be trained."

I could see his point but maybe they thought the animals were friendly because they weren't in enclosures, like at a zoo. "I guess it's important to remember that most people who visit here have never seen bison or elk or undeveloped land."

Steam billowed out of the geyser vent.

He continued, "Most people don't interact with the environment even if they get out of the car, watch Old Faithful go off, and buy an ice cream."

"For people who are inexperienced with nature," I countered, "there are threats here that would keep them in their cars. For one, the ground can collapse and burn you to death."

At the geyser mound, water boiled out of the earth. Each ejection went higher. As tall as a five-story building, I guessed. And in similar succession, the spray subsided. Half the people departed the ground-level observation area en masse before the eruption was over. I supposed they only cared to see how high the water went. Maybe some were anxious about keeping to a schedule or avoiding lines in the restroom. Still, it saddened me that they had traveled the distance to get here and then turned their backs on the display.

I took a picture of the people leaving, the plume of Old Faithful behind them.

The cyclist and I continued our discussion. Old Faithful returned to a white mound in the distance.

"I need to get moving," I said. "I know you weren't following me." I paused as a replacement for a wink since neither of us could see the other's eyes through our sunglasses. "But thanks for finding me and saying hi."

He looked at me, and his smile twinkled.

"I'm Heidi, by the way." I extended my hand toward him.

"JD." He gave my hand a firm, single shake before letting go. "Do you want to ride together?"

I couldn't tell if JD was hitting on me or just being friendly. "I don't want to slow you down." If JD was being friendly, of course I should ride with him. If it was more than that? I didn't know. Would Daniel care if I rode with JD? Did it matter? Daniel was following along on my blog and sending me occasional e-mails but hadn't signaled wanting more than our casual arrangement. What if I found someone new on this ride? Did I want that?

"Let's just see how it goes. We should go at a pace that works for both of us. If it doesn't work, we're free to go our separate ways."

"That sounds sensible."

JD had only a few big gears on his bike. Big gears are hard to pedal, and they move a bike farther with each pedal rotation than smaller gears. Even though I expected JD would ride faster than me on the hills, I felt like a puny girl as he climbed and lengthened the distance between us. But on the downhills, I shifted into high gear and shot past him.

After two climbs, I let go of my inhibitions about riding with JD. My slowing him down didn't seem to be a concern he shared.

When I reached the crest of Craig Pass, JD was slathering sunscreen on his arms. His bike was parked against the sign CONTINENTAL DIVIDE ELEVATION 8262. We traded cameras. I took a picture of him with his bike. I intended to stand in front of the sign without my bike, but he encouraged me to include it in the photo. There was a short slope, and at the top, the front of my bike with its loaded panniers tipped and fell. I struggled with the weight, resituated my bike, and posed with a big smile.

JD chuckled.

"That was embarrassing," I said.

"I got it," he showed me the blooper shot.

"Ha! That's pretty good. You also got the posed shot?"

He advanced to a picture of me with an on-top-of-the-world smile in front of the sign. "Says it all." He handed the camera back. A smile crooked half his mouth.

As the dividing line between the Pacific and Atlantic watersheds, the Continental Divide is the nation's spine and follows the Rocky Mountains. Ten miles from Craig Pass, we came to our second crossing of the Divide and took pictures without the bikes. Eight miles farther, we came to the third crossing on a downhill and didn't stop.

With traffic concentrated in the hot springs and geyser area, we had open road. We spent the day passing each other and stopped twice for snacks and to talk. He said that he was completing a move to Jackson, Wyoming, and that he had lived and worked seasonally in Lander, Wyoming. He was a National Outdoor Leadership School (NOLS) instructor.

Alone for a stretch on the road, feeling saddle sore and ready to be done pedaling for the day, I glanced at my watch. There was plenty of light in the sky, but 6:00 PM was past dinner.

I caught up to JD at a pullout. He had parked his bike against a dumpster and lay on the pavement eating a brown ball out of a plastic wrapper.

"Want one?" he asked.

"What is it?"

"It's like a Larabar. Dates, almonds. A friend made a bunch for me before I left."

"Yeah. Thanks." I stood on the pavement staring at him blankly while he rummaged in his bag.

"Here." He handed me a wrapped ball and then lay back on the pavement. "You should lie down."

"I'm afraid I won't get back up if I do."

He stretched from head to toe and let his body relax. The hard, gravelly pavement called to me. I didn't care that it was next to a dumpster. Gravity pulled me down.

The ball was real food, oily on the outside but soft and sweet with nut chunks. Gravel dug into my shoulders and backside. The dumpster wafted Glad bags and sour milk.

I was in heaven.

Eventually, JD broke the silence. "We should get up."

I didn't hear him move. "I'm not ready." I kept my body still. "It's so pretty here."

"We should get up." He didn't move.

"To what end?"

He took a deep breath and let it out. "Well, we could get a camp-site and make some dinner. I have a stove and some rice."

"That sounds nice. That would require getting up, wouldn't it?"

He stood and brushed the gravel off his backside. I tried to sit up, but nothing happened. JD reached a hand to me. I lifted my arm and grabbed his hand. He helped me to sit and then stand. I brushed off the gravel that had stuck to me.

After pedaling only half a mile, we turned at Colter Bay where there was a campground and grocery store. We split the cost of the $14 campsite and passed several other hiker-biker campers en route to our site.

"You take the bigger spot since you have a tent," JD said.

"You're sure?"

"Yeah. I just have a bivvy bag."

I set up my shelter and changed into non-biking clothes. I emerged dressed in double layers to fend off mosquitoes.

We walked to the store for rice accompaniments.

"You know you have a hitch in your giddyup?" he asked.

"Yeah."

"What's wrong?"

"I don't know. My left hip zaps me if I straighten my leg."

"Would you rather ride?"

"No. I've had enough today. Does it show when I ride?"

"Yes."

I was touched that he noticed, and we left it at that. I didn't want to be perceived as weak or foolish, and I already had a lot to over-come being a woman alone. The issue with my hip was one more thing, and since I didn't have a diagnosis, it hadn't seemed worth mentioning. I wasn't raising awareness about people with physical disabilities or adaptive recreation. My cause was rural communities —keeping them on the map and improving access in ways that maintained their charm and uniqueness. The Interstate System had altered rural America. Small towns that had once been rest areas found themselves bypassed and in decline, their economies struggling. New infrastructure grew at Interstate interchanges where travelers' stops were short, impersonal, and predictable. Bicycle tourism, because it was slow and avoided the Interstates, had potential to boost economic activity in these small towns. The experiences in these towns were varied and authentic.

At the store, we bought frozen vegetable medley, sausage, tomatoes, and onions. JD sequenced all the cooking in one small titanium pot. I dug in my panniers for my bowl and spoon. Voilà, dinner.

We talked into the dark.

JD sat on the picnic table and talked while I flossed and brushed my teeth. When I finished, I said, "I wish I had the energy to stay up all night, but I can't even sit up anymore. Would you like to share space under my tarp?"

He was quiet a moment. "Yeah."

I had just squiggled into my sleeping bag when he appeared with his sleeping pad and bivvy sack. He settled in and talked.

"Please don't take it personally if I fall asleep," I said.

"What if we just fall asleep?"

"Okay," I said softly. "I'm just about there."

He crinkled in his bivvy, and then the thick silence of the campground descended.

10.

See You Down the Dusty Road

The next morning, I had difficulty opening my eyes. I climbed over JD, who didn't stir, and visited the restroom. Mosquitoes had bitten my eyebrows, and it looked like I had a mosquito bite on one eyelid. My right eye was swollen half shut.

When I returned to camp, JD was arranging his gear.

"Why do I feel like yesterday was a long day?" I said.

JD looked at me, his hair standing straight up like a shock of wheat.

I liked that he was at ease with his impressive bedhead. I was self-conscious about my eyes. "Please ignore the fact that I look like I've been punched in the face," I said.

He gave me a long, quiet look. I stood there uncomfortably, looking back at him. "Do you want any hot water?" he asked with a smile.

"Yes, please. Thank you."

While JD heated water, I checked my map. "Eighty-eight miles," I said with some surprise. "So, yesterday was a long day. Sorry if I cut your adventure in Yellowstone short."

"You didn't cut anything short." He poured boiling water into my bowl, and I dunked my tea bag a few times.

I hadn't asked him what he was really doing in Yellowstone. Probably, he didn't know. Like him, I had a pat answer for what I was doing on my bike—riding to a conference in Washington, DC, and researching bicycle tourism and rural economic development—but that project wasn't really why I was on my bike. I was forcing a change in my life. I had hopes—a leaner body, career, partner—but I couldn't know what the outcome would be.

Given everything unexpected on the trip already, I could rely on being surprised by my own change.

I enjoyed JD's company. I liked how catching up to him was like a dance. How I started to understand that he didn't ride ahead of me to make me feel puny but that he really wanted to ride with me. Or maybe he didn't even want to ride with me but since that's what I was doing, he came along. I couldn't believe someone would want to join me. I didn't want to have to consider someone else's needs, but he didn't ask anything of me. If anything, he gave me help where I needed it, like the sweet ball at the dumpster and encouraging me on simply by being out there with me.

If JD hadn't said hello, I would have pedaled away from Old Faithful and maybe stopped for a photo here and there and a five-minute break to eat a Builders Bar. I would have arrived in Colter Bay an hour earlier, maybe two, eaten at the restaurant, looked through my photos, thought about what I would write in a blog post, and fallen asleep before dark.

But he did say hello. What came next?

I scanned the day's route. Dubois was the closest town with full services and lay sixty-six miles from Colter Bay. To get there, I would climb Togwotee Pass—fifteen miles and 2,600 feet to the Divide crossing at 9,658 feet. Only the first six of those sixty-six miles would overlap with JD's route to Jackson.

I sipped tea. JD ate oatmeal.

One of the other cyclists staying at the campground, Mike, whom I'd met in Twin Bridges, stopped by. He was about my age, wore glasses, and his tall, slim body looked ready to ride in black cycling shorts and a fluorescent yellow wind jacket.

"I'm going to take the pass slow," he said, "stop a lot, take pictures."

"Cool," I said. "Sounds like a great approach. See you down the road."

JD and I packed up camp not long after. We pedaled and talked. At a viewpoint, we took pictures. Everything between us felt comfortable and easy. Less than a quarter mile from the viewpoint was his turn to Jackson. We stopped.

"Well," he said, "that was fun."

"Indeed." I wanted to say something that captured how much I enjoyed our time together, that conveyed how much I didn't want to say goodbye, that hinted at what it might be like if we could continue our adventure together, but I couldn't scrape together more than the one word.

We hugged. He smiled.

"See you down the dusty road," he said and pedaled on with a wave.

"See you down the dusty road," I called after him. The inside of my throat thickened and the skin at the top of my cheekbones tingled.

I pedaled toward the pass. I felt a pull to follow JD. A tear squeezed out the corner of my left eye. Then my right.

I caught up to Mike within a mile from where JD turned, and we rode together.

"Look, a bald eagle!" I squealed. Mike stopped to take pictures of it standing in its nest, and I continued pedaling.

"Elk!" I squealed. I grabbed my camera from its storage pack on my top tube and took a picture in motion.

While I took a break at Togwotee Lodge, Mike caught up to me.

"Here," he said. "I stopped at the ranger station to get some information on camping in Wyoming. I got a map for you."

"Thanks," I said, touched by his thoughtfulness. I looked at the map and then tucked it into my red go-bag.

"The road is under construction. There are some gravel segments, and we may have to ride in the pilot car."

I hoped that wasn't the case. Being driven up the pass seemed like cheating.

Mike and I pedaled away from the lodge together. When we came to the first construction stop, flaggers instructed us into the pilot car. I was irritated to have no choice.

During the car ride, I took some action photos. The selfies were bad and reflective of how I felt. I would post one. It seemed real.

After the second of three pilot car rides, Mike and I pedaled to the top of the pass, an unsigned, mauled mountainside. We didn't stop, didn't take a picture.

After the third pilot car ride, Mike and I split up. I watched him descend out of sight on his way to a campground past Dubois.

I stood astride my bike. Hot wind plastered my riding jersey against my back. The soil matched the color of the sagebrush that lumped the landscape. The insides of my nostrils tightened. I knew this Wyoming—it broke people.

One westward-traveling cyclist told me that the first car ride he'd taken was in Wyoming to get through the headwind. He paid someone to drive him from one town to the next.

Not me. Not today. With my back to the wind, I flew.

When I reached Dubois, the Facebook post wrote itself.

 A motel lured me in with BIKERS WELCOME on their sign along with WE HAVE WIFI. It was across the street from the laundromat. I was sweat crusted and reeked. I bit hard.

When I walked across the street to the laundromat, the wind blew dry my hair.

11.

Lander

The road out of Dubois was eerily empty. Warm air touched my face. I welcomed its softness. In my freshly laundered riding clothes, I armored my skin against the sun's intensity across this mostly treeless state. My face, neck, and fingertips were the only exposed skin but with sunscreen. The day would be seventy-four miles, mostly downhill and through the Wind River Indian Reservation. Lander, my evening destination, sat 1,700 feet lower than Dubois just outside the reservation.

Cloudless blue sky. Pale green grasses and lumps of sage dotted rust-colored slopes. Pinky orange rock cliffs seemed soft like nougat and made me want to bite into them.

By early afternoon, I arrived in Lander—population nine thousand—a large town compared to most I visited. I rode the main street and passed a bike shop and a climbing shop. Downtown's storefronts were occupied with businesses, and the historic buildings were in good repair.

"Bookstore with pastries. There." Sometimes I needed to say something aloud to remember my voice worked. I pulled over and leaned my bike against the wall. To my surprise, NOLS was across the street, and I went there first. I hoped I could send mail to JD. The tan woman at the reception desk couldn't find him in her database.

Disappointment filled my body.

"He said he works here?" the woman asked.

"He said he *worked* here. Maybe it's been a while." I doubted JD would have lied about being a NOLS instructor.

"Yeah, I don't know." She straightened her head and shrugged.

"Thanks for looking."

At the bookstore, I opened my laptop at a table with a view of the street and my bike.

I checked Warmshowers.org for lodging. Warmshowers is an international online network of hosts and bike tourers. Hosts offer lodging—yards, floors, couches, spare beds—and either provide kitchen space or feed guests. It's a free, pay-it-forward service. Not every host has to be a bike tourer, but it adds to the experience to stay with people who have also toured.

Ever since Linda in Halfway surprised me at the library with an invitation to her home and mentioned that she and another household in Halfway were on Warmshowers, I'd been tempted to try it in a place I didn't think would have hosts. My guts did a little cartwheel when search results returned one host, Jim. Jim's profile mentioned wanting a day or two of notice. I sent an e-mail requesting lodging and apologized for the late notice.

While I waited for a response, I blogged about Yellowstone and then wrote a note on the paper backing of a sticker JD encouraged me to buy in Colter Bay. I sealed it in an envelope I made with a piece of paper and the black masking tape from my art kit. I slipped it into my journal, not sure when or if I would ever send it.

"Wow, you're going light," Jim said when I met him outside the bookstore. "Impressive." He was also on two wheels and had just finished work for the day.

"Two panniers isn't much volume, but they're not light."

We pedaled through streets lined with cottonwoods that made a complete canopy.

"How long have you lived in Lander?" I asked.

"Twenty-five years. I came here after I finished school because I got a job that fit all my criteria. I'm a CPA. Now, I'm the deputy treasurer for the county."

"That sounds like important work. How's the county doing?"

"Well," he said. I thought he was collecting his thoughts but then realized he'd spoken it with a period at the end, not a comma— *Well. The County is doing well.* "Wyoming is a mineral-rich state, particularly in gas and oil, so when things are going poorly for the rest of the country, we tend to do okay. Conversely, when the rest of the country is doing well, we often don't."

At the house, I met Julia, a tidy woman with shoulder-length graying blond hair and glasses who welcomed me warmly. She gave me a quick tour.

I took a shower and emerged to the aromas of Jim's hamburger scramble. We dined in the lush backyard. All the greens in the salad came from their garden.

After dinner, Jim left to till someone's yard, and Julia and I chatted over the dishes. She recently retired from teaching math and science, partly because of a head injury she sustained from ice skating two years prior. She grew up in Lander and earned a PhD in engineering from the University of Wyoming.

"My dad was a dentist," Julia said, "and when I was growing up, he used to wrangle me into being his assistant during emergencies."

"Mine too!" I practically interrupted her.

"I wonder if they knew each other."

"Let's find out." I e-mailed Mom, and she responded.

No kiddin! Bill directed the marginal dental program for years and Dad provided a great deal of care for marginal patients.

When we first moved to Cheyenne, Bill gave dad some very astute business advice: "Charge what you need to, to meet your costs."

Ahhhh Wyoming. Small town with very long streets.

Love,

Yomomma

Julia and I were tickled by the coincidence.

Jim returned from his good neighbor task and joined me and Julia at the dining room table. He mentioned that the woman whose yard he tilled had been selected for jury duty.

"Oh, she'll be really good," Julia said. "We need good jurors."

"What kind of case?" I asked.

"Murder," Jim said.

"Murder?" Lander seemed safe. "I didn't think you had homicide issues in small towns. Everyone I've talked to so far has mentioned the absence of crime being one of the reasons they live rurally."

"With the reservation close, we get a fair bit of conflict," Jim said. "The Shoshone and Arapaho were warring tribes, and now they're on the same reservation. Also, the reservation has an incredible amount of mineral resource, and groups come up and try to take advantage of the riches, which also causes conflict."

"Generally, we find it safe here," Julia said. "Lander is a mix of independently wealthy to welfare. Having NOLS in town changes the demographics of the place. And if you go to Riverton—it's part of the Reservation, and it's not—things are different. As a teacher, I would hear all kinds of things, the kind of stuff you wouldn't just hear around town. I would ask new kids why they came to the area, and sometimes they would say, 'To live on welfare.' They didn't know what that meant. Their parents wouldn't tell you that's what brought them here."

After conversation that steered us away from the murder case and welfare, we went to bed.

12.

Blood

In the morning of day twenty-three, I discovered my period had begun. I wanted nothing between me and the chamois of my bike shorts while I bled, not even a string. I was afraid of abrasion. My menstrual cycle generally didn't produce intense flow, and the chamois in my riding shorts was designed to disperse moisture. The padded area was sewn to black Lycra, which wouldn't show blood if it soaked through. I could rinse my shorts out in the evening.

With a full quantity of water, sun protection, and energy food, I pedaled out. I didn't feel any cramps, which meant I wasn't bleeding much.

As I left the last shade I would likely see until the southern border of the state, I recalled Jim's words that morning: "It will be up and down and then a climb up Beaver Ridge. When you get to the top, be sure to look back. It's beautiful."

I pedaled through the searing, gusty landscape southeast of Lander toward Beaver Ridge. Sagebrush tacked the earth down across the expanse.

Three hours from Lander, I stopped at the Beaver Ridge interpretive sign and looked back toward the odd, green patch of Lander in the distance—not unlike a desert oasis. The wind snatched the air before I breathed it.

I turned from the vista and faced the sagebrush. The vast landscape in this direction was beautiful in an uncomfortable way, like witnessing someone bawl.

Cramps crimped my abdomen and tensed the muscles in my lower back. Most of me wanted to get fetal. My girl body wanted to take the day off. My inner taskmaster refused. The desolate, lidless July day scorched, compelling me onward, but I needed to rest.

Sweetwater Station, the nearest place with water and toilet paper, was twenty miles away. I scanned the terrain for a place to shit.

Atop the bluff, I searched for a crack or swell—a shield from the cars that probably wouldn't pass by. I mostly didn't care if anyone in a car saw me with my drawers down.

I leaned my bike against a fence post and crossed between the lines of barbed wire, careful not to get snagged.

The imprint of growing up in Wyoming pressed on me here even though it had been seven years since I last drove through the high plains. The simple motion of crossing through barbed wire brought back childhood memories with a clarity that surprised me, my brother stepping on the lower line and lifting the upper line, making the opening larger for me. Though I liked to think I didn't need his help getting through the fences, he probably saved several pairs of pants from being ripped.

I saw my brother and me outside after a thunderstorm had passed. He was eight, and I was six. We collected worms that were escaping the storm's gush and dropped them in a pile on the sidewalk. All those worms wriggled and stretched in a shiny mass on the sidewalk.

I stood there in my pink shirt, jeans, and pink shoes looking down at them, wondering why they came out when it rained. The mound started to flatten as the worms began their trek across the sidewalk.

My brother used the edge of his hands to sweep them back together and then pushed me away.

"Stand back," he said.

He kicked his foot into the pile. Again and again, he smeared the worms between his shoe and the sidewalk.

I was horrified. It happened so fast, and I didn't expect it. I couldn't save the worms, couldn't stop him.

As a child in Wyoming, I felt a constant need to catch up, to compensate for being younger and a girl, to be as strong as my brother, to give him an experience of the hurt he inflicted on me. No matter how I fought back, I could never hit him as hard as he punched me. I could never outrun him, my shirts pulled and stretched in his hands, my long hair ripped, my shins and arms bruised. Over what? Because I wouldn't do what he wanted. Because I tried to take back the colored pastels he stole. Because I rolled double sixes when we played Parcheesi.

I tended to forget the ways he cared.

When we were kids, we made forts in the basement and watched TV in the hot tub in the greenhouse until our palms pruned. Sometimes, he invited me on his trespasses to catch snakes.

One weekend, the summer after my first year in college, we were both home at the same time. The two of us set off on mountain bikes to meet his friend Dave at the park. We started out on our old grade school walking route—across the undeveloped field to the west and then south down the hill. Montclair Drive cut near the base of the hill, and Davis Elementary sat on the south side of the road.

We gained speed descending toward Montclair. He flew down the dirt track ahead of me, rising and falling as the terrain flattened and then dipped again. At the bottom, a flat grassless area collected eroded soil. At the last dip before the flat area, I leaned left to avoid a gully, hit a small berm, and caught air.

I flew over my handlebars and landed on my left eye and cheek. Kent was waiting for me at the bottom of the hill. I didn't move or breathe. A boy had followed us and ran back up the hill to get help. Someone with a cell phone, a rarity in Cheyenne in 1994, was driving down Montclair, saw me crash, and called 911. My brother was about to give me rescue breathing when I took my own stuttering breath. In less than three minutes, emergency responders were there. They stabilized my head and asked me my name. I thrashed and told them to fuck off.

Dad rode with me in the ambulance. Mom and Kent met us in the emergency room.

"What day is it?" someone on the care team asked me.

"Tuesday," I replied.

"And what were you doing before you came here?"

"Fishing at Miracle Mile." Miracle Mile was a three-hour drive from Cheyenne and never a day trip. Later, my family would chuckle over my responses, but at the time they were scared.

The left side of my face was bruised, and the tissue around my eye was purple and swollen shut. X-rays showed that I hadn't broken my orbit or cheekbone. A nurse cleaned the abrasion on my left arm with a plastic scrub brush. I writhed but did not scream.

Dad asked me what I was reading. I didn't know. I could remember the story about a man taking a shit and who fantasized about eating a kidney, but I didn't know the name of the book. It was fat and had a soft cover. The title was written in black block letters vertically up the front, a white background, topped with a hat. What was the word? I looked at Dad. Could I actually read?

He looked back at me. "You can't go home until you remember."

I looked at the book in my mind's eye. I stared at the title. I knew each of the letters. How did they go together? What sounds did they make?

"*Ulysses!*" I belted out.

When we returned home that evening, I went straight to bed.

The next day, my brother and I put together a jigsaw puzzle on the kitchen table. We didn't talk much as we worked on the puzzle. I had the feeling he was watching me for signs of normal me-ness. But maybe he was in a post-traumatic state himself, replaying images of me lying in the dirt not breathing. Maybe dead. Whatever was going on with him—I never asked—he spent the day at the kitchen table instead of seeing his buddies. He put together the buildings and carriages. I pieced in the sky and trees.

Intense cramps brought me to the present as I searched for a place to relieve myself. I headed toward some bushes. They grew in a water scar. Water couldn't penetrate the earth, and it left marks where it beaded and chained on the hydrophobic soil. Not an ideal location, but my mess would dry and flake away before water came here again.

I picked up some sticks and rocks. I didn't carry toilet paper, ever. Weight, space, necessity—no reason was compelling enough for me to carry it when I could make do without. Glancing left and right toward the empty road, I pulled down my cycling shorts and squatted.

Blood had seeped into my shorts and dispersed across the chamois.

I didn't use to bleed. I took birth control for twelve years; it gave me amenorrhea and erased my emotions. Four years prior, I quit using the drug. After it left my system and my body started to readjust to itself, my cycle returned vengeful and erratic, my emotions, too—neglected, punishing. More than the blood, I had one emotional flood after the next, unprepared, unknowing, unpracticed.

I used the sticks and rocks to wipe, grabbed the waist of my shorts and pulled them up as I stood.

Pushing the barbed wire down, I stepped through the fence.

"Weakling," I heard my brother say.

My abdomen clenched. I stood tall in the wind, and it buffeted me. I breathed for my little girl self. She grew up in this harsh climate.

Gusts rammed my arms and legs, swirled around my neck, grabbed my breath. As I pedaled away, I looked back toward the bushes.

When the blood came, I liked to see it, to let it out, messy, like splattered paint. In its expression and irregular form, beauty.

The bluff fell to meet the treeless plain. This landscape, like the sea, had no edge, no masts.

Back in the bushes, exposed and untethered atop rock, my mark on the landscape, my love letter to this place.

13.

Nothing in Nothingness

The ibuprofen I took when I stopped to relieve myself was working, but I was being sizzled alive. Cloudless blue above. Sage ripple below. Searing interface between. Forceful wind pushed everything, including me, east.

I pedaled the straight line of road with my blood and sweat volatilizing. Whatever I was unconsciously running from, I ran straight into it on this hot griddle of land, past my six-year-old self, into a different life, a place where the physical, psychological, and cosmological mixed. These wounds were hurts from my brother, the terror of rabbits screaming in the night, hate crimes, violence to the land. The injuries reached beyond my lifetime and included the pioneers and people of the Shoshone, Cheyenne, Ute, and Arapaho tribes. They existed in soul space, where, like Prometheus chained to a rock, an eagle ate my liver every day. I didn't have conscious knowledge of what my body sensed, but I knew it happened here, in Wyoming.

My attention turned to the unwavering line of road ahead. There was no looking back in this austere beauty of nothing and not-nothing. There was the road that few vehicles traveled, the barbed wire fence that paralleled the road, the snow fence. I passed a cluster of trees, the only ones in the whole expanse. A contorted family of five in complete isolation.

After Sweetwater, which was nothing more than a rest area, twenty miles of this container-less burn extended to Jeffrey City. Pioneers on the Oregon Trail must have seen this place as hell, although Sweetwater, true to its name, would have offered profound relief to thirsty people and animals. I could sense layers of previous lives, certain that I had endured traveling this wasteland on foot, accompanying oxen with cracked hooves that toiled to pull a wagon full of grief.

I crossed to the north side of the highway to read an interpretive sign. A solo woman in a Prius also stopped in the pullout—straight, shoulder-length light brown hair, gray T-shirt, navy blue shorts, tennis shoes, about my age.

"Are you headed cross-country?" she asked.

"Yeah. Are you?" She had Virginia plates. Unusual for Wyoming.

"Yeah."

She seemed as unable to make conversation as I.

"Do you need any water?" she asked.

I had just refilled at Sweetwater. The uncanny feeling of being a pioneer in the future disoriented me. I knew where I was, but I was less certain when I was. A cackle formed like an egg in my throat, but nothing was funny. "All good," I rasped, "but thanks for asking."

"My road bike is in the car," she said.

It seemed weird to me that she would say this. I could tell she was trying to make a connection, that she could empathize with me as a cyclist in this hot, dry, windy place. But the biking wasn't the intense experience here. Specters ranged the expanse, howling their frustration and pain in the wind. I was being touched by these traces of lives. I couldn't find any words. It was almost as if I couldn't breathe.

"Do you want any blueberries?" she asked.

"Okay. Thanks," I said, but my voice didn't speak from my body.

"Take a big handful." She held the bag open.

I reached in the bag, then popped the berries in my mouth one at a time. They tasted sweet, fruity, and out of place.

The woman watched me eat. It seemed she was assessing me for hyperthermia and dehydration. I wasn't thirsty, too hot, or in need of a snack, but I wasn't okay. How could I tell this stranger that my life force seemed diffused into the thin atmosphere? I was the physical residue of a long-lived soul, returned to a place of wounding, bleeding.

If she had pulled over and asked me whether I needed water and wanted blueberries before I reached Sweetwater, I would have been able to say yes and yes. I wanted to tell her how much I appreciated her stopping and checking on me. Or maybe I did tell her and wasn't aware of saying so. She stayed until I finished the blueberries and then departed. The only reason she stopped, it seemed, was to check on me. Were people actually that nice? I'd been visited by an angel in the most godforsaken part of the whole state. Who knew angels traveled in Priuses?

I read the interpretive sign about Ice Slough. It was a unique depression of land where water collected. Cold nighttime temperatures meant that people could find ice by digging about two feet below the ground surface, even in the middle of summer. While Ice Slough no longer made ice, the fact that pioneers could find frozen water in this desolate, seared land seemed as unlikely as the angel's blueberries.

Back on my bike on the right side of the road, the tailwind blew me east.

Way off at the horizon and almost too tiny to see was Split Rock, a distinctive notched rock formation that served as a landmark for Indians, trappers, pioneers, messengers, and other travelers.

The pioneers came through this dry expanse because of a flattish crossing of the Continental Divide at South Pass, a gap between the Northern and Southern Rockies and thirty miles west of Sweetwater.

I was moving much faster than the pioneers could have traveled on foot. Even so, being unable to escape the scorch of sun made me appreciate the hardship they endured—the inexorable inching forward in hot, desiccating wind toward something cold and wet and thirst quenching.

Many towns in Wyoming had extremely small populations. Highway road signs would name the town, its population, and elevation. There were towns with populations in single digits and double digits that began with one. I would pass two of them the next day. I was in the heart of the state's unpopulated center.

Away from Wyoming at college, the spare boundlessness of unpeopled landscape crooned to me from the gray, closed-in winters of New York. I wrote poems about these flyspeck towns and painted the landscape. On one canvas two-feet tall by one-foot wide, I painted a thin line of yellow ochre on the bottom of a field of gradient blue. I wanted to capture the verticality of the sky, its immensity in relation to the land. My painting professor suggested I try another version, much larger.

I envisioned a wall-sized painting of the sky with just a hint of land at the floor, of walking into a room and being surrounded by the sky. At room-sized scale, I could begin to express the solitude of being in Wyoming, what a population density of six people per square mile felt like, especially allowing that the population of Wyoming wasn't evenly dispersed across the state. People clustered in towns, which meant most of the state had no people whatsoever.

I blew my art supply budget on two eight-foot squares of canvas. I stretched the canvas directly onto the painting studio walls using hammer-in staples. Since I couldn't afford the quantity of artist's paint I would need to cover the canvas, I bought quarts of hardware store wall paint.

The painting failed. The sky looked striped. I couldn't blend sixty-four square feet of blue before the paint dried and didn't attempt a skyscape on the second canvas.

Blue. It stopped my breath, the color, yet I wanted to breathe it in and fill myself with it. I wanted to become the atmosphere. I took a picture. Like my college painting, it failed to convey what I had hoped. But it was blue. I imagined my blog readers would find the picture silly. I wished I could make the image big enough to blow the ceiling out of a room, to explode the dome of awareness and perception, to give my audience a glimmer of what it felt like to be nothing in nothingness.

I dissolved in it.

Alone.

On a bike.

For miles and miles and miles and miles.

I positioned myself at Jeffrey City's roadside interpretive sign so the wind wouldn't push me over. Jeffrey City had boomed as a uranium mining town in the latter half of the twentieth century, but once the mine closed in 1982, most residents left within three years.

I hadn't heard anything good about the town even though my map made it seem like a bustling, service-laden community compared to everything else between Lander and Rawlins. Even Jim thought Muddy Gap would be a better overnight option than Jeffrey City. From previous family road trips, I knew Muddy Gap was a gas station at the T-intersection of two highways. Could Jeffrey City be so miserable that Muddy Gap was the better choice?

A library sign hung on unit 6 in a complex of derelict apartments. It said open but didn't seem so.

Two dogs cough-barked when I passed a trailer.

At the school, the rubber seats of the swings were intact, but there were no bare patches in the grass beneath them.

The bar's front door was open, venting a howling wail.

Scared, I scrambled to the highway shoulder. The wind pushed me east.

A slim person in long, pink shorts and a white tank top walked on the shoulder ahead of me. I rolled past her.

I stopped in front of a sign that was a top hat perched on the word MOTEL. The hat appeared moth-eaten. Was it possible the building behind the sign with boarded windows that looked like an oversized vehicle maintenance garage was the motel? The woman came up behind me and said a friendly hello.

"They opened the motel for us," she said with a Dutch accent. "We're with an Adventure Cycling group. I'm sure you could stay here if you wanted. It's not so bad."

"Good to know. I thought I would get some food at the bar, but it sounded like someone was having a hard time inside. I didn't go in." Whoever howled inside that bar knew Jeffrey City was a ghost town and didn't give a shit if I went in.

"I went looking for a store. There's not much here."

I didn't see a reason to stay, and she offered to take my picture. I handed her my camera, and she stepped into the middle of the highway and lined up the shot with the motel sign.

The wind blew my hair and jersey. I steadied my bike with one hand. The grass rose and flattened with the gusts.

"Thank you so much," I said. "I'm going to accept the wind's invitation and keep going."

"Yes. It's a hell of a lot better than fighting it at three or four miles per hour the whole way."

I didn't have to pedal to start moving. My bike rolled as soon as I lifted my feet. I waved to the woman. "Enjoy!" A gust yanked the word from my mouth.

The shoulder had wide, jarring cracks every ten feet. The wind blew me straight toward Split Rock, and I pedaled fast in my biggest gears, even going up the hills. It was like riding on a widely spaced cattle guard for twenty-two miles. What a place, Wyoming. Any joy came with misery. I mustered a small gratitude: There wasn't much traffic in that desolate place. I periodically swerved around the rumble strips to ride the road where the cracks were filled with tar.

14.

Looking My Truth in the Eye

Muddy Gap didn't have cell service or Wi-Fi. I scoured my brain for vocabulary to describe what seemed like miserable but hospitable conditions. I drafted a Facebook post for the next day when I would have a connection.

> Paid $12 to pitch my tarp on the gravel "lawn" at the Muddy Gap gas station. Shelter minimized regular dustings from the wind, amplified and concentrated the sun's heat. Made roast cyclist. Had gas station convenience store dinner, the dining option of last resort: 2 quarts bottled water, orange juice, and unheated straight-out-of-the-microwavable-container Chef Boyardee ravioli (with congealed fat). Bon appétit!

I didn't have the option of a shower, so I didn't change out of my salt-crusted and blood-soaked biking clothes. My lower legs were sheathed in gray socks with purple and pink polka dots. The socks matched my riding outfit and my creative side's circus-like attire preferences, though the artist in me had been under cover for close to three and a half years. The descent was sudden, but clawing my way to the surface was slow and fraught. I hoped this ride could get me out.

On January 3, 2007, my art show installation, *AltarPsyche*, had opened at one of Eugene's downtown galleries, where I also had a contract fundraising job. *AltarPsyche* represented the secret underside of human experience—the taboo, unseen and opposite. The work encouraged viewers to interact, to touch, to read up as down, hidden as exposed, ugly as beautiful, imagined as real. The gallery room was loaded with art objects, everyday items, kitsch, and knickknacks: door-sized black-and-white photographs, a suspended altar table made of black walnut, fridge door, vanity, armchair, Persian rug, books, lamps, plants, little red wagon, tarot cards, wooden fire truck, small wooden chairs, mirrors, pillows, train case full of sex toys, plaster body casts, two little girl outfits, magnetic poetry kits, and thousands of small objects.

Most elements in the show I borrowed, was given, or purchased cheaply. I spent thousands of dollars amassing the collection with money I didn't have. *AltarPsyche* was Persephone's living room in the Underworld. It was an altar to Pluto, and I invited the energy to inhabit me. It did, and something of the Underworld came with me after the show.

A week after the show, I lay on the floor next to the gas stove in my living room with my eyes closed. It was 9:37 AM. The stove ignited with a *woof* to warm the house. Soon, it ticked with heat. I opened my eyes. Tears streamed into my ears. After all the effort to bring the art show together, all the people who came to the opening, all the changes I saw people had made to the installation when I visited —the show was everything I hoped for, but I couldn't turn it off.

It felt good to lie on the floor in the quiet house, undisturbed. I was cold though, but I couldn't sit up. Since before 4:00 AM, maybe 2:00 AM, my thoughts were ablaze over my greatness as an artist. The stove fan clicked. I lay under the pale blue heart of my open sleeping bag as if I were a clutch of eggs. The bag's lofty down and silky nylon settled over me like a mama hen.

I had suspicions about the tears.

Suspicion one: I was detoxing from birth control. I had quit taking the drug the year before, at age thirty-one, and looked for some sign that it was out of my system and my hormones had normalized, such as the return of my menstrual cycle or any emotion. No blood came. But on the winter solstice before the art show opened, I abruptly ended twelve years of veganism—I ate yogurt, then lamb, and relished both. I was a vegan during the same twelve years I used birth control. Vegans were disciplined. Discipline equals control. I was no longer vegan.

Suspicion two: I was manic. Hyperactive, heightened creativity, sleeplessness, impulsivity, racing thoughts, spending sprees, sense of grandiosity. I rolled these symptoms around in my mind like marbles, shooting them at one another.

David, my artsy, eccentric, sixty-two-year-old friend of five years who gave me $1,000 in December for the art show, dropped by while I was crying on the floor. He knocked and let himself in. He sat on the floor, his back against the wall. He listened to my monologue on Pluto's transit of my Mars and what I believed was my awakening.

He encouraged me to sit up.

My head was heavy, and my whole body seemed tied to the floor by resistance bands. I collapsed.

He left soon after. Since he wasn't concerned about me, maybe I was okay. I could always call him. Had I called him?

I called Kaz. He had loaned me the Persian rug for my show and was active in several arts-related revitalization enterprises downtown. I hardly had a relationship with him. I talked for eleven minutes straight.

When I finished, he said, "I can't comment, but I heard you."

We hung up.

Tricia, my good friend and past housemate, called during her lunch break, concerned about bleeding with her new IUD. I loved her. I told her about my empty bank account and the mysterious $632.81 that appeared there, how I thought the bank was watching me. The phone cut out.

Tricia and I tried to reconnect. Couldn't. We must have been calling each other at the same time. She left me a message: "Wow, sometimes you never know what you're going to get. The last I heard was 'The bank is monitoring me.' Let's talk again soon."

I called my naturopath's office. The woman on the line asked, "Are you okay now?"

"I'm not sure."

She put me on hold.

When Dr. Umber came on the line, I told her, "I haven't slept. I've been crying since 4:00 AM. I'm paranoid about the bank watching me." I heard a click on the phone. My hands shook. I panicked, hung up. Dr. Umber called back. I answered, and we didn't talk about the bank.

She didn't confirm or deny anything I said but gave me an assignment to get cod liver oil and take two tablespoons right away.

I hung up with Dr. Umber, and Mark called. Mark and I had met three years earlier at a yoga potluck. He loved hugs and naked hot-tubbing. I loved wrapping my body around other people.

"Did I call you earlier?" I asked.

"No. What's up?"

"I can't tell what's real."

He convinced me to come over to his house. I arrived crying. I told him how I couldn't sleep, my mind racing with insights, the art show, suspicion one. I kept suspicion two to myself. I told him about the bank: how I was broke, that money mysteriously appeared, that I answered a survey and they had my personal information, how the phone kept cutting out when I said these things.

"Whoa, whoa, whoa," he stopped me. "Don't leap to conclusions."

I sat on his sofa, mute, face wet. I trusted his insight about the bank.

He broke the silence. "Have you eaten today?"

I shook my head.

He offered to buy me dinner after I ran my cod liver oil errand.

I drove to the market, pretending I felt fit to operate an automobile. Vitamins and supplements lined the shelves of the mental health section, but I didn't see fish oil.

"Can I help you find something?" a slim, white-haired woman in an apron asked me.

With tears streaming, I turned toward her. "Yes. I need Carlson's cod liver oil, lemon flavored."

"That's over here." She led me to a shelf with rows of green glass bottles. She must have known why I was getting this.

"Are you a Beavers fan?" she asked, referencing Oregon State University. "Or do you just like orange and black?"

In Eugene, home of the University of Oregon Ducks, green and yellow were the proper colors to wear. The Ducks and Beavers were fierce sports rivals.

I looked at myself. Coral-colored yoga pants, a turtleneck sweater the same color with horizontal stripes of brown and white, black high-collared cotton duster jacket, bright orange scarf. I didn't give a shit about sports. Between tears, I got out, "I just like orange and black."

At the register, I paid $29.95 for the oil with two twenties, the last of my cash and the last of all my money if there was some mix-up with the $632.81 that appeared in my bank account.

I drove home. The oil went down like water. I put it in the empty fridge and returned to Mark's house.

At Lotus Garden, a girl at the neighboring table turned in her seat and looked at me, nudging her mom with a question, "Why is that lady so sad?"

I wasn't sure I was sad, but I was touched by the girl's concern. I had no appetite, but I ate, the food forming a sticky paste in my mouth. I felt like a freak, but I was with Mark, and somehow that made it okay. Over the course of dinner, my tear flow lessened.

By the time we returned to Mark's house, the tears had stopped. As weird as it was, I attributed the tears stopping to the cod liver oil. Dr. Umber was so certain that was all I would need.

At Mark's house, everything happened in slow motion. We took a hot tub.

"Thanks for being with me today," I said.

"You're welcome."

"Now I'm actually tired."

"Success."

We got out, dressed, and had a long hug.

"I need to get home," I said, the left side of my face against his chest. "Sleep."

"You do that, Heidi B." His right cheek rested on the top of my head, and his hands gently massaged my back.

"Thank you."

At home, I crawled under my sleeping bag. Blue flames in the stove pulsed light on the walls and ceiling that I matched to the beat of my heart. My mind observed the dark, quiet space and rested.

The darkness that pulled me down during the art show seemed to be something Dad and I shared—suspicion two. I was in graduate school in Fort Worth, Texas, for English in 1999, when Mom called me to say Dad had seen a psychiatrist. They didn't know what Dad's issue was, but they worried I might have it, too. She wanted me to read the book the psychiatrist recommended. Kay Redfield's memoir, *An Unquiet Mind*, arrived a few days later in a slim manila envelope. From it, I learned about the experiences of mania and depression and how they were a higher volume of normal behaviors, good days, and bad days. I took mental notes and stashed them in a fold of my brain.

In May 2001, I bailed out of my PhD program and left Texas to climb mountains. I wanted to reembody myself after the cerebral excess of school. While I liked riding my bike then, it would be eight years before my first bike tour. I practically lived in the mountains and dulled my intellect with pot, psychedelics, and alcohol.

June 2002, my parents and I moved to Oregon. I had an outdoor gear sales job in Eugene and biked for transportation. My parents bought a house in Corvallis—fifty miles north.

I pursued adventure and intoxication. I feasted on adrenaline and endorphins—climbing, dancing, yoga. I built my work life around these bodily joys, neglecting intellectual aspirations and suffocating them in pot smoke.

In June 2007, five months after I disassembled *AltarPsyche*, Mark was away for a month, and I was tending the garden at his house. Since my contract at the gallery ended in March, I'd been trying to find direction for my life. I felt a strong urge to disappear, yet the thought of vanishing hurt. I had already cleared out my precious attachments at home and thrown out remainders from the art show. Old research from graduate school went into the recycling bin as did a 263-page draft memoir.

Jack Cat trotted into Mark's backyard where I sat weeding the sandy between-places in the flagstone patio. Jack slowed, head high, ears alert. Crows muttered in the tall fir next door. Bees searched the fuchsia and anemones. A beetle lumbered across a corner of the patio. Jack swiped my leg and lay on a flagstone within reach.

"How do you do, Jack Cat?" I put on a pleasant air, hoping by pretending that I could feel it. "Mighty fine day in the neighborhood."

He looked up at me and blinked.

I stroked his orange head and fluffy mane, rubbed the side of his face, and scratched under his white chin. I assumed Jack had a home somewhere, a house with few rules, a place he could always go.

Visits by Jack Cat were the high points of my day since I rarely had company. He didn't care that my body was getting softer and fuller than it had been when Mark helped me through my tearful day in January.

Since I spent my days in the dirt, I didn't have reason to wear my brightly colored artist clothes. Fewer of them fit, and I didn't want to draw attention to myself. If no one saw me, I couldn't be embarrassed by how I'd gone out of control.

"I'm glad you're here, Jack Cat," I said. He supervised my work from a concrete bench by the hot tub.

This summer garden scene seemed wrong—delightful, but wrong. Inside, I felt heavy, like sticky tar. When I biked away from my house that morning, I considered ways to kill myself. I was more probing than plotting, and by the time I was two blocks from Mark's house at the busy intersection with Highway 99, I had dismissed the imagined scenarios as either too horrific or impractical.

Then something propelled me into the three lanes of stampeding automobiles.

My body didn't get rubbed like an old eraser beneath all those tires, leaving dark streaks on the pavement. My backpack didn't go flying, disgorging my water bottle, rubber work gloves, and dandelion tool. My lunch container of rice and veggies didn't explode on the asphalt like a vomit splatter. My bike didn't twist and crumple into a swirly-eyed fish like wire in Alexander Calder's hands.

Hours later, I was in the garden, alive, but I didn't feel any better than I did when I departed home that morning.

Jack Cat left.

Crossing Highway 99 that morning, I experienced my death. That scare showed me I didn't want to die. And yet, I didn't know what to live for.

I sat in my own *jus* in Muddy Gap. Sweat trickled down my back. Riding across the country had direction and purpose and felt like what I needed to find a way out of the Underworld.

There were too many factors operating in the buildup to my art show and the crash that came after to attribute what happened to one thing. Dad was never diagnosed as bipolar, nor was I, but Redfield's description of mania and depression matched my experience. While I never sought a mental health or mood assessment, naturopathic care was a cornerstone of my recovery. My prescription was a daily supplement of cod liver oil, regular exercise, adequate sleep each night, and low stress—challenging to follow.

I couldn't have consciously presented myself with a better way to look my truth in the eye than riding my bike across the country through my home state. One thing was certain, I couldn't look away. My past was everywhere.

15.

Carnage, Girl Talk

I pedaled south from Muddy Gap around 6:15 AM.

The highway had more traffic than the one I rode the previous day. Two lanes, no middle lane, four-foot shoulder. Less than a mile from Muddy Gap, a hawk-sized owl dead in the shoulder stopped me.

I picked up the owl the way I would a live raptor, my hands over its back, wings folded aside its body like pot holders. It had gray-brown feathers, a large beak, huge eyes, and a bare, bloodless gash on one side of its head. It felt warm, but feathers could deceive. Like the little owl in the Ruby Valley, I rescued this one from the roadway.

Not far from the owl were the remains of a deer that looked as if it'd been blown up. Dead deer littered the road, shoulder, and embankment. So much gore in less than ten miles.

My antennae were up, tracking vehicle speeds and traffic volumes, counting exploded deer. I gripped my handlebars and hoped I wouldn't become the next body of raw meat smeared across the road. There were no other route choices.

Road conditions were shit. The shoulder from the fog line to the road edge was half eaten with rumble strip, and the remaining eight inches of rideable area were broken-rough-cracked-pocked-strip-of-junky yuck next to another eight inches of base road with tarred cracks. Trucks passed with oversized loads that I guessed were bank vaults, combines, wind farm rotors, nuclear reactors, and bridge I-beams. One had a police escort.

A tiny bird on the shoulder brought me to a stop. It wasn't a hummingbird but precious all the same. Like the owl earlier, I moved it. A sun-bleached jawbone lay on the gravel on the roadside. Then, a decaying antelope.

Nearing the crest of a hill, I saw something on the shoulder I never expected in the desert scrub: a turtle. It looked as if it were about to take a step, except for the broken carapace.

I rolled into Rawlins under a cloudless blue sky. In a café downtown, I ordered a sandwich. After swallowing half of it in two bites, I realized I hadn't washed my hands since the evening before. I hadn't even removed my cycling gloves. These were the same gloved hands that touched dead birds that morning. I picked up my camera and documented my hand holding the last bite and then ate it.

The forty-five-mile afternoon ride from Rawlins to Saratoga was hot and shadeless. I was motivated to tough out the heat and distance because I would meet my childhood friend, Cara, in Saratoga and spend two days with her. I hadn't seen her for seven years.

I pedaled past a massive oil refinery in Sinclair and followed the biking route onto the shoulder of I-80. At first, I was nervous about being on the same road as freight traffic and vehicles traveling eighty-plus miles per hour, but I soon adjusted and found it a better ride than the highway I'd pedaled to reach Rawlins. The shoulder was as wide as a highway travel lane and freshly paved. While there were blown-apart tires, twisted pieces of metal, dead animals, and rocks to navigate, there was room to keep my distance from the semitruck slipstreams.

Thirteen miles later, I exited I-80 and continued on a lesser-traveled highway to Saratoga.

Wyoming has limited roads, and present-day highways tend to follow historic travel routes. South Pass was a key reason people traveled through Wyoming on the Oregon Trail—it was the easiest place to cross the Rocky Mountains with a wagon. Northeast of where I was are the National Historic Landmark Guernsey ruts, wagon wheel tracks carved five feet into the sandstone.

On my way to Saratoga, I crossed the Overland Trail, a historic route used by animals, tribes, emigrants, the military, Pony Express, and stagecoaches. The Overland Trail crossed the Continental Divide at Bridger Pass. Later, Union Pacific Railroad, Lincoln Highway, and U.S. 30 would follow this same route.

Nearby water from the North Platte River greened the landscape. Wildflowers dotted the prairie. Birds sang and insects buzzed. The wind stilled. I could see why Cara suggested we meet here. The place breathed ease.

Cara and I were four years old when our parents met. In 1980, Cara's dad began working for the U.S. Embassy, and they moved from Cheyenne. My first letters to her went to Washington, DC, and then Rabat, Morocco. After Morocco, she and her family returned to Washington, DC, and then moved to Japan.

We'd seen each other in Cheyenne the last days of July 1985. Cara had been visiting her grandpa in Laramie when a freak storm hit Cheyenne, and twelve people drowned. In what became known as the August First Flood, a carousel of twelve tornadoes set sirens wailing while six inches of rain fell in three hours. Hail, some larger than golf balls, pelted the city and fell in such quantity that snowplows were used to clear the streets. Also in that storm, the house on the hill where Cara and I played as children and that my parents still owned was struck by lightning. The lightning hit my old room. Incredibly, no one had been hurt.

I saw Cara again in 1991 after she and her family were evacuated from Zaire and transitioning to their next assignment. Zairian troops had rioted in Kinshasa, a city of 3 million, attempting a military coup of the Mobutu dictatorship. Most of the city, including its water infrastructure, was destroyed. During that visit, we sat on the concrete landing outside the front door of my house and had girl talk.

After that, our letters to each other became less regular. I addressed envelopes to Korea, Maryland, Virginia, and North Carolina. In early 2003, it had been ten-plus years since I'd seen Cara when I stopped in Laramie where she was attending law school at the University of Wyoming.

Now, reuniting again in Wyoming, she'd married, moved to Cheyenne, had a daughter, and was pregnant again.

As kids, Cara was the worldly adventurous one who brought me experiences and insight about life beyond Wyoming. I'd been the homebody who knew what it was like to go to school with the same kids from kindergarten through high school. Even now as an adventurer, I wanted stability, although I wasn't sure that settling down and having children the way Cara had was for me.

"I'm pretty sensitive to my body," Cara said during our steak dinner at the Wolf Hotel. "I can even tell which ovary I ovulate from."

I stopped cutting my meat and looked at her. "How do you know that?"

Cara talked about the subtle sensations of internal discomfort on a given side of her lower abdomen.

I told her how dislocated I'd felt from my reproductive body while I was on birth control and how normal that seemed. I didn't even know I had an emotional life I hadn't experienced. In retrospect, my lack of long-lasting romantic relationships likely resulted from this emotional disconnection. Since quitting birth control, I'd been learning how to operate in a more flexible, emotional space, and I'd been more frequently in relationships. But I couldn't claim romantic success. I was inexperienced, lacked confidence.

Cara looked great at breakfast, and I took a few pictures of her for my blog. I liked how it felt being with her, the familiarity and intimacy—the gem of our friendship. When I raised the camera to take another picture, she said, "You're killing me," and sipped roughly at her orange juice.

I had no idea how nauseated she was feeling and assumed I was being too upbeat and pesky with the camera.

"Sorry to do this to you," she said abruptly, "but I need to go back to the hotel. The breakfast burrito will be coming back up."

As soon as we returned to the room, she went to the bathroom, closed the door, and turned on the faucet. Outside, I ripped up National Geographic magazines I found in a local free box.

I collected the pages I wanted to carry with me and the discard pile and tentatively went back inside. Cara sat on her bed leafing through a magazine as if nothing had happened.

"How are you feeling?" I set the dismembered magazines on my bed.

"Eh. Okay."

We walked to the Hobo Pool, the free hot springs in town. On the way, I stopped in the post office. When I came out, Cara said, "My mom just called while you were in there. She wanted to know if you were really doing this and by yourself. I told her, yes, you really are that crazy."

I smiled. For me, riding solo was normal, but I could see how nuts I seemed to other people. What sensible woman would put herself in danger and set herself the challenge of riding across the country and enduring hardship?

"I am certifiably crazy," I said, pleased.

The Hobo Pool was an open-air, rectangular pool about three or four feet deep with a sandy floor. We put our feet and lower legs in.

The hot water stung. I sat on the concrete edge of the pool, yoga pants rolled above my knees. "Wow. Not sure I'd be able to get all the way in even if I had something appropriate to wear," I said, looking over at Cara.

She was looking down at her own feet in the water. "This is plenty for me."

"The sting feels strangely good." I swished my feet in the water.

We had a long lunch and a comfortable, rambling chat before it was time to head our separate ways.

"Can I drop you off somewhere?" Cara asked.

"Nah, I'll ride from here. It's only twenty miles to Riverside." She didn't look reassured, but it seemed silly that she would drive me such a short distance.

Years later, Cara would tell me how she watched me pedal away from her, getting smaller on the road. She cried as she considered how little and vulnerable I looked.

Me, I pedaled as I had so many days previously. I had a hard deadline to reach the East Coast in time for the mid-September conference and more than half the country with all its unknowns yet to cross.

But one thing was different, a subtle feeling my body wasn't used to. Was it satisfaction? As I pedaled, I explored the feeling with curiosity. What could it teach me?

16.

Daniel

Day twenty-six. I pedaled toward Riverside in the hot, sunshiny afternoon. Daniel had texted asking if it was okay to call me that evening, and I was excited to talk to him.

Daniel and I met seven months earlier in mid-December. We lived in the same apartment building and had friends in common. One day outside the building, a slim, nicely dressed man walked toward me and waved. I looked behind me and saw no one. When I turned back, he smiled and said, "Heidi! I'm Daniel." His freckly face, dark lashes and brown eyes, and the auburn flecks in his beard charmed me. Something about how he held his body, his gestures, his dress, and his voice made me think he leaned toward gay. I was instantly attracted.

While I hadn't felt confident about my physical desirability since my art show, I was certain I'd make a good girlfriend and longed to share my life with someone. I was looking for someone brainy who liked touching and being touched, and ours became a friends-with-benefits relationship. The physical attention after three years of none seemed precious, hard-earned.

My $8.50 Lazy Acres campsite was adjacent to the main road on lush lawn and included unlimited hot showers in the community house and a decent Internet connection.

I learned from my neighbor, Lisa, that a group of women were at Lazy Acres for a vintage trailers and fishing retreat. Lisa pointed to a cluster of trailers parked in the campground's center. I rarely encountered women on the road, and I appreciated there were other women out there bucking gendered expectations for outdoor recreation. I felt kinship with them even though I didn't have a vintage trailer and never had success fishing.

Lisa and I sparkled at each other, and then she jumped in her jeep and headed back to Denver.

Daniel called just before the light fell. It was strange to hear his voice, and I wasn't sure what to say. Most of what seemed like news I'd been sharing in my blog and on Facebook, although Daniel wasn't on Facebook. We talked about twenty minutes. He gave me some highlights from his adventures and told me how cool my journey was.

He asked if he could call me again. I said yes.

The sky was dark.

I texted Daniel sexy pictures of my body from the shower room. He replied with a picture of his face and one word: "orbiting." I was disappointed he hadn't engaged my sext with a cock shot or something similar. As I looked at the picture, I remembered that he referred to tripping on acid as being in orbit.

I lay in the dark under my tarp. I had mixed feelings about the call and sexting knowing that Daniel was tripping. I liked that he wanted me to be part of his experience, but I thought he was Daniel during the call, not Daniel on drugs.

One of my pothead friends had a saying that people who couldn't function while high needed to practice more. That philosophy never worked for me, but I supposed it worked for Daniel. He sounded normal on the phone. But would he remember the call? Would he remember that he'd reached toward me?

One night back in the spring after watching a film, Daniel and I tried a sideways scissor sex position. This approach touched lively channels in me. I touched a finger to tiny horn, hoping I might reach orgasm, too.

I closed my eyes and concentrated on the sensation's velocity. My orgasm was like a night-train driven by an improvising engineer. I listened from the station to its faraway rumbling as it went to the right. I pressed with my finger and felt the train loop back, nearer, louder but still at a distance. It crossed my vantage point, chuffing speedily to my left. With urgency, I held tightly to Daniel's motion and pressed again with my finger, willing the train back. It turned toward me, close, in line with the station, the rhythm of wheels rolling over rail joints, the rush of air pushed ahead, the warning horn blasting in a sear of red light and hissing brakes as it drove abruptly into the station.

The next time Daniel and I rendezvoused and were getting naked, he asked me with teenage-seeming eagerness what preferences I had for sex.

"Let's do what we did last time when I came," I said, keen for a successful repeat.

Even with the lights out, I could see his empty expression. He usually had a couple tumblers of vodka while I was with him, and I hadn't noticed it negatively affecting him. Now, I saw that it did.

Having an orgasm had felt like a sign that we were opening up to each other. I could ask for something I wanted instead of being someone who said yes to whatever was offered. It hurt that he had no recollection of the experience. Rather than calling him on his lack of memory and sharing my disappointment, I said, "On our sides, you behind me."

Did he think I'd been having orgasms? What was it like for him to have no memory of sex? Was it exciting to try it afresh every time? Was it frustrating? Did it even matter? Would he even remember this exchange?

Distracted, I pulled away from him and lay on my back. It seemed futile to try to call a train into the station. He climbed on top, came, and fell asleep.

That hurt was months ago, and here he was reaching to connect despite our physical distance. Were we building something? By phoning me while he was tripping, wasn't Daniel communicating that he felt safe with me? Trusting me while high was significant, but if he couldn't remember how we got to this moment, what did we have?

I looked into the darkness under my tarp. I wished I had maps for relating like I did for my bike ride. I closed my eyes. The darkness looked the same.

17.

Century Day

Twenty-eight miles separated Riverside from the Colorado border. The shoulder was cracked, not unlike the stretch I had pedaled between Jeffrey City and Muddy Gap. The travel lane was freshly chip sealed. The shoulder hadn't been chipped but had a thin coating of oil.

I wasn't sure what hazards the oil presented, but the wide cracks in the shoulder would be annoying to hit every ten feet and could cause a flat.

Riding on chip seal sucked. The treatment prolonged the life of asphalt. A tar layer on the road prevented water from seeping into cracks and served as glue for a layer of rock "chips" that provided traction. As vehicles rolled over the chip seal, their weight pressed the rocks into the tar and wore down the chips' sharp edges. Fresh chip seal was like riding on cobbles, and loose rocks could be shot from tires with enough force to break windshields.

There was no good place to ride. I used the shoulder only when a vehicle approached. I was thankful there was hardly any traffic, which reduced my risk of injury from flying chips.

Grassy foothills flanked the roadway. Low mountains in the west had the purplish cast of dead trees. Evergreens were hardy yet susceptible to pine bark beetle infestation. Beetles bored into pines, laid eggs, and protected their clutches by introducing blue stain fungus. The fungus prevented the flow of water, nutrients, and pitch. Between larval feeding and the fungus, the rice-grain-sized beetles starved trees to death.

Around 10:00 AM, I entered Colorful Colorado.

I pedaled over a short rise. Tall blue mountains appeared, and the landscape rustled with trees, flowers, grasses. The road surface and my ride improved.

In a wetland area, pelicans floated. Cows gathered on green slopes.

Fifty miles into my ride, I stopped for water at a gas station in Walden, population 734 and gateway community to Arapaho National Wildlife Refuge. Vacant storefronts dominated the main street. The grand two-story courthouse building had paper cutout ghosts in the upper windows. I couldn't tell if the building was open or the exclusive domain of the ghosts.

Outside the gas station, a woman smoking a cigarette asked me, "Are you staying here tonight?"

"I was thinking of pushing on. It's only one o'clock."

"It's sixty miles to the next town."

"Sixty?" It was farther than I expected. "It's a little early to stop. I think I can make it. It'll be a big day."

"There's a hill."

Her dry mention of Willow Creek Pass amused me. I'd already climbed 1,000 feet from Riverside and had another 1,500 feet to climb to top that "hill." "Yeah. Looks like the grade is pretty low though. How long have you lived here?"

"Since eighty-one."

"What do you like about living here?"

"Nothing."

Her quick response surprised me. I expected she would have liked something about a place she'd lived for twenty-nine years.

"Wanted to leave for a long time," she said. "Just haven't been able to. There's no work here. It's a struggle to make a living."

"What's the big industry?"

"Ranching and hay. There was a to-do about getting a pellet factory with all the dead timber from beetle kill. That was about a year ago. I worked there, and then they closed. We all got laid off."

"I noticed the dead trees."

"We're having an epidemic. We told people a while ago that there was a problem. No one did anything."

"The beetles don't have natural predators?"

"No, they get under the bark."

"Woodpeckers can't get them?"

"No. They say a really cold freeze would kill them, but it hasn't gotten to fifty below yet, and the things seem pretty resistant to cold. The only thing that would really kill them is a big fire. If there were a fire, Walden's down in the valley. They say the smoke would settle here, and we'd all have to evacuate."

"Then you could move!"

She smiled, and we had a conspiratorial moment. "When you go down the road . . ." She gestured lighting a match and throwing it.

We exchanged names. Caroline wished me a safe trip.

A couple miles outside Walden, I stopped to snack and read refuge interpretive boards at a covered kiosk. Some swallows had built nests among anti-nesting devices inside the kiosk roof. Rebels. Opportunists. Artists. A bit like me.

Out on the road, raptors circled overhead. The interpretive boards suggested these birds were peregrine falcons and not red-tailed hawks, the raptor species that dive-bombed me in Montana. After my experience in Wisdom, I was wary of birds of prey, but I was so excited to see peregrines in the wild, I didn't care if one attacked me.

When I was a child, California condors, bald eagles, and peregrine falcons were headed for extinction from wide-scale use of DDT, a pesticide meant to kill mosquitoes. The pesticide concentrated in animal bodies as it traveled up the food chain. In birds of prey, this toxin thinned eggshells. Raptor populations plummeted because the birds crushed their eggs during incubation.

In grass on the roadside was a dark-feathered roadkill with big eye sockets, tan body feathers, and chocolate-colored wing feathers. It looked like a peregrine, and I took a picture to confirm my identification later. It disturbed me that peregrines had escaped the human-caused threat of extinction and now on a National Wildlife Refuge could still be killed by humans driving cars.

Around 3:15 PM, I stopped for juice and water in Rand, a one-building outpost on the mountain. I sat on the store's porch and let my heart mingle among the wildflowers, ride the wheel of a windmill, and steer through the sunny sky atop a puff cloud.

Back at my pedals, I climbed past enormous teepees of dead trees. I wished I could ask Tom, the forester from Halfway, about forest ecology and the beetles. Could the few living trees fight off infestation long enough for a deep cold snap? Was starting over from fire better?

After a nine-and-a-half-hour day of climbing, I flew down the road from the pass, my eighth crossing of the Divide. Air roared in my ears. Delight filled my chest.

I rolled into Granby, population 1,525 and the western gateway to Rocky Mountain National Park, at 6:00 PM, exhausted. I checked in at a motel and headed out for dinner. I was stinky and sweat-crusted but didn't want to risk the restaurants in town closing if I took a shower first. I also doubted I would have energy to get food if I didn't do it right away.

While I waited for dinner, I slouched in my chair with my map to count the day's mileage. I recounted. I ate and counted again. Each time I came up with a different number more than 100 miles and less than 110 miles. I waited for dessert and considered that this wrung-out, can't-sit-up-straight, and unable-to-do-simple-math state was what it felt like to pedal 100 miles in one day. My body seemed boneless. I played with some ideas for a Facebook post over berry cobbler, and first thing when I returned to my room, I wrote a quickie to my friends.

A century virgin no more! Today I pedaled more than 100 miles in one day. I know some of you out there might be concerned. Please be assured, I used protection . . . wore my helmet all day. There was no blood. I experienced ecstasy. (Is that possible?) And now, I am mollusk.

18.

High Point

The next morning, I flew twenty-eight miles downhill on roads with almost no traffic that wound through dramatic mountain scenery and deposited me at the Colorado River.

The river was swift and wild. It extended 1,450 miles from La Poudre Pass to its mouth in the Gulf of California and, along the way, shaped notable landscapes such as Horseshoe Bend and the Grand Canyon.

I felt small.

One human pedaling by the magnitude of this river.

Hoover Dam, among other engineered structures, regulates the Colorado's flow. Along its journey to the Gulf, the river's water is diverted to meet agricultural and domestic demand. Since 1960, the Colorado River has been dry at least one hundred miles upstream of its mouth.

How could this raging froth at 7,300 feet not reach the sea? What would the river say about the claims humans had on its water?

What would the river say if it could say anything?

Once I reached the outskirts of Silverthorne, situated at nearly nine thousand feet, my attention scattered into the distraction of traffic, businesses, and streets. My fuel tank was empty.

I turned onto Rainbow Drive. The hostel where I had a reservation was near. The street disappeared into a series of linked mall parking lots. I was rudderless and disoriented in the sea of automobility. As if by magic, a visitor information booth appeared, and I found a local map that helped me navigate the parking lots.

After getting settled at the hostel, I went out for food. My head felt as if it were floating three inches above my neck. Probably low blood sugar. I walked along a path, appreciative that one existed and kept me out of the parking lots.

I ate too much of my rice bowl and snail-walked back to the hostel. My head had returned to its usual position, but my body was entangled with a python named Sleep, which hooked its needle fangs into my eyelids and pulled them down. My internal body pressed against my outer body. So this was what it was like to be eaten by a snake. Barely back at my room, I passed out.

I departed the hostel in an adrenaline-fueled rush, as if I were late for my first day of work. Between Silverthorne and Breckenridge, my route followed a scenic bike path, and the pounding in my chest shifted from anxiety to my body's response to climbing at altitude.

The path skirted Dillon Reservoir and flowed with fun ups and downs. It was like an amusement park ride minus waiting in line. A touring cyclist approached, and I slowed, anticipating conversation. We stopped, and he chattered with questions, tips, and stories of his adventure. We moved our bikes to the edge of the path to allow room for others to pass between us.

John wore an Oregon jersey and was on his way home to Portland. He'd started his journey on the TransAm from Yorktown, Virginia, twenty-three days prior.

"I came over the pass this morning," he said, referring to Hoosier Pass, the highest point on the route at 11,542 feet. "Breckenridge has great food. I had greens. Like, for real, fresh spinach. And a latte."

My tummy rumbled. I hadn't eaten since before writing my blog post, and it was now past noon. John didn't seem in a hurry, and since we were on the topic of food, I ate a Builders Bar.

I was self-conscious eating in front of him. He was slim with veiny arms and muscular legs. Even though I felt good about what I'd been asking my body to do and had been pedaling almost every day for four weeks, I didn't feel accomplished or badass in his presence. I felt exposed, especially around my waist where my flesh bulged over the top of my cycling shorts. When he told me how many days he'd been out riding, I nearly choked. He'd probably finish in forty days or fewer, half the time I planned. "Holy smokes! You're moving," I managed to say.

"You have a pretty quick pace going, too, if you're averaging about 75 miles a day. I rode with this one guy on the Western Express. You won't catch him. He was doing about 180 a day. I rode with him for a couple of days. Did 140 one day, 120 another." I registered his compliment of my ability, but his crowing put me right back to worrying over my midsection bulge.

He asked what I was doing out on bike. In response to my "studying bicycle tourism and rural economic development," he said, "You tell those people: Buy something. In the small towns, they keep these little stores open just so people will get something. These young riders come out of the stores and say, 'All they had was Coke.'

I say, 'Well, did you buy one? Even if all you do is give it to a kid outside. Leave a couple of dollars or something if there's nothing you want to buy.'"

It heartened me that he understood, that he could appreciate the perspective of someone trying to keep a business afloat in one of these tiny towns, that as cyclists we had a role to play in supporting the businesses so they'd be there for future riders of the route. It was a good reminder for me, too, to always buy something, no matter how small, when I went into a business.

"I should let you get to the pass," he said. "Thanks for letting me bend your ear. It's been a while since I talked to someone."

I pedaled onward. Conversation wasn't anything I missed. I talked to people all the time who were riding with me in digital space. For the pace John was keeping, he probably wasn't blogging and on social media. Different styles.

I stopped in Breckenridge after 1:00 PM. I needed to break a hundred dollar bill and figured anywhere in the ski town could handle it. Earlier on my ride, I tried to break the bill at a small-town grocery store thinking that my twenty-five-dollar purchase would be enough to make reasonable change at the register. It wasn't. I bought bicyclist fuel for the ten-mile climb to Hoosier Pass at a gas station and pocketed my change, pleased with my preparedness to buy drinks, snacks, postcards, and other little things in the small towns ahead.

I was the only cyclist on the road to Hoosier Pass that afternoon. The grade was moderate, the shoulder narrow to nonexistent, the cars plentiful.

I stopped at a sign four miles to the summit to catch my breath and drink water. Extra hydration was the remedy for altitude sickness, and keeping my fluid levels high was the best prevention. With the moderate grade, four more miles seemed reasonable. No, that wasn't the right word. Pedaling four miles uphill at more than 10,500 feet above sea level wasn't reasonable. It was fucking insane. I drank more water. If I thought this was reasonable, I was probably suffering from cerebral edema. A swelling brain. Not a swollen head. There was a difference.

Several yards ahead, the grade changed, and the road switched back. Switchbacks could be difficult to climb in any circumstance. On low-traffic roads, I followed the shallowest part of the slope, which arced through the middle of the road. With all the traffic, I couldn't safely do this. The first switchback was an inside turn and scary steep. I stopped to catch my breath before taking it on. I went for it, pedaling fast in a low gear and then standing to get up the slope. After I made it through the turn, I sat on the saddle and ped- aled, giving one leg and then the other an opportunity to recover while I stayed in motion, sucking air. On the outside of the next switchback, trucks on the side of the road blocked my way. I stopped and waited for them to get back on the road, welcoming the rest.

Clouds built up overhead. I wound my way up the pass and stopped periodically to breathe. During one stop, I took a picture of Quandary Peak, one of Colorado's mountains that reached over fourteen thousand feet. I pedaled another set of switchbacks and rested in motion as I did earlier.

The pass came into view, a parking lot with a big sign. I pedaled slowly to the top, breathing hard. A car passed me and parked. A man got out and took a picture of the sign as I arrived.

"You made it!" he enthused. "Do you want me to take your picture?"

"Yes, please. Thank you." I could hardly breathe but was ecstatic that someone was there to witness my accomplishment. I panted. "Give me a minute."

"Sure thing."

I handed him my camera, and he waited while I rolled my bike to the sign, drank some water, and climbed onto the rock base. My watch read 3:15 PM.

We talked, and then he returned to his car and continued on.

I stayed at the pass. Even though I'd been at higher elevations in my mountain-climbing days, I always started at a high elevation. To reach Hoosier Pass on bike, I climbed every foot of the 11,500 feet it took to get there.

My view east featured dramatic mountain scenery. A dark gray rain cloud hovered close but held its spit. I sat on the lumpy ground and gloated.

A thunderhead boiled up from the west slope of Hoosier Pass— round, dusty lobes extended from menacing gray. The storm butted the air with its upslope advance.

I put on my windbreaker and remounted my bike, cutting short my triumph on the pass. My break at the summit had been enough for me to stop sweating, but my jersey was damp. I needed my windbreaker to prevent convective heat loss on the long, steep descent. I hoped to outrun the storm on the way down.

Less than half a mile from the summit, cars waited in a long line at a construction zone. I rolled down the shoulder to the flagger, frustrated that the storm might hit while I waited.

The flagger shifted his weight from foot to foot and held his body at odd angles. His neck or back didn't seem to flex, and one leg bent toward his midline at the hip. When the storm hit, he would have to take whatever the clouds dished out.

He asked me where I was headed. After I responded, he said, "I broke my neck two times riding mountain bikes. Split my skull open. Don't ever put a backpack over your handlebars."

Did he say he broke his neck twice? Like he put a backpack on his handlebars two different times and broke his neck each time? And then he realized it was a bad idea? "Thanks for the tip. I won't."

"Yeah, one of these days I'm going to have to ride across the country."

"Well, be safe doing it. There's no need to break your neck again."

"Maybe."

I gave him a steady look.

"You're out by yourself?"

Maybe changing the subject was as much of an acknowledgment as I'd get of his daredevil approach to biking. "Yeah," I said, still stoked about reaching the pass.

"Adventuress! Are you single? You're my kind of girl."

I liked the nod to my adventuring spirit but not his recklessness. The light in the sky fell as the clouds drew close. "How long do we have to wait here?"

"Until they say it's okay to go. When I get the okay, you can ride down the new pavement first. You won't have to share it with cars."

Unusual consideration. I liked it. About a minute later, he gave me the go-ahead. I wished him well and glided down miles of blissfully smooth, fresh pavement. I tucked. My windbreaker flapped and snapped. Air roared in my ears.

19.

A Curious Sign, Skeletons

Day thirty. I rolled downhill through a buildingless landscape and sunny, mild morning. Evergreens dotted grasslands. Tall blue mountains on the eastern and western horizon bookended the traffic-less road.

I climbed a pass, my body comfortable with the effort and appreciative of more oxygen. I sweated, working my legs in direct sun.

Ten miles on the downhill side of the pass, I stopped at a standard bike crossing sign with a small panel below that read GUFFEY. I knew there was a town named Guffey with lodging, but there were no buildings nearby. I consulted my map. The town was a mile off route. It was nearing 1:00 PM, and I had plenty of daylight and downhill ahead of me. The next town with full services, Cañon City, was thirty miles downhill, which I guessed would take an hour and a half to reach.

Curious, I turned toward Guffey. I hoped a visit to the town would help me understand what the sign meant. The road climbed around a hill. Hardly a quarter mile up the road, my lower back strained. I sweated. This was too much effort for a minor curiosity.

I expected the road would bend down around the next curve.

It didn't.

As I labored, I thought about the westward touring cyclists who climbed three thousand feet over thirty miles from Cañon City to Guffey. I imagined they might be desperate for lodging, exhausted, suffering from the effects of altitude. They would climb this hill. They were badasses. I would climb this hill, too.

Guffey nestled in a hollow where the road leveled. The first building in town was the Freshwater Saloon. Sagging buildings lined the road beyond the saloon. I leaned my bike against the saloon's patio railing and walked in, uncertain what I might find.

A young, attractive brown-haired woman behind the bar asked if I wanted something to eat.

"I'm not sure. Maybe." In this town of ninety-eight residents, I wanted to buy something, but I didn't know that it would be food.

The woman placed the menu on the bar in front of me. "Our specials are on the board. Here's our menu."

The bar was dark compared to the brightness outside. I couldn't see with my sunglasses on, and I couldn't see without them. "I'm a bit visually impaired," I said and looked down at the menu on the bar while I fumbled for my glasses.

"We have a green chili burrito, and a chicken-fried steak special."

With my glasses on, I scanned the menu and saw they had cherry pie. "Sure, I'll get something to eat," I said and sat down on a barstool. It was lunchtime—I couldn't only have pie.

In a dinky town such as Guffey, it surprised me that the saloon had business. There was a couple at a table inside and a group of eight dirt bike riders out on the patio. From my seat, I had a view of the patio hummingbird feeder, abuzz with birds. "You have some regulars here, don't you?" I said to the bartender and nodded toward the feeder.

"Crazy little birds. They showed up when it was still snowing this year."

The bartender, Birdie, was like a hummingbird, too, buzzing in and out between the patio, the bar, the kitchen window, the table behind me.

She lived four miles up the road and had come from Florida to escape hurricanes and the power outages they caused.

"What do you like about Guffey?" I asked.

"The locals are idiots," she said with the same tone she used with the hummingbirds. "Have you heard about the Chicken Fly? It's what we're famous for here in Guffey, if we're famous for anything."

"Tell me."

"Every year on the Fourth of July, they build a stage with a mailbox on it. The mailbox is open on both ends. Everyone who comes gets to pick a chicken. You take your chicken and stuff it in the mailbox. Then you hit the chicken in the ass with a plunger, and whoever's chicken flies the farthest at the end of the day wins."

I sat in stunned silence. I doubted the chickens appreciated being ammunition for a game of chicken cannon. If I were there for the Chicken Fly, I would want to pick a chicken that took the "boost" of the plunger and kept flying toward its freedom and never came back.

I filled up with hot tea, iced water, burrito, and pie. My belly stretched uncomfortably, and the band of my bike shorts cinched my middle. I was too full to pedal.

"How many days are you out doing this?" Birdie asked.

"I've allowed eighty days."

"How do you get that much time off work?"

"I'm in school right now and work on roadway tourism projects for the county government back home. I'm studying bicycle tourism and rural economic development. Not exactly taking time off. I'm doing fieldwork." I considered everything I was doing on the ride that was work: making notes in my journal, collecting receipts and

maps, taking photos, updating a spreadsheet with the businesses I
gave window decals, talking to riders and people in the communities, adding notes on the Google Map of the towns I went through,
and especially documenting my experiences in the blog.

For cyclists, staying at a motel or hotel was the biggest daily
expense unless they were also doing some other activity such as
river rafting. But few of the riders I met were doing anything other
than biking. For some, "bike tour" was synonymous with camping,
whereas others no longer liked sleeping on the ground. The reasons
cyclists were out and the experiences they wanted seemed as varied
as the individuals I encountered. One man I met in Idaho was essen-
tially homeless. He would pedal until his money ran out and then
work as a cook until he got the itch to continue his journey.

Bicycle tourism and scenic byways went together. Bicyclists
loved scenic routes, and byways tended to have less traffic than direct routes. Motorcyclists loved byways, too. Apart from gasoline,
motorcyclists needed what cyclists needed, and a scenic byway was
an asset to any community on or near one. Scenic byways were also
usually historic roads that were designed to flow with the landscape
and built in the time when vehicle wheel bases were at least seventeen inches narrower than today's—the experience of a scenic byway
was like a hug from or playtime with nature.

Historic sites, like national parks, were important destinations
within historic route networks. But the landscape was a kind of a
palimpsest of travel routes. Over time, new roads reached these destinations and overwrote the old routes. Sometimes the old routes
were still there, and sometimes only traces remained.

"You need to talk to Bill," Birdie said. "Tell him what you just told
me. If you go down the street to the garage, he'll be there in a black
T-shirt and black cap. He has a white ponytail."

I entered the garage's dark interior and walked into an alligator head with a fake hand in its mouth. "Hi," I said. "I'm looking for Bill."

One of two men who was deeper in the garage said, "I'm Bill."

To the alligator head, I said, "Birdie sent me. I'm studying bicycle tourism and rural economic development." The garage was cluttered with bones and old things. "This is neat stuff."

I couldn't tell if Bill was friendly but figured Birdie wouldn't send me to an axe murderer. I went back outside and took pictures while Bill finished with the man.

Bill handed me a key on a rough ring in the shape of a heart and belched. "Here," he said, "you should go look in the museum at the town hall. Just leave the key here when you're done."

"I like this, it's great," I said, gesturing to the reptilian skeletons arranged on the hoods of cars rusting in the grass next to his shop. It was as though the cars and creatures had died in place, a kind of aboveground cemetery.

He pointed across the street to a building with an ANTIQUES sign and old furniture, stoves, cabinets, water heaters, wooden wheels, and other items arranged on the building's porch and in the grass in front.

"That's the old stage stop there. Eighteen ninety-six. Right next to it is the original Guffey jail. You have your camera?"

I held up my camera so he could see it.

"Yeah, go into the museum. The Bikecentennial certificate is up and to the right after you walk in."

"What's with the bike sign out on the highway? What does it mean?"

"We had to fight and fight to get that. Lots of people pass by here, and then they end up in the middle of that." He gestured in a way that conveyed "fucking nothing." "It lets cyclists know that we're here."

The services were sparse in the seventy-six miles between Fairplay, where I stayed after my climb of Hoosier Pass, and Cañon City. It would be easy to miss the turn for Guffey.

I thanked Bill and walked through the museum. It seemed like an extension of his personal collections. The centerpiece was a skeleton riding a rocket that looked to be made from a stovepipe and ducting pieces. The skeleton wore a yellow construction helmet, had a red bandana tied around its neck, and held a plastic lightning bolt aloft like a decathlete with a javelin. Under the rocket on the sculpture base reclined a Raggedy Andy–like stuffed rooster. On the wall behind the sculpture was a gun rack made from a mounted deer head, its antlers the cradle for the gun's barrel. Everywhere, odd objects were hung or piled.

Tacked up on the ceiling was Bill's Bikecentennial certificate. He was one of four thousand people who participated in the inaugural ride of the TransAmerica Trail in 1976. The Bikecentennial ride was an act of patriotism, a way to celebrate the nation's two hundredth birthday and independence. It wasn't about bike advocacy but seeing and experiencing the country in a way that made it easier for riders to interact with the places they traveled through and with the locals they met.

I took my time in the museum, appreciating the kooky installations and playfulness. Bill was an artist. For all of Guffey's strangeness, I felt welcome. It was worth every foot of elevation and every drop of sweat it took to get there.

20.

Outrunning the Storm

On the main road east of Guffey, the landscape was light on buildings and passing vehicles. Rolling plains were edged with blue mountains and big sky.

A storm darkened the western sky and cast a green shadow on the tawny grassland. The creeping darkness made the day seem close to sunset even though it was 3:10 PM. The air was without breeze or cooling wind.

After a few miles, the road pitched down. I flew.

"Wheeee!" I hollered to the expanse. The descent of nearly three thousand feet on traffic-less, no-pedaling-necessary, curvy, and smooth road brought me an hour later to an intersection where I turned onto a busy road.

Thirty more minutes of quick pedaling downhill brought me to Cañon City. The western sky seemed nearing sunset although it wasn't yet 5:00 PM. I continued pedaling. Florence was nine miles farther east, my stop for the night.

The sky darkened, and lightning struck. I pedaled faster. Large raindrops splattered on me and seemed to evaporate on contact. I didn't stop to put on my windbreaker. Warm and wet was nothing to worry over even if being soggy wasn't pleasant. Lightning, however, was worrisome.

I raced. Six miles to Florence. Four.

Ahead was a railroad crossing with the gate arms down, lights flashing, and a line of stopped cars. The crossing bell clanged. No train in sight. I considered running the barricade but dismissed the thought. It seemed bad form for a cyclist to run a railroad crossing in the same way it seemed bad form for a cyclist to run a red light.

Large raindrops fell. I hoped the storm would not intensify while I waited. Not a moment later, the arms went up. On the other side of the rails, I cranked hard on the pedals and shifted into high gear.

Out of big raindrops, I rolled into Florence with an internal hoot. I rode along the main street looking for lodging but saw only large, well-kept historic homes and mature trees.

The wind picked up, and then the sky opened. Rain and hail tracked across the road in sheets.

I needed to shower and wash my biking clothes, but I hadn't planned on doing both at the same time on my bike. I was grossed out, riding in an envelope of dirty Heidi.

Having grown up in the west, I knew storms could be short-lived. Violent perhaps, but brief. I stopped under a large tree. After two minutes, I realized this storm wasn't letting up, and I wasn't safe from lightning beneath a tree. The wind lifted and twisted the leafy branches.

I continued pedaling.

Rain splattered my glasses, and I couldn't see the road. It seemed as though I were riding a stationary bike in a shower. A loud crack sounded to my left, and a gigantic limb fell on a side street.

Ahead on my right was a gas station. I stopped under the awning at the pumps. A lightning bolt flashed white and then red. I flinched with the instant crack of thunder. The gas station awning and most of the adjacent building was made of metal. On top of gasoline. The whole place could explode. It seemed less safe than the tree.

Across the parking lot was a Chinese restaurant where I stood under the entry roof and kept the gas station in view. If the station were hit by lightning, I could hide behind a car or part of the restaurant to avoid flying glass or building shrapnel. Water frothed in the restaurant's roof gutters and ran over the sides.

I was drenched but not cold.

Sheets of rain and rapids in the street were all I saw. No downtown. No motel.

An SUV pulled into the restaurant's handicapped spot, and a man got out. He used a cane-like trekking pole and didn't seem to mind the rain. He had white hair and wore jeans and a blue button-down shirt. He asked me where I'd come from and was going to. I filled him in and mentioned I was hoping to find a hotel that I thought was nearby when the rain let up. He went inside. A woman came out of the restaurant. "Would you like a cup of tea?"

Tea wouldn't hurt. I accepted.

"Please, sit," the woman said.

I didn't want to track water and cycling stew into the restaurant or put my body against anything that would absorb water. "I'm sopping."

"It's okay. Here." She gestured to one of several vinyl-covered chairs in the lobby.

Even these chairs would need clean up, although a swipe with a rag would do the trick. "It's not really cold out there, just wet," I said, sitting.

The man who talked to me outside gathered his takeout. He turned to me. "Do you want a ride? The hotel is on my way home."

The woman who invited me into the restaurant handed me a cup of tea.

I took the cup. I hadn't imagined taking a ride for weather-related reasons, and it didn't seem burdensome to wait for the weather to abate. Still, I didn't know where the hotel was. If this man knew, that would be helpful. I thought of Alfred at the RV park in White Bird, Bill in Twin Bridges with his airplane, and the Sweetwater angel in the Prius. People seemed curious about me. And many seemed inclined to offer me things. Water. Conversation. Blueberries. Information. Airplane rides. The offerings came from a place of generosity even if they weren't exactly what I thought I needed.

"Okay," I said to the man.

The woman who had given me the tea was still there. "Thank you," I handed the cup back to her. "It looks like I have a ride. I'm sorry about getting everything so wet."

"It's no worry," she said.

I loaded my bike into the back of the man's SUV. As I was about to get into the front seat, I asked, "You're sure you don't mind me getting the seat wet?" My clothes were saturated, and water ran down my scalp and face.

"It's fine."

I climbed in, and he started driving. Our glasses and the inside of the windows steamed up. He pulled over. I slid my glasses to the tip of my nose.

He adjusted the fan and defroster. "Are there any napkins over in the door? We're not going anywhere unless I can wipe my glasses off."

At the base of the door in the map holder was some folded paper. I reached for it and found the familiar texture of paper napkins. "Yes. Here."

He took the napkins and handed one back to me, "Have one for yourself."

My eyes burned from dissolved sweat and sunscreen. I took my glasses off and used the napkin on my eyes and face.

He started driving again. Water ran down my back.

Two minutes later he said, "Here it is," and pointed at a two-story stucco building. "And it stopped raining. Figures." He sounded disappointed that his rescue had fallen short of dramatic delivery of his waterlogged charge.

I thanked him and asked his name. Joe accepted my offer to photograph him. I could recognize his kindness by letting my blog readers know who had helped me.

A small, middle-aged blonde woman with a French accent greeted me at the Riviera's front desk.

"Do you have room for one?" I asked, hoping I wouldn't make a puddle on the floor.

"Yes. We have a special rate for cyclists. You are by yourself?" I told her I was.

"Brave."

I shrugged. "Do you get many cyclists coming through here?"

"Yes. Usually lots of French, German, other cyclists. Not so much this year."

I nodded.

"We have laundry."

"On-site?" Such luck.

"Yes. Coin operated. Just there, outside." She pointed to a room next to the office.

Laundry was a superb bicycle-friendly amenity.

"Here." She handed me a key. "You're in room five." She pointed across the motel parking lot. "It's a big room. I think you will like. We have coffee here in the morning. Only coffee. You are brave. Be careful."

As soon as I entered the room, I took a selfie to document my epic dousing. Then, I peeled off my wet clothes and took a shower.

Dry clothes were a joy to put on. I slipped into my Mary Janes and went out for quarters and the Wi-Fi code. The innkeeper ducked into the side yard right as I came out. Another hotel guest stood outside his room, smoking a cigarette.

"Did you stay dry?" I asked him.

"Yeah."

"Nice. I got totally soaked. Are you on vacation?" Not far west of Cañon City was the Royal Gorge and rafting.

"I'm here visiting family."

He had a melancholy air about him. I didn't want to pry or make assumptions about what his family situation was. "Do you know the Wi-Fi code?"

"No."

With the conversation shut down, I went looking for quarters at a convenience store. As I walked, I considered that the grumbly man was visiting family at the prison. Florence was home to the federal supermax prison, which held people such as Timothy McVeigh— until his execution in 2001—and Terry Nichols, the Oklahoma City bombers, and Ted Kaczynski, the Unabomber. It couldn't be easy for anyone who had family there.

For 6:00 PM on a weekday, the town center was quiet.

I returned to the hotel office.

"I just went and looked in the garden," the innkeeper said, "and everything is fallen over. What a mess! And so much work to clean it up. But we need the water. It hasn't rained for three weeks."

"Well, you got three weeks' worth all at once! May I have the Wi-Fi code?"

She wrote the code numbers on an index card and handed it to me with quarters. I started laundry and connected.

The next morning, I loaded the panniers on my bike and rolled out of the Riviera's parking lot. I planned to rendezvous with a friend in Pueblo that afternoon and spend time with friends of the family the next evening. I was excited to see familiar faces and talk about things beyond my bike ride.

Pueblo was forty-five miles away, an easy ride that would take me about three-and-a-half hours.

The air and road were hot, and it wasn't even 9:00 AM. Despite the rain the previous evening, the landscape looked parched.

Less than two miles from the Riviera, I passed the prison. Dry, treeless lawn surrounded the facility. A building was set back from the road, and tall security lights surrounded it. No wonder the ground cover was fried. Anything that could have provided shade would have obstructed clear view of the grounds. Barbed wire fencing with NO TRESPASSING signs defined the road edge. Later, after searching for information about the prison, I learned that inmates had windows in their cells, but the windows were only four inches wide and didn't give prisoners a view of any orienting landscape features.

After passing the prison, I settled into a pedaling rhythm. I sweated and sipped warm water as if those sips could rehydrate the landscape. The sun's rays baked the top of my head through the vents in my helmet, but I didn't care.

I looked back to the west. From this vantage, the distance between me and the mountains seemed impossible to cover on bike in one or even two days, but I had. Beyond the mountains I could see, I had pedaled almost two thousand miles, climbed thousands of feet of elevation, and crossed the Continental Divide eleven times. I had pedaled more than one hundred miles in one day. I had survived the Idaho log trucks, a driver who swerved into me, mosquito attack in the Big Hole, raptor attack, camping on thorns, convenience store dinner, and tearing the Band-Aid off my psyche and spirit in Wyoming. I wasn't still on Hoosier Pass, but I felt on top of the world, nonetheless.

Whatever was next, I was ready.

Part 2
HEAT

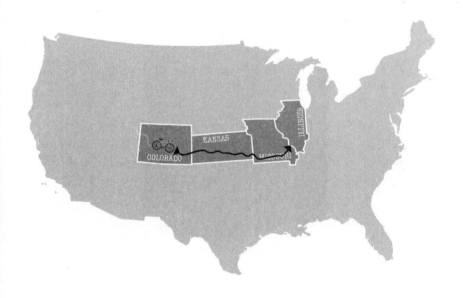

21.

Prairie Horizon

Day thirty-four. On the road east of Pueblo, Colorado, hot wind blasted my face. The wind was a harsh welcome to my new reality. I strained at the pedals. Sunflowers whipped the air. The terrain was flat with tall grasses, agricultural fields, and the straight road.

I fought my way through hot wind to Boone, a town of 323 people, and stopped at the store, a windowless utility shop. Next to the OPEN sign was a sheet of paper with WELCOME CYCLISTS! above the PRAIRIE HORIZON TRAIL logo. The store didn't look welcoming, and I wasn't sure I wanted to go in. I heard John from Portland's voice in the wind: "Did you buy something?" I took a deep breath and entered.

The shopkeeper looked like a movie cowboy. He wore a black cowboy hat; gray, long-sleeved shirt buttoned all the way up; black leather vest; worn blue jeans; and mauve neckerchief tied in a cowboy cravat. His bright blue eyes bore into me. A blond handlebar moustache covered his mouth.

I placed bottles of refrigerated juice and water on the counter and said something about the weather. The cowboy stood stiffly as he rang up the drinks and didn't respond. As I collected my purchases, he practically croaked. His gravelly voice seemed to come from underneath his neckerchief, "You're welcome to sign our cyclists' logbook, if you so choose."

The notebook had the Prairie Horizon Trail logo on its cover. When I finished scribbling, I asked, "What is the Prairie Horizon Trail?" He didn't give me a direct answer, so I asked how long he'd lived in the area.

"Fifty-nine years," he said. "Born and raised here in Boone, Coluhraduh. I was born in 1951. July tenth."

"No way. That's my brother's birthday. Wyoming's birthday, too."

"Where'd you grow up?"

"Cheyenne."

"I been there a time or two. My name's Jeff Earhart."

An American flag hung from the wall behind him with a display of convenience store drugs. "Jeff, may I take your picture?"

Jeff gave a slight nod and leaned his hands on the counter. It took me a moment to realize he was posing.

After I took the picture, we went outside.

Traveling on bike seemed flag-like in its symbolism for many people I encountered. I had observed that bicycling for transportation was perceived as impractical in rural America, and I imagined that us loonies who did were assumed to be urban dwelling Democrats. People couldn't see I'd grown up in Wyoming. They didn't know we had commonalities. I had to rely on conversation to share this.

Jeff lit a cigarette and told me his story. "Ten kids in my family. I'm the middle boy. The kids range in age from seventy-three to forty-six."

"That's a big family."

"There would have been thirteen of us if they all lived. I'm married now and live on the same land my dad had. He came out here in 1917." Jeff pointed behind the store with the cigarette. "That place is the original Boone homestead. Daniel Boone's grandson, Harold, settled on that spot. There used to be a three-story brick school building where the park is." He pointed toward the west. "I went there to third grade, but they had all the way up to graduation. After third grade, they built that new school over yonder, and I went there."

A vehicle pulled up. "That's my wife." Jeff smiled under his moustache. "My shift's just ending, and she's taking over." A blonde woman got out. "Hi, Hotcakes. Just here chattin' with this lady, tellin' her some history."

Hotcakes greeted him with a kiss and said, "Did you give her a map?" She opened the shop door, grabbed a map from the counter, and handed it to me. "Here, this will help you find your way around our area." She went inside. Jeff finished smoking his cigarette and gave a little wave to match mine as he reentered the store.

A railroad paralleled the road from Boone. Miles of graffiti-painted livestock freight cars sat on the tracks, a linear art gallery that broke up the monotony of the road and treeless grassland. Cabbage butterflies courted one another in twirling flight. Their dead bodies colored the road edge with sulfur yellow. I passed two towns ten miles apart, each with a prison.

I arrived in Ordway in the early evening. The town of 1,248 residents seemed deserted. I entered Martin's, the only open eatery in town.

The restaurant was empty, but every table had a paper RESERVED tent.

A woman dressed in hot pink greeted me. "We have a party of sixty-five coming in soon, so if you want to sit, we have a couple tables there." She pointed. "You order at the bar."

I took the menu.

"Oh, and here's our cyclists log." She thrust a fat notebook toward me. "If you would please sign it."

I took the notebook and read the menu. "Does the Slopper come in a bucket?" I asked. It sounded like something a person might feed hogs.

"No, it comes on a plate. The burger patty is on mashed potatoes with gravy over it. There's no bun."

"I see. What's the difference between a regular and smothered burrito?"

"The smothered burrito has shredded meat in it."

"So what's the difference between a smothered burrito and a Garbage Pail?"

"The Garbage Pail has shredded beef and shredded pork in it. The smothered burrito just has one kind of shredded meat in it."

"So the Garbage Pail is like the Kitchen Sink?"

"Yeah."

I ordered a smothered burrito, and the woman filled me in on the logistics of cycling in the area. The local map had information about area businesses, including hours. Most places were closed on Sunday, so I should take extra water. Cyclists started their days at 4:00 AM to beat the heat. In town, Gillian hosted cyclists for free.

I appreciated the woman's advice and planned to leave early in the morning. "How long have you lived here?" I asked.

"A few years. I grew up in Arkansas but have lived in Colorado for a while."

She and her husband had come to Ordway because of the cheap real estate. They bought a 1920s farmhouse for $20,000 that didn't require much work to upgrade for their needs.

When I finished dinner, which burst with meat and tasted fresh with a gentle bite of green chili, I looked through the logbook. Most cyclists reported eating a Garbage Pail. One rider wrote, "Wow, three kinds of slow cooked animal."

After Martin's, I went to the grocery for water and instant oatmeal packets, which I would eat dry for breakfast.

Outside the store, an older man dressed in worn jeans, sun-bleached T-shirt, and a trucker cap and whose shoulders curled toward his sternum stopped me. "Where's the rest of yeh?"

I looked at myself. "Here's my feet, my hands"—I touched the top of my head—"I got my head on. I think I'm all here."

"You're just one, are yuh? Well, have a good time."

"I will. Thanks."

When I entered Gillian's compound, I passed a pen of goats abutting two trailers. I rode around the modular home looking for Gillian and followed the sound of voices. Several people were having a party in a pool.

"I'm looking for Gillian," I said.

A head popped out of the water. "I'm Gillian." It must have been obvious to her why I was there because she offered, "Go around to the gray trailer. You can stay there. It has a green porch and a veggie garden out front." She had a Kiwi accent. "I'll show you around when I'm done here."

I felt uncomfortable arriving without notice when there was a party underway. The trailer had several mattresses stacked against the wall. Gillian mentioned she was going to put bunk beds in there, but at the moment, it was just a shell with a carpeted floor. A table and chair stood at one end, and a few things were plugged in at the other on a nonfunctional sink.

Gillian's son oriented me to the compound. "Mom used to be a cyclist," he said. "She knows it can get expensive staying places. She wants to help however she can."

Gillian and I talked while I waited for the shower to open up and she polished the furniture with lemon oil.

Lying on the floor in the trailer, I watched a stripe of light angle in from the window. I couldn't fall asleep. My left hip was cranky. My lower back was fatigued. I didn't have a pillow. I was hot.

In a fit of exhaustion over not being able to sleep, I opened my eyes. I scanned the unfamiliar room and realized I had been dreaming I couldn't sleep. My watch alarm had woken me. It was 4:45 AM.

I left Gillian's before anyone had risen. Ordway looked like a ghost town as I pedaled through that Sunday morning. The sky was overcast, but the ambient air temperature was probably eighty-something degrees. No people. No vehicles. Main Street's storefronts looked derelict.

I skipped blogging that morning and experimented with an early departure based on what the woman at Martin's had shared. Pedaling past the not-yet-open grocery store, I turned onto the route. Empty stock transport cars lined one side of the road. Electric poles and flat, open landscape defined the other. Everything stood in self-composed portrait: windmills, grasses, fence posts, power lines, roads, clouds, grasshoppers.

After hours of pedaling, Eads appeared like a dirty smear on the horizon.

I settled into a booth at JJ's for Sunday brunch. A grandma, mom, and two girls sat at the booth adjoining mine. A woman came to their table to talk to the mom. After a short exchange, the woman addressed the older girl, who was wearing an aqua-colored T-shirt and pink skirt, and said, "You look like a boy with your hair cut like that." The woman wished the mom luck with her fiancé and the move to wherever they would be stationed and then left.

While no one at the table responded to the comment about the older girl's haircut, I thought it was mean, like a comment one of my classmates in sixth grade had made. She said I looked fat in the stirrup pants I was wearing. Once home, I took the pants off and never wore them again. Since then, and even on this trip, I evaluated every picture of me—did I look fat?

After lunch, I pedaled to the Travelers Lodge and didn't leave my room until the next morning.

Day thirty-six. The sun blinded, and the air was already hot at the Eads post office at 9:00 AM. Sweat trickled down the small of my back.

Daniel had penned me a two-sheet, double-sided letter on yellow legal pad paper and apologized for his poor spelling and handwriting. He wrote in all caps, and I didn't notice any misspellings. He referenced how long it took him to stop adding an "e" to "bowl." He explained: "bowl and bowel—very different things." I chuckled. It felt good to laugh. I liked where we were going. Maybe we needed the distance to drop the sex so we could learn new things about each other.

East of Eads, there were no services for fifty-eight miles. I had two water bottles on my bike and two reserve liters—enough to get me through the service gap.

Fifteen miles east of Eads, I could detour south forty miles on pavement to Camp Amache, a World War II Japanese internment camp, or north nine miles on a dirt road to the Sand Creek Massacre National Historic Site.

Sand Creek was the likelier of the two sites I might visit because it was closer to the route and I'd written a poem about the massacre in college. In 1864, Colonel John M. Chivington, a Methodist minister, led the U.S. Army attack on a community of 750 Cheyenne and Apache Indians wintering on Sand Creek.

As I approached the turn to the site, I was afraid of how I would feel seeing the place where the mutilation of about 230 people—mainly women, children, and elders—occurred. I was afraid of the voices I might hear, afraid of the restless spirits I might encounter.

I envisioned the Sand Creek site as an expansive area with a sparkling creek and flower-dotted prairie. I imagined the Cheyenne and Apache camped in winter. Boys would learn how to hunt rabbits and bison. Girls would mimic older women in camp craft, break ice in the creek, and haul water. Dogs would bark. Horses would stand close against the cold wind and chew grass near a bluff. At night, the people would stargaze and tell stories, fight, make love, sleep. The people had what they needed here, even in winter.

Prairie grasses rustled in an untilled field.

Pain rose in my body as I sensed the past violence.

I didn't go to the site but continued east.

22.

God's Place

The landscape had four variations: young cornfields, buzz-cut wheat fields, bare soil, and grasslands. The grasslands swished in the wind.

The few built structures were cones, cylinders, boxes. Rectangles, triangles, parallelograms.

A royal blue sign with a skipping star welcomed me to Kansas.

The road surface improved, mostly.

The wind swirled and batted the front of my bike.

Clouds dotted the sky above a flat horizon.

There was no roadkill, excepting an occasional small bird. No bees, no butterflies, no moths, no mammals, no snakes.

I pushed through the wind and stopped at the edge of Mountain and Central time. There was a sign to mark this invisible line, and weirdly, a shadow. On one side of the sign, it was 2:00 PM, and on the other, 3:00 PM.

A town welcomed me with a billboard message from God. In red letters on a white background, it read, "Will the Road You're on Get You to My Place?" and "—God" was in blue. Did the TransAmerica

Bicycle Trail take me to God's place? Whoever made the billboard had chosen the colors of the American flag.

Back in Pueblo, one of my Facebook friends from school in Eugene who had just graduated in the Class of 2010 commented on a post, "You should consider carrying an American flag on your bike as you go through the middle of the country. For safety." His comment perplexed me. I wasn't on a political mission. When people asked what my cause was, I said, "Keeping rural communities alive."

Out on two wheels, I didn't see political messages in the landscape, nor did the people I encountered talk politics. I assumed people were like me and unaware of current events. I didn't read news, watch TV, or listen to the radio. I didn't know what was going on in the country beyond this trip.

If I had a flag, would it mean God was with me? Wasn't Spirit everywhere all the time? Wasn't that God's place? Didn't that make a billboard or flag unnecessary? Chivington, who led the charge to massacre the village at Sand Creek, was a Methodist minister. He must have thought he was in God's place. Did he ride with a flag?

What about the Japanese Americans who were interned by the U.S. government during World War II? The government sent them to some of the most unpeopled and difficult-to-reach places in the country solely because of their heritage. Were the Americans who tore these Americans from their homes and livelihoods in God's place? Were the internees in God's place?

America.

In God we trust.

I am a white American—spiritual but not religious. The Sand Creek Massacre and Japanese Internment were part of my Americanness, my history, which was wrapped together with the flag and

God. America had been won by stepping on other nations and by exterminating, devaluing, and diminishing other American people. How could I fly the flag with pride when I couldn't see past the wrongs my nation had and continued to commit against Americans? As a person of privilege, how did I reinforce, question, or challenge the Othering of Americans? As unsettling as it was, I owned my complicity in these atrocities and discrimination. I didn't like it. How could I do and make better?

My thoughts knotted. I kept pedaling.

The hot crosswind tired me. My hands grew numb.

I was surrounded by America's breadbasket and what looked like America's agrichemical heartland. The infertile land of plenty.

When I read Michael Pollan's *Botany of Desire* on first moving to Oregon in 2002, I finally understood what organic meant. It was the whole sphere of life that surrounded the cultivation of food. Soil was dark brown, almost black, full of dead and decaying matter that fed insects, worms, nematodes, and fungi that in turn enriched the soil with nutrients and moisture. This soil ecosystem created food for plants. With this fertile foundation, organic farmers grew food plants among others that attracted pollinators and predators of pests.

Industrial agriculture was yoked to businesses that sold fertilizer, herbicide, pesticide, and seeds that could germinate and grow in the presence of poison.

Many of western Kansas's fields stood naked in the sun, devoid of life. The soil—perhaps "medium" was a better word—looked gray, corpse-like.

The wind buffeted me. Ten miles from my destination for the night, I pulled over at a roadside picnic area and lay on a table. Five minutes passed. Ten. I scolded myself into continuing.

In Leoti, pronounced by locals as *lee-oat-uh*, I went to the Dairy King. The hot wind had sucked me dry.

The Dairy King was a drive-in where people parked under a carport and ordered at a walk-up window. There were places to sit under the carport. The kitchen had a couple of people in it who slid windows up and down to talk to customers but who otherwise kept the windows down and the cool air inside.

I sat under the carport drinking iced water. A bang on the window let me know my food was done. Dinner was a grilled chicken salad, fried okra, and a limeade. The wind kept blowing the lettuce off my fork and threatened to blow the salad out of its container. I went back up to the window for a banana. I could only get a banana with ice cream, so I ordered the boat.

"It's challenging to eat in the wind," I said to the teenage guy behind the window.

He nodded.

"I guess that's why people have cars." I looked at the vehicles under the carport where people were eating without issue.

He smiled and nodded with one eyebrow raised as if to say "Duh."

I hoped to sleep in the park, the likely camping area. My map said a hospital across the street from the park had bathrooms campers could use, but a sign on the hospital door indicated NO PUBLIC REST-ROOMS. I went to the motel where an innkeeper insisted everything I needed I could get there.

He'd been in Leoti about thirty years and had come from Nebraska.

"My family bought this place," he said, "and my wife and I came down here to run it." He leaned back in his office chair. "I put you in the handicapped room. It's the last room I have on the ground floor. Is that okay?"

"Will no one need the room?"

"Usually if they do, they call ahead. I think you'll be okay."

"Okay."

"You know, you could always take the bus if you didn't want to ride in the wind."

My exhaustion must have been obvious. Maybe he understood the psychological distance I'd traveled to get there. Locals seemed to understand bike touring better than I would have guessed. Because I didn't encounter them out on bikes and because many of them made comments that referred to the difficulty or scariness of bicycling, I didn't think they rode bikes or would understand my experience. But they—Bill in Twin Bridges, the innkeeper at the Riviera in Florence, and the proprietor at Martin's in Ordway—knew how to support my experience before I even arrived.

I wasn't the first person to visit these towns on bike. People had been pedaling the TransAm for thirty-four years. That was a lot of opportunity for conversation. This man had offered lodging for thirty of those thirty-four years. He would know. He'd probably talked to hundreds of people who had the same weary presentation I did.

"That would be one way to do it," I said. "Is there passenger train service around here?"

"Down in Garden City, south of here. But the bus is better."

I wasn't ready to give up on pedaling, but I liked knowing there were options.

23.

Tortillas, a Flat, Cobbler

I departed Leoti aiming to overnight in Bazine, where there was a bicyclist camp. If I made it, I would pedal nearly one hundred miles that day. I got moving by 8:00 AM, later than planned but reasonable for my first morning in a new time zone. It was pleasantly warm but not hot. A gentle breeze stirred. I pedaled quickly, taking advantage of fresh legs and ideal riding conditions.

Twenty-five miles from Leoti, I stopped at the grocery store in Scott City. A man in shorts and a T-shirt with salt-and-peppery brown hair approached me in one of the aisles and said, "I have to ask. Where'd you start?" After I told him I was from Oregon, he ranted, "You, Oregonians —"

Was he the kind of person who would sideswipe a cyclist to make a point about safety and society's best interest? Thankfully, our exchange was in the public space of the grocery store.

"What possessed you to ride your bike across the country?" His tone was sharp.

"I'm going to a conference in Washington, DC, and I thought I would ride there."

"A conference, huh? That must mean you're intelligent."

"Some say that."

"Yet you're riding your bike across the country?"

My anger rose. He was my brother calling me names. The smarty-pants conference was only a destination. Something buried in me propelled this journey. I had glimpses of awareness, but whatever creature or energy motivated me was inaccessible to my intellect. I shot back at him, "I'm crazy, too. I was that way before I left."

Light danced in his eyes, but his tone didn't change when he said, "Well, if I'm going to Dodge City, I get in my car and go. It's quick. Takes only forty-five minutes."

I was done with the conversation and looked at the boxes of tea without saying anything more. If I wanted to get somewhere fast, biking might not be my first choice. It would depend on where I was going. Getting to Washington, DC, wasn't about getting there quickly.

"Well, be safe out there," he said and exited the aisle.

The exchange felt antagonistic, but he parted on a note of safety. A contradiction. Was he playing?

I stood there, irked. I assumed the goodness in people. If they made an attempt to talk to me, that was a sign of friendliness. I didn't think I was giving off the "vulnerable female" vibe, and I expected anyone who might mess with me would be intimidated by my strength or craziness and would steer clear—unless they were emboldened by the protectiveness of a motor vehicle, ignited by rage, and unencumbered by a conscience.

When I left the store, the man was waiting for me outside.

"Here." He pointed to a pack of tortillas on a stack of boxes. "These are what I bring here to the store." The edge in his voice was gone. He handed the pack to me. "Take this. They're good energy food. Put some peanut butter on there or something. They don't need to be refrigerated."

I breathed relief. I took the tortillas and thanked him. He got in his truck and drove off while I fiddled with packing my purchases and the tortillas in my panniers, grateful for his kindness.

Beyond Scott City, the road was lined with cornfields, and the plants' wide leaves brushed one another in the breeze.

Cornfields transitioned to feedlot. I first noticed mounds of black soil. Something alive! But my excitement waned when I smelled the manure.

A ruckus in the feedlot caught my attention. A cowboy approached a cow on the ground. A lash cracked. A low groan. The cattle that had been near the one on the ground scattered. The cowboy raised a cudgel over his head and brought it down on the cow. The cow moaned but didn't move. I knew little about raising cattle. The cowboy might have been trying to save the cow's life, but it didn't look that way.

Sign after sign along the road advertised premium beef. I sweated in the heat and battled the crosswind. The day was a repetitive patchwork of genetically modified crops, lifeless landscape, and feedlots.

A wind farm did little to lift my mood. The water in my bottle was hot. Kansas sucked.

Then I saw a turtle run along the roadside and laughed.

In Dighton at the Frigid Creme, a drive-in like the Dairy King, I sat at a tall table under the carport and opened my map.

If I wanted to stay in Bazine, I needed to call ahead. I turned on my phone and dialed.

A gentle female voice answered.

It seemed unreal to me that I only had to follow directions on the map and would be matched with a place to sleep and breakfast at someone's house. In July 2010, Airbnb was still in its infancy. Elaine was ahead of her time in offering the Bicycle Oasis B&B. For $15, I could camp in her yard and have breakfast. Two other women would also be staying there that night.

I'd pedaled forty-nine miles to reach my perch in the shade. Now that I had a reservation with Elaine, I committed to going another forty-four miles in the hottest part of the day.

I poured the ice cubes from my cup into a water bottle and pedaled into the assaulting heat. Sweat salts showed on my clothes. I needed to be attentive to hydration and electrolyte intake. The road was a shadeless inferno. The sun baked me from above. The road sautéed me from below. The hot wind sucked moisture from my body.

East of Dighton, the terrain rumbled in places. There were fewer corn and wheat fields but more hayfields, oil derricks, and grasslands. And birds and grasshoppers. And a monarch butterfly! A kindred journeying spirit.

Trees shaded a roadside turnout with a historical marker.

I pulled over and turned on my phone. It was 2:18 PM. I e-mailed Daniel:

> ✉ I'm standing in the only shade for miles at an interpretive panel about George Washington Carver's KS homestead. My bike just got blown over. It's hot, whew.

My hair blew in the wind. I took a couple selfies. Eventually, I hefted my bike from the ground, remounted, and pedaled toward Ness City.

Four miles shy of Ness City, I got a flat tire. I sat in the partial shade of some bushes that lined a driveway and fixed the flat. I was hot and cranky and skinned my knuckles reseating the tire on my wheel. My arms went wimpy as I worked to inflate the tube with my hand pump. The fix took forty-five minutes. I was back on the road but grouchier.

At the Ness City Frigid Creme, I was crabby—probably dehydrated and low on electrolytes. Bazine was twelve miles farther east. I ordered iced water, a hamburger, and spicy pickle spears. Pickles sounded cold—even if spicy—and full of electrolytes. The staff handed me a thirty-two-ounce Styrofoam cup of iced water. I sucked on the straw, sat on a bench in the shade, and turned on my phone.

After receiving a refill on my water and before I could ask what the hold up on my *fast* food was, the young woman inside slid the window down and turned away. Unsure how long I might wait, I pulled my laptop from its pannier and updated Facebook. I finished my water refill and checked my watch. Twenty-five minutes seemed an excessive wait for a burger.

Another water refill would tide me over, but neither of the two women inside acknowledged me. I stood for five minutes in the sun, empty water cup, waiting, seething. When the window finally slid up, a paper bag came out.

"Sorry that took so long," the woman said. "It's my fault. I messed up your order and we had to remake it."

Cool air cascaded from the window.

"How much do I owe you?" I asked.

"Don't worry about it."

"What?"

"Really, don't worry about it. Be safe." She slid the window down and turned away from me.

I should have felt appreciative, but I was cranky. I took my bag to the bench. The burger was good and basic. Perfect. The pickle spears were fried. Horror of horrors. What sick fuck thought it was a good idea to abuse pickles in such a way? They were spicy, oily, and hot as hell. I burned my mouth. I was repulsed but ate them anyway.

As I started toward the road, one of the women came out and called after me, "Be safe."

"Sure thing." I waved.

At dusk, I approached some buildings and haying equipment and passed a sign made from a bicycle. In seconds, the buildings disappeared, and the road ahead was vacant. I had passed through Bazine. I looped back. I pulled into the driveway at the bicycle sign. There were two bikes with touring gear along the fence. A fit-looking man wearing a ball cap stood in the garden.

"Excuse me," I said.

He didn't hear me. I leaned my bike against a picnic table, looked at the door, and saw a card indicating Elaine's Bicycle Bed & Breakfast. I walked up to the door, and just as I was about to knock, the man came over.

"You made it! I was beginning to wonder if I should go look for you." He gave me a big hug and ushered me inside. I was still wearing my sunglasses and tripped on some low steps and the threshold into the kitchen where three women in orange sat.

"I'll be right back," I said.

I retrieved my glasses and reentered the kitchen, dazed. Elaine, a slim woman with glasses and strawberry blonde hair, brought me a glass of water, and I drank. The man I met from the garden, Elaine's husband, Dan, put a bowl of apricot cobbler with ice cream in front of me. Across from me were the two other cyclists, who appeared to be between twenty and thirty-five years old.

Meaghan and Rita had arrived at Elaine's separately. Rita, the slighter of the two, with long brown hair, came from Massachusetts. I never figured out where Meaghan came from, only that she was moving. She had a curly brown bob similar to mine and wore an orange dress that barely contained her breasts. She started her trip in Seattle, had something to do in New York, and was ending in Connecticut.

"Why did you decide to do this ride?" I asked Rita.

"I always wanted to go across the country, but I don't like driving. It seemed like the way to do it."

"Had you ever been on a bike tour before?"

"No. I did an eighty-mile ride before I left but never an overnight. How far did you go today?"

"I don't know." I pulled the map from my jersey pocket and pretended I could do math. "About ninety-three miles." I was pleased with the number.

Both Rita and Meaghan were prepared to pedal more than a hundred miles the next day. Meaghan had been out since June 1, zigzagging the country. I shared my plans for reaching Washington, DC. Meaghan and Rita set up their camps while I took a shower. When I emerged from the shower, Elaine and I decided on breakfast for 6:30 AM. I brought my punctured tube into the living room. Two fans kept the air moving, and I couldn't find a hole. I would deal with it in the morning.

On the lawn, I sprawled on my sleeping pad. Little things kept biting me. I twitched and covered my legs. More little bites. I abandoned my sprawl and made sure no part of me extended over the pad. Still, little bites. Things rustled under the pad. By midnight I sat up, unsure that I'd slept, intent to find a less buggy spot.

The picnic table beckoned, and I put my gear on top. It was like lying on a bed except for the airiness underneath. No bites. No rustling under my sleeping pad.

I fell asleep, woke when dogs barked, went back to sleep, and woke again just before 5:00 AM when Meaghan and Rita packed their tents. On the table in a stupor, I sat, knowing I would not sleep more, and watched them go, lights blinking in the dark.

At 6:30 AM, Dan, Elaine, and I sat at the kitchen table for breakfast. Bazine seemed smaller than small, and I asked how they had settled on living there.

Dan answered, "Elaine grew up here. I grew up in Minnesota. We met and married in Colorado. Then we came here."

Elaine added, "The town needs help. We need young people. They move away and don't come back." Her answer was like Linda's assessment of Halfway. Probably there were other similarities. "Is agriculture the main industry?" I asked.

Dan responded, "Primarily, but oil, too."

I didn't get the feeling they were economically strapped, and they had real concerns about the longevity of their town. "So what motivated you to start taking in cyclists?"

Elaine answered, "We kept seeing them here, a lot of them in quite a desperate way. We wanted to do something to help. People kept telling me I was crazy to let strangers into my house, but cyclists aren't going to steal things from you because they have nowhere to carry anything. And I've found them quite an interesting group of people."

I ate my eggs, nodding over the similarities between Elaine's feeling about people on bike tours and what Bill from Twin Bridges had said, that touring cyclists were fascinating and stirred him to help accommodate them.

Elaine continued, "Everyone has different reasons for going on a trip like this. I like being here for the people who really need help, who come in and are ready to quit. Sometimes all they need is a place to stay, kind people, food, and some inspiration. It can really turn things around."

When I showed up the night before, I was spent. Water, apricot cobbler, and some rest met my immediate needs, but I saw the thin line between my crabbiness and exertion and quitting. I hadn't seen just how thin until she mentioned it. I had wanted to quit.

After breakfast, I was antsy to get on the road. It was 7:00 AM. Rita and Meaghan had been gone long enough to cover twenty miles.

My tire was flat again. Damn.

At the picnic table, I set aside the tube that had been in the tire, suspecting a leaky valve. Dan brought a floor pump, which made things easier. The tube I thought had a puncture from the previous day held air, so I put it back in the tire and loaded up the air pressure, hoping yesterday's flat was a fluke. I departed Elaine's oasis at 7:45 AM aiming for Larned forty-four miles down the road.

As I pedaled, I strategized about my blog. I hadn't had a chance to write between yesterday's delayed dinner, the socializing at Elaine's, and the flat tire. Since Larned was close, I could write and publish two posts while I was there. The first one would be important to let my followers know I was okay. My parents and Daniel weren't on Facebook, so the post was my best way to let them know I was on my way for the day. The second one was more of a housekeeping matter since the blog was my main field notebook. Remembering two days' worth of conversation and observation was easy for me, but I didn't want to get further behind.

Larned's downtown streets were paved with brick. On the uneven surface, my rear tire went flat again. I was hot and tired. I walked to an espresso shop and ordered a chai. The chai was like hot eggnog, not what I hoped, but I sipped it anyway. Daniel had e-mailed.

✉ Hey you, still typing? Or just having a day of leisure? Or............................... :0)

Leisure? As if. I was short-tempered. The tea was weird.

✉ I'm having KS.

In Larned now. Plan is to get a spot and write. Must deal with flat too. Temp fix is all I can do. Heat's up there. Ugh.

I pushed my bike to the Country Inn, where my first question of the gray-haired woman behind the desk was "Do you have Wi-Fi?"

"Not today. The rooms are good though."

I couldn't complain about thirty-five dollars for a room with air-conditioning even if it didn't have Wi-Fi.

We discussed the relationship that brought her to town, the friends who were her reason to stay, and how the opportunity at the hotel came to her when she needed a change. While we were talking about my work, someone came in for a room, so I went to #16 to deal with my flat.

Before I showered, I called Mom to research overnighting a new tube to Larned. She answered on the first ring. Hearing her voice reduced my distress. I hadn't found anything that would cause a puncture in the tire and didn't know why a tube that held air could suddenly go flat.

Mom was available to help with anything at any time, and she treated every request with urgency. Usually, I phoned to check in when I had cell reception and space in my schedule, often during rest days. When I rang out of the blue, such as this call about the tube, it was a time-sensitive matter. For requests that came during sleeping hours, follow-ups from I-need-something calls, or other updates and communications, we used e-mail. I had the impression Mom was glued to her desk, ever ready should the phone ring or an e-mail arrive from me.

By the time I finished my shower, Mom had left a message. Her research was thorough, the news not what I hoped. Overnighting wasn't possible in Larned, and even express delivery to a nearby town took two days. There was a bike shop on my route seventy-one miles east of Larned in Hutchinson.

I could reach the Hutchinson bike shop in one day, but if I got a flat before I reached it, I would probably have to walk miles on the hot road in the middle of nowhere and risk dehydration before I could get help.

I went out on foot for an early dinner.

Cycling clothes hung on the railing outside a room two doors from mine.

Back at the Country Inn later that evening, I was looking for a puncture in the tube when my brother called.

"Hey, Kid, Delcie and the kids are in Kansas. We're trying to figure out where you are to see if we can arrange a meetup."

"I'm in Larned." I heard the curtness in my voice as if those three words could say, *It's fucking hot and windy, I have a flat tire, and I'm exhausted. Get me the hell out of this wasteland.*

"That doesn't look very big," he said.

"What do you mean? It has two state jails and is bigger than most towns I've been going through." The community's size didn't seem germane to intersecting with his wife and kids.

"Huh" was his only response. "They're south and east of you. Is there a place you could meet in the middle?"

We settled on breakfast in Macksville. With an early start, I could pedal the twenty miles off route to Macksville and avoid some of the day's heat.

I returned to my tube, which was in the sink.

How unlikely. Intersecting with family in Kansas. My niece was the one I'd blogged to about tough girls. The excitement I had to see her was dampened by my duress. I feared Sonora would judge me if she saw I was having difficulty. It didn't seem the time or place to talk about how tough girls could have a tough time. I said yes to whatever life dished out and took it. I didn't know I had the option to say no. I was already overburdened. Meeting with family was an additional weight.

A line of bubbles revealed a pinhole in my tube. I patched it and prayed the pinhole was the only problem.

I woke at 4:00 AM. The morning's blog post put me forty-five minutes behind schedule, and I departed Larned at 7:15 AM. I planned to make up the time by riding fast.

Under cloud cover, I pedaled south. The air hadn't cooled overnight, and the land radiated heat. My skin was sticky. My body absorbed the heat like my water bottles. Filled with cold water in the morning, the bottles would sweat for twenty minutes and then turn hot.

I pedaled hard in the headwind. Sweat squeezed from my pores.

Moisture collected on me from the air. Wind agitated the hot, wet film that coated my body. My leg muscles burned. I wouldn't make Macksville by 8:30 AM. I stopped and texted Delcie, "Late start and headwind. 9 more realistic." Without waiting for a response, I stashed my phone and kept pedaling.

At 8:45 AM, I intersected with Highway 50. I texted Delcie again, "Hwy 50 heading east. Now it should only be a crosswind." Seven miles to go.

Without the wind in my face, I rode faster.

At 9:15 AM, I rolled onto the sidewalk outside Macksville's downtown café. Sonora popped out of the café in a streak of pink and orange, her brown bob flapping. Aidan was like a faintly smiling fence post behind her in navy cargo shorts and blue T-shirt. I leaned my bike against the wall and hugged them. "How long have you been here?" I asked.

Aidan responded, "About fifteen minutes, but it's felt longer than that."

In the dim interior, Delcie sat at an oval table. She wore a brown T-shirt and tan shorts, and her shoulder-length brown hair was tidy. We greeted each other. She and my brother met in college, and they'd been married eleven years. Since Delcie had graduated from college, she'd had various roles as an educator, and once my brother started his own design firm, she balanced cooking and parenting with the firm's operations.

A boy about two or three years old toddled over to Aidan and Sonora with delight in his eyes. I understood why Aidan thought the wait was long. The boy was persistent. I appreciated when the proprietress told the boy to let us enjoy our breakfast. I had last seen my family in December when the idea to ride to DC was still fresh.

After we ordered, the woman disappeared.

"How did you end up in Kansas?" I asked Delcie, unsure how this needle-in-a-haystack reunion came about.

"We went to my great aunt's ninetieth birthday in Cleveland."

I didn't know she had relatives in the Midwest. The conversation bumped along. It was awkward to pick up our thread as a family in a café that was someone's living room.

My breakfast burrito arrived. It was smaller than a frozen burrito, and the cheese was an American cheese single partially melted over the top. I touched my fork to it. It didn't inspire confidence, but I ate everything on my plate and the egg that came with Sonora's bacon that she didn't want.

I settled up at the counter.

We walked down the street in direct sun and suffocating heat to a park with a playground. I welcomed the opportunity to see my family and be seen by them, but it felt like a new trial to put aside everything that pressed on me and play with kids in oppressive heat. They wouldn't be here if I weren't, and I wouldn't be here if they weren't. I cooed over the toad Aidan caught, pushed the merry-go-round, and engaged Sonora with a dead cicada I found in the grass.

We wound down the visit at the gas station store where I purchased two big bottles of water, an orange juice, and a little bag of cookies. I had sixty miles ahead of me, and it was almost noon. The temperature was probably in the nineties but felt like one-hundred-something degrees from the humidity.

We sat in the shade while I guzzled my drinks and ate the cookies.

"Wow," Aidan said, "you drank that whole thing already?"

It didn't seem worth explaining what riding in the heat felt like, how little I wanted to be in the muggy oven of Kansas and incinerated on the shadeless highway. "Yeah. It's kind of like filling up the car with gasoline. The fuel goes in me." I hoped it would also cool me down so the first mile or two might feel like a warmup.

Sonora piped up, "Grandma said I should ask you why you spend money."

Did my mom think my niece would care about or understand what I was doing? It didn't matter. I liked the challenge of articulating my research to a six-and-a-half-year-old. If she didn't care, she didn't care.

My response was the most I'd said in the three hours we'd been together. Sonora held my gaze and then said, "You're weird."

It sounded like something my brother would say. Regardless, it was the segue we needed to end the visit. I squeezed Sonora hard, a tough girl hug. She made a noise and then said, "You're choking me." I couldn't tell if she was joking or serious, but I felt badly for not being gentler. Just because my brother squeezed the shit out of me when he hugged me didn't mean I needed to do it to my niece. But, all that family stuff aside, I hoped the squeeze created a positive transference of badassery.

I pedaled out on the highway as they piled into the car. I waved. They waved back. I smiled and turned my attention to the road ahead. With that turn, everything I'd pushed aside during their visit sling-shotted back. An average pace would get me to Hutchinson in six hours, when the shop closed. I needed to hustle. My anxiety mounted. Could I handle the physical demands? What if I got a flat?

24.

Feeding the Hungry Heart

Highway 50 had a wide shoulder that offered smooth riding. Large vehicles traveled at higher speeds than the roads I'd been pedaling, but I was a comfortable distance from them and felt a modicum of ease.

Still, the oven-like heat pressed. How was the landscape green and lush? I was brining in my own salt. My hands sweated a hot slime on the inside of my cycling gloves, and they slid like a five-headed slug toward the fingerless openings. The glove seams pressed into the tissue that connected my fingers no matter how I held the handlebars.

My head roasted.

The air steamed, and along the roadside were bogs and ponds. The heat asphyxiated.

Stretches of road were littered with flattened frogs. I counted armadillos that were like deflated basketballs—stiff, textured, round, the skins sometimes shattered into tortilla chips. I also rolled by dead turtles, squashed opossums, and fragmented raccoons.

Amid this backdrop of death, red dragonflies flew in all directions, and monarch butterflies fluttered. Countless piles of scat sat on the road eight inches from the edge. The precision was stunning.

I fueled up briefly in Stafford. I'd made good time. From there, wind blew from the southwest. Part tailwind. Part crosswind. I pedaled hard. My rear tire stayed inflated.

I counted mileposts and checked my watch. If I maintained my pace, I would arrive in Hutchinson by 5:00 PM, an hour before the shop closed. Hutchinson's cyclists-only lodging was at the Zion Lutheran Church Hostel. My map indicated that I could pick up the key at the bike shop. Another reason to reach town before the shop closed.

To distract myself, I set a goal to pedal consecutive five-mile segments. It was challenging to remember which mile marker I started counting the increment. My mind wandered.

Growing up in Cheyenne, I had often walked a two-and-a-half-mile loop around Sloan's Lake. As a high schooler, I tried to run this same trail to train for an Outward Bound course, but I didn't have the fitness or determination to do it without walking.

I sampled running again near the end of college. Several of the women I lived with ran. The activity made me cough and turned my face bright red. I got better at it. By the time I moved to Eugene, running was a regular part of maintaining my physical conditioning. But once I started practicing yoga regularly, I ran less.

Now I was unable to run because of my hip. I missed the body I had when I was vegan, doing yoga five to seven days a week, dancing once or twice a week, and working as a landscaper. People thought I was sexy in that body, and it was the first time I felt sexy in my body. But even then when I looked at myself, I was a bit heavy, and nearly all the women around me were slimmer.

Then, I quit being vegan. I quit dancing. I quit doing yoga. And I quit doing physical labor. Those changes were slow-falling dominoes that started at the time of my art show, persisted through my depression, and continued into the Recession. I got softer. My clothes were tight. I was embarrassed by my body. If people thought I was sexy in this softer body, they had to be lying. And if they didn't find my body sexy, they confirmed what I already knew.

A few months after my all-day crying event after my art show, my therapist recommended I read Geneen Roth's *Feeding the Hungry Heart*. I cried over the pages and the dramatic transformation that was possible for the women in the book when they came to love who they were, as they were. They looked different to other people when they thought more generously of themselves.

Roth's book had been one source of aid through that dark time, and while I could grasp the benefit of loving myself, I couldn't do it. Gentleness made me soft. Gentleness could not get me over the Rocky Mountains or through this heat. Gentleness would not have led to biking across the country and certainly not with a bum hip.

I was proud of my physical effort and persevering, but admiration of what I could do didn't translate into loving my body. I still saw myself as fat. I couldn't even tell if my body had gotten smaller. How could I love this thing that didn't respond to heroic effort?

I rolled into Hutchinson at 5:00 PM and stopped at a traffic light, something I hadn't seen since Pueblo, Colorado, six days and 405 miles earlier. I made it!

A man at the bike shop helped me with the tubes. While browsing, I found HALT!, cayenne spray dog repellent. I'd been cautioned about dogs in Kentucky by several cyclists. During my conversation in Bazine with Rita at Elaine's place, I asked about the Kentucky dogs. Rita confirmed the dogs were aggressive. She'd been chased by them. Repellent would be handy.

"You have everything here," I said to the man in the shop.

He nodded. "We've been around for a while. Since 1964 at this location. Other bike shops have come and gone."

I set my purchases on the counter. "I'd like to stay at the hostel. How do I do that?" Now that I was in Hutchinson, my tiredness weighed.

He rang up my items and placed a key on the counter. "It's down the street three blocks. When you leave, put the key on the table there."

I descended stairs to the church's basement door and let myself in.

Two double beds were set up on the basement stage. A curtain hung between them. Each "room" had a shelf with sheets, a TV, and movies. Making the bed made me happy, like being at home.

The hostel was air-conditioned. I could get Wi-Fi across the street at the library. Deluxe. I luxuriated in my privacy and called Daniel. We wished we could meet somewhere, but the logistics of doing so were impossible. Nonetheless, we fantasized about a sexy encounter.

Right as I pressed the button on my phone to hang up, Daniel said, "I love you."

I looked at the dark screen. Did he mean to say it? I tingled.

After washing the day's salt and slime from my body, I headed out for dinner. The recommended Mexican restaurant was a distance from the hostel. While I wanted a break from my bike and worry over a potential flat, my hip wasn't up for a long walk.

When I finished a zesty *arroz con pollo,* I remounted my bike and discovered my back tire was flat again. I walked, dismayed. What could be causing the flat?

I returned to the hostel at dusk in a cloud of exhaustion. I hadn't done any writing. Couldn't. My thoughts were atwitter with Daniel's "I love you." It seemed automatic, like maybe he said it accidentally. Yet, that kind of slip wouldn't happen if he didn't feel something for me. Unable to focus, I took a nap and woke sweating in the stuffy basement.

I turned the AC on. As the basement cooled, I wrote Daniel a letter and closed with "Love." I took another two-hour nap and got up to write a blog post.

The library Wi-Fi was weak. I walked the parking lot until I found a stronger signal from someone's house. It was after 6:00 AM. The cloudless morning brightened.

In the air-conditioned basement, I dealt with my flat. Before I put a new tube in the tire, I wanted to make certain there wasn't something in the tire. I ran my fingers carefully along its inside and discovered a wire shard poking through. It was tiny and difficult to remove. It had to be the source of my recurring flat. Sweet relief.

I inserted one of my new tubes from the bike shop and departed Hutchinson in the morning's growing heat.

25.

Road Rage

Day forty. Not far from Hutchinson, I stopped in the shoulder at the front of a line of cars at a construction zone. The flagger nodded. I was in full sun and running on three nights of minimal sleep. I stood for a few minutes and then shifted my feet, which cooked in my cycling shoes.

Five minutes passed.

Ten minutes.

I roasted and fumed.

Did none of the construction crew recognize I was frying? Did they not understand that the only water I had was already warm and becoming hot? Did they not consider that I could ride on the shoulder and keep far away from their equipment and mess?

I doubted anyone in the line of stopped vehicles understood my anxiety and frustration. They were bathed in air-conditioning. They were not hot, so no one else was. If they had any thoughts about me, I was certain those thoughts highlighted my foolishness and how it served me right to wait in the heat.

The sun roasted my head. I looked at my watch. Fifteen minutes I'd been waiting.

The shoulder called. Everyone's attention was on the men in the road. I shifted on my feet as my inner rule breaker took charge, clipped one foot into a pedal, and steadied the front of the bike. The flagger said something into his radio and moved. The movement startled me. The flagger stepped back and swiveled his sign to slow. I darted forward.

At the end of the construction area, I came to a short, two-lane bridge with no bike lane. I took the lane. Vehicles backed up behind me. I could feel the press of exasperation from outside my body and within. Drivers told me off by revving their engines as they passed.

On the other side of the bridge, I steered into the wide shoulder where I pedaled and drank. The water in my bottles was hotter than my tongue.

My body was too hot. I wanted to scream.

I was on alert. Heat illness was serious. I might not be able to do anything if I recognized myself in distress. The progression from heat exhaustion to heat stroke to death could be quick and faster than I could find cell service if I even had presence of mind to call for help.

Drinking hot water amplified my rage, but I did it. I planned to stay alive. If I had enough sense to hydrate, I was still okay.

Another construction zone stopped me. One lane was closed while the work crew patched cracks. The flagger nodded to me but didn't say anything. I stood on the road preparing for another fifteen-minute roast. Hot air blew on me like I was standing in front of a giant coil heater on the highest setting. I swore heat waves blurred the edges of my shoes.

Shortly after I arrived, the flagger waved me through. Perhaps he'd been out there long enough that morning to appreciate how hot

I was. The traffic released in the direction of travel opposite me. A guy in a big truck yelled, "Buy a car!"

Did the mere fact of me on the road insult his manhood? Did he realize the profound lameness of what he yelled at me? Buy a car?

I pedaled and raged, wishing I had the capacity for an appropriate come back. I wanted to yell, not so much at the man but the whole fucking state of Kansas. I wanted to yell at the people who told me I would hate Kansas—they were right, goddamn it. I wanted to yell about how hard it was to get up day after day with little sleep and pedal the monotonous roadway and write my blog and Facebook posts that made it seem like everything was easy breezy, funny mishaps, ironic adventures, scarcely averted dangers, woman power, and wasn't-it-so-great-the-neat-things-I-was-seeing.

Fuck America.

Bootstrapping was a sham. There was nothing here. No money. No life. No mercy. America didn't just break dreams, it crushed them, ground them into the dirt under its giant radial tires, gassed them with diesel, and then lit the mess on fire.

Up in flames. Poof.

Melt the glaciers.

America didn't care. About me or my dreams.

I wanted someone to turn off the damn heater. I wanted to yell my hot water cold.

I rolled at a low boil for miles. Was the man who yelled at me uncomfortable to see me red-faced and frizzling on the road? Did he appreciate how delicious his air-conditioning was? Was his comment aimed at talking sense to my apparent lunacy? Was he insulted that a woman was out there riding a bike and taking the heat, doing something he couldn't or wouldn't do because it was too difficult?

"Buy a car." Fuck that. I did. For $4.99 in Austin Junction, Oregon. I wasn't driving it either. I was carrying it.

When I looked up from my rant, I was passing a field of bushy plants. Then a freshly tilled field. Then a grassland with cattle.

My science brain activated. Here was crop rotation in real life. The land seemed alive compared to western Kansas. The tilled fields were deep brown and buzzing with bugs. Under the soil's surface, I imagined the earth was a living culture, like yogurt.

The bucolic scene contrasted with the feedlots, never mind the insulting truck driver. The hot grass smelled of honey. The cattle looked happy. They wallowed in wet spots, flicking their dripping tails. They clustered under trees, buddying in the shade.

The cattle might have been hotter than I felt, but they seemed to enjoy the now. I hoped I, too, could accept the now and find the place where what I was doing was everything I wanted in the moment— freedom, movement, vitality, beauty.

I pedaled next to a still pond with dead trees. I stopped, not sure what I was seeing. Perhaps the heat was melting my brain. The trees appeared as darkened bundles of floating neurons. Did the heat make me see things differently? More of the monstrousness? More of the beauty? Both? I took a picture. I would check myself later, after I cooled down.

At midday, I rode into Newton, population 17,190. The downtown had cared-for historic buildings. I parked my bike against a tree outside Prairie Harvest and entered its sanctuary of cool. Health food in rural Kansas. Was I still seeing things? Had I entered a wormhole? I ordered two salads from the counter and a bag of organic spinach.

After lunch, I went to the bookstore next door where I sipped an iced soy chai. The burn of salt on my skin reminded me that I smelled even though I couldn't detect my own reek.

Young people and professor types came and went. I liked the college town vibe. The place was alive like the dark soil in the fields. Something I couldn't see made it sing.

Connected to Wi-Fi, I learned that the bushy crops were soybeans, a field rotation that returned nitrogen to the soil. Kansas was a top-ten producer of soybeans in the nation. I enjoyed the irony that the Kansas I experienced, Newton excepted, eschewed things hippy and earth friendly while being a leading supplier of the base ingredient of tofu.

After an hour at the bookstore, I pedaled to a motel.

I wanted sleep, shower, and Wi-Fi.

Once in the room, I showered and conducted my first experiment with hand-washed bike clothes. I filled the sink with warm water and submerged the clothes. I squeezed. The water turned cloudy gray. I squeezed some more, drained the sink, refilled it, squeezed, drained, and then I wrung out each item. I just rinsed, afraid soap would leave a skin-irritating residue.

Outside was hot but humid. Inside was cool. I hung the clothes inside. Worst case, I would put on damp clothes in the morning.

I lay on the bed and passed out.

I lifted out of my coma two hours later, refreshed and eager to iChat with Daniel.

He looked adorable with his lopsided smile. "Gosh, it's good to see you," I said.

He didn't say anything right away, but I watched his eyes track around the computer screen. "What are those tan points on your forehead?" He said "forehead" with an East Coast accent, *far-head.*

"Those are from the vents in my helmet. I put sunscreen on every morning, but the sun is pretty intense from above."

I told him about being yelled at. In the cool of my motel room, it was easy to see the ridiculousness of the exchange that had so aggravated me. I retrieved the Thunderbird and showed him. "See, I already bought a car."

We talked about the "I love you" he said the night before. He had been surprised that it came out, too, that it was automatic, but he also meant it. I told him I was up in the middle of the night and wrote him a love letter. Something to look forward to.

Then we had sexy talk.

"I love you," he said.

"I love you, too."

My screen went black when he disconnected.

I walked circles in the space between the desk and bed. It felt strange to say I love you because I wasn't certain I meant it. But maybe what I felt wasn't uncertainty but the discomfort of doing something unfamiliar. Underneath those unsettling feelings was excitement, like maybe Daniel was who I was looking for.

26.

Mary and Dermot

Before leaving my motel room in the morning, I psyched myself up for a hot, sunny, humid day. My eyes and head were heavy with tiredness, but my sink-washed biking clothes were pliable and cool when I put them on. My mood was lighter without having to wear the previous day's sweat.

I was on the road before 7:00 AM in hazy heat on a quiet rural road without a shoulder. Tall grasses with pearly ballerina seed heads danced in the breeze on the roadside.

At 10:10 AM, I reached Cassoday. The town, population 130, was near I-35 and had a convenience store with a restaurant in it. On the wooden rail outside stood two bikes with panniers. I welcomed the cool indoor air. Two riders sat at a community table drinking coffee—a man with short, gray hair and a sunburned face wearing a red long-sleeved jersey and a blonde woman with tan arms in a white tank top jersey with pink trim and flowers.

"May I join you?" I asked. I had ordered breakfast.

"Certainly," said the woman. She had an accent.

My hip zapped me as I sat down, interrupting my breath. The man sat with his back against the table. "Where did you start your ride?" I asked.

"Florence, Oregon," the woman said. "Are you riding the Trans-America Trail?"

"I am. I left from home in Eugene and am heading to Washington, DC."

"Are you by yourself?" she asked. I guessed her accent was British.

"Yeah. I'm doing research and couldn't imagine asking anyone to join me."

"We saw you in Hutchinson," the woman said, looking at her partner, who sipped his coffee. "You have a distinctive bike with only front panniers."

"Yes! The orange one."

She nodded. "You're going light."

"You know, it's funny." I leaned forward. "The rack weighs almost as much as my bike, and I have everything in those two panniers. They're not light."

"Are you staying in motels? You don't have camping gear," the woman said.

The man continued to sip his coffee, engaged in the conversation with his eyes.

"I have camping gear. I'm studying bicycle tourism, so I'm trying everything—camping, motels, hotels, hostels."

"Well, you can't have much. What do you have? A sheet or something?"

"I have a sleeping bag and sleeping pad. I don't have a tent, but I have a tarp shelter. The shelter doesn't have a floor, so it isn't very good in buggy places."

The man's eyes widened, and his eyebrows rose. "Really?" he said. "You have all that with you?"

He had a gentle voice and an accent. I wasn't convinced I was hearing British accents though. "I do. But I'm not carrying cooking gear. Since I was limited to two bags, I used highly compressible gear."

"That's impressive," the woman said. "We're staying at motels. It's easier to get a good start in the morning after sleeping in air-conditioning. Plus we don't have to carry as much."

Their approach sounded sensible. The man set his empty cup on the table. "Your accents are British?" I asked.

"Irish," the woman said. "I'm Mary. This is Dermot."

Once she said Irish, I heard it.

"It's lovely chatting with you, Heidi," Mary said. "We're going to get moving, but I'm sure you'll catch up to us."

"I look forward to it."

Mary and Dermot were probably the ones at the Country Inn in Larned with their biking clothes over the railing. I liked them.

When I caught up, we pedaled and talked and had the road mostly to ourselves.

"Where are you from in Ireland?"

Mary responded, "We live in Wales now, but we're from Galway."

"What prompted you to do this ride?"

Dermot responded, "When I was about seven, I was getting my hair cut and had a *Time* magazine with a picture of a hairy, weather-worn man on the cover. He'd just walked across America. I wanted to do that, too. I drove across the country one year, but it wasn't the adventure I imagined, so we thought we would ride."

Although I hadn't read it yet, I had the same man's story in my panniers from one of the *National Geographic* magazines I picked up in Wyoming.

"Do you cycle much at home?" I asked.

"Not really," Mary said. "In November, we decided to do this trip and got these secondhand bicycles and started to prepare more."

I could hardly believe they were riding across the United States on secondhand bikes. Yet, they both seemed delighted with their adventure. Why was I having such a tough time? Would it feel different if I was on vacation instead of working? Was it all the things I asked of myself that made it difficult—the lack of sleep, the pressure to blog, the aloneness? Maybe they had similar challenges but put on a happy face to the world like I did on Facebook and my blog.

We rode to the next convenience store and went in. I purchased a bottle of water. Mary asked, "Why do you buy water when you can get it for free from the soda dispenser?"

"I'm studying economic development from bicycle tourism. I want to be an ambassador for bike tourists and support the businesses that are out here by buying things."

They wanted to sit, and as much as I enjoyed their company, I wanted to ride. We said goodbye again.

I arrived in Eureka in the early afternoon with tiredness pulling at my eyes.

I'd been dreaming about sleeping in air-conditioning since Mary mentioned it. My thoughts were stuck on how tired I was.

Food was my first priority so when I got a room, I wouldn't have to leave. I found a Mexican restaurant and enjoyed a quick dinner.

At the Carriage House Inn, I discovered Mary and Dermot's bicycles outside a room. Dermot came out. "Hey! You want to go get a beer in a little bit?"

"Probably not. I just ate, and I'm looking forward to not going anywhere for a while."

"If you change your mind, you know where we are."

"Thanks," I said with more enthusiasm than I felt.

I went into my room and didn't come out until I was ready to roll the next morning.

27.

Cadaver

I'd frozen my water bottles in the mini fridge in the motel room. An hour down the road, there wasn't any ice left, and the water was warm.

I hoped to pedal about a hundred miles to Girard that day. A century had been possible in the western states and a huge boost to my confidence. Here in Kansas, my body was in better physical shape than it had been those first times I'd come close to a hundred miles in one day, and the terrain was flat and at low altitude. The distance was within reach. All I had to do was pedal. Yet, seventy-five miles had been impossible since Elaine's. The fewer miles I covered each day, the more miles I needed to pedal the next for timely arrival in Washington. Low-mileage days also meant less opportunity for a rest day. I couldn't get ahead of my exhaustion.

Along the road in the middle of nowhere were a few scattered residences. I passed one that had medium-sized American flags attached to fence posts.

Since my friend's recommendation when I was in Colorado that I ride with an American flag, I'd been looking to buy one. I hadn't found one in the stores I visited, which perplexed me. American flags were abundant in the landscape. I'd seen flags in yards, as part of decoration on houses, as stickers on trucks, and hanging inside the Boone store. I expected to find flags in the convenience stores at the checkout counter as part of the display of Slim Jims, breath mints, gum, lighters, and energy elixirs. I hadn't even found one at the Hutchinson bike shop where they seemed to have everything a touring cyclist needed.

Would a flag ease my difficulties? Help protect me?

Somewhere in Kansas or eastern Colorado, the ride stopped being fun. Each day I returned to the road, my focus was on survival. Having death as my constant companion did not make me joyous or grateful that I could spend the time riding my bike, seeing the country, appreciating that my body worked well enough that I could do both things, or even that the calorie burn made it possible for me to eat with abandon. No brownie sundae was worth pedaling toward the straight road's vanishing point in this steamy, agricultural hell.

Sisyphus and Prometheus had it better. Well, at least they knew why they were fettered to a daily task of extreme endurance. When I started this ride, it was about transportation and skills that would distinguish me in the job market. It was about seeing America. It was an antidote to a sedentary lifestyle. If I was going to have difficulty, it wasn't going to be in the flatland unless a tornado came through. But here I was in the flatland. It wasn't tornado season. I was in great physical condition. And I hated the feeling of pushing myself to go another day, to the next town, or even five miles when I didn't want to.

On the right side of the road, a driveway curved to a house. The yard was fenced, and two brick pillars stood on either side of the driveway. Spaced every six feet the entire length of the driveway on both sides were American flags.

Near the driveway, I stopped, grabbed a water bottle, and squeezed hot water into my mouth. The flags were exactly what I was looking for. Were the people who lived there warmhearted and welcoming like Elaine and Dan? Were they cranky like the man who yelled at me on the road? I squeezed more hot water into my mouth.

I needed a flag.

Trespassing was a no-no. I wouldn't go onto someone's property for anything, even shade. Especially not to filch a flag. But there were two flags outside the fence. If I took a flag, would it be less obvious if they were both gone? I didn't need two flags. I reracked the water bottle and rolled my bike into the driveway apron. I stopped within reach of a flag and decided it could be spared for a traveler in need. That's why it was placed outside the fence. I bent forward and plucked it. Just as quickly, I held the flag to my handlebars, turned my bike, and pedaled down the road, heart pounding.

Had the people who lived in the house watched me steal their flag? I imagined that they offered me a forgiving prayer: *God is with you now.*

Out of view of the house, I stopped at the edge of the road. The flag was eight by twelve inches and attached to a wooden dowel about twenty-four inches long. I draped it over the top of my left pannier. It would be visible to people who might pass me from either direction. I continued pedaling.

A few miles later, I stopped at a rest area and went inside to cool down in the air-conditioning.

A woman and tattooed man were cleaning. Across the man's throat was a dashed line with little scissors at the end near his ear like on clothing patterns. He stopped polishing the water fountain and turned to me. "Do you cyclists tag team riding?"

"No. I'm just out by myself."

"A couple came by earlier."

He spoke English, but his voice was drawl, gravel, and phlegm. Maybe his throat had already been cut, and the tattoo covered the scar.

"Are you from nearby?" I asked.

"I grew up in a town of fourteen, and that included the six of us in my family."

"What do you like about living in small towns?" I didn't think I would be happy in one that small.

"We're in the country. If we need anything, it's only six miles in any direction."

As I departed, he said, "I'm just saying, bicycling makes you look good." I turned and waved to him and then focused on the road ahead. Was he saying what I never expected people to say of me, that I was good-looking? Did he respond the same to Mary and Dermot? The appreciation felt genuine, like a gift, and I accepted that he meant it even though I didn't believe it myself.

Six miles past the rest stop, I arrived in Toronto. Since I had cooled down and replenished my water at the rest area, I didn't stop at the convenience store with the sign that announced: STOP - EAT - GET GAS.

In the oppressive atmosphere beyond Toronto, my humor transformed into something putrid. I struggled to pedal, and services were sparse. There was a gas station twenty-nine miles from Toronto, and eleven miles beyond that was Chanute, a town where I could find air-conditioned lodging if I couldn't go farther.

Almost twenty miles from Toronto, I stopped in Coyville. The community had a population of seventy-one and seemed to be decomposing. It smelled of mulch, mold, and bad breath. The traces of human life seemed choked on the fecund vegetation.

At the main intersection in town, signs identified a cemetery to the right, bike route to the left. I wanted to turn right. My stink suited the odor in the air, and I felt dead.

I turned left.

Out of town, I passed listing power poles. They were failing in the air's hot soup, too. Or was it just me?

The heat suffocated. I wanted to stop and give up but called on friend Tricia's inspiration from a letter I received in Eads: "One pedal stroke at a time." Instead of the next services or the next mile marker, I fixed my attention on turning the pedals.

One. One. One. One. One.

Dad had also sent me a letter in Eads. He wrote that he was with me on each pedal stroke.

One. One.

It was eerie to think that Dad was with me as I counted. Was he dead? Was I dead? I pedaled and cried.

One. One. One.

A full rotation of the pedals was a small milestone, but I didn't lose count. I could achieve it. It wasn't twenty miles, or fifteen or five or two.

Just one. And another. Again.

One.

One.

One.

I cried. Death couldn't come for me yet. I wanted to have sex again.

On the roadside, I saw myself crashed in a heat coma. I looked down at my dead body. Me-who-stood-looking appeared the same as me-on-the-ground. And if I was looking at me-who-stood-looking *and* me-on-the-ground, who, what, and where was I? Was I in the *bardo*, that between-place where reality is interrupted, and you don't know if you're alive or dead?

In this state of fractured consciousness, I pedaled for miles. Too hot, more hot, hot hot.

The lone gas station came into view. I crumpled, thinking about the cool interior, refrigerated water or juice, cooling myself inside and out simultaneously. The pedaling became more difficult as I approached. The gas station sign read LENNY's, my dad's name. He really was with me on the ride. I cried hot tears.

The station's awning shade offered small relief. I noticed there were no cars parked outside. The interior looked dark. I rolled to the door. Lenny's was closed on Sundays.

"Dad!" The outburst of my own voice burned. Hot tears slicked my cheeks. I took a small breath. "This is not helpful," I whispered.

I stood in the shade. Dad couldn't be the gas station. He wouldn't do something so cruel as encourage me to this place but deny me access. He would give me hope and something to aim for. But Dad had nothing to do with the gas station even though his name was on the sign. I needed help, relief. What was my expectation of what this journey would be? Had I not acknowledged it would be punishing? Did I believe I was not allowed to have good things in my life unless I first ran a gauntlet? Did I simply want to feel something? Why did it have to be pain? Could I not feel anything else?

My map showed eleven miles to Chanute. Services. Air-conditioning. Fewer miles than I had pedaled between Coyville and this gas station. I gave myself permission to stay the night there.

My reserve water had been cooking on top of my right pannier all day. I drank nearly half the liter in one go and dumped the rest into a bike bottle. I stowed the empty reserve container, drained another half of the water in my bottle, and headed on.

I rode in a timeless repetition of turning pedals. Heat, humidity, sweat, tears, tearlessness. Steam, soup, slime.

I dropped away from my body. I don't know where I went.

At 2:04 PM, I arrived in Chanute. I stumbled into an open restaurant and sat at a booth, thankful to suck down iced water in air-conditioning. I had lunch. Ordered the large. The waitstaff made sure I had enough water and replenished my bottles before I left.

Mary and Dermot's bikes were outside a tall, buff-colored brick hotel, maybe seven stories, but I couldn't count. It looked expensive. I didn't want to pay extra for a room I couldn't bring my bike into. All I was going to do was sleep.

At the edge of town, I checked in at the Guest House Inn. I showered and then rinsed my cycling clothes in the sink.

After I hung my clothes to dry, I crawled into bed and phoned my parents. Even though I'd eaten and washed, I wasn't sure I was any more alive than I had been on the road to Lenny's. My body seemed on auto; my thoughts were mush. As I lay in bed, the mush slid to the back of my head.

"Where are you?" Mom asked. She had the speakerphone on, and Dad was on the line, too.

I closed my eyes and poked the mush. "I'm in Cadaver."

"Where?"

"Cadaver."

Dad made a noise. Shifted his body, said something? I couldn't tell.

"Are you funnin'?" Mom again.

"No. I'm in a town that starts with C, and I'm dead."

Dad's voice, "How do you know you're dead?"

"I'm lying down, and my eyes are closed. And I'm talking to you."

"Are you outside?" Mom asked.

"No. I'm inside. There's air-conditioning."

"Maybe take a nap and call us a little later?" Mom offered. I heard concern.

"Okay. I love you."

"Love you, too," Mom said.

I was inches from napping, but I had my computer in bed and e-mailed Daniel. I still couldn't recall the name of the town I was in and added:

✉ Today I wanted to quit.

I fell asleep for two hours.

When I woke up, Daniel had e-mailed.

✉ heidi, baby, what's going on in that town that starts with C? or what happened on the way there? wanted to quit!? what's up? kisses, hugs, licks, sucks. these are a few of my favorite things.

Sleep refreshed me. I looked at my map. I still couldn't remember the town's name, Chanute.

28.

Road-Closed Route

I departed Cadaver before 7:00 AM. In fewer than four miles, I saw Dermot and Mary. They started their day later than planned. I wanted to know how they had fared the previous day. After some small talk and without prompting, Mary said, "I had a very hard day yesterday."

What relief. I wasn't alone in the struggle. "I did, too," I said. "I wanted to quit."

"With the heat and running out of water and everything closed . . ." Mary trailed off as if she were looking at the horror.

"I don't know what it was about yesterday," I said, "but it seemed to take forever to get anywhere."

"There was a headwind," Dermot said matter-of-factly.

"Is that what it was?" I looked at him. His eyes were trained on the road ahead. "I thought it was a furnace blowing hot air on me."

Dermot nodded in my direction, hinting a smile.

"I left my gloves under a tree," Mary said, "and Dermot went back for them later. When we got to that gas station, and it was closed, I wasn't sure I would make it. I'd run out of water."

I nodded. I couldn't articulate the state I was in at the gas station.

And where had Dermot found the energy to backtrack for Mary's gloves?

Mary asked, "When did you get in?"

"Right at two. I was so dead when I arrived, I couldn't remember the name of the town."

"I couldn't either."

The three of us pedaled together in silence. Dermot steered us through our route's left turn. A mile farther, a man in a truck told us the road ahead was closed.

Dermot called to me at the truck where I was getting the detour details. "Heidi. We'll be fine. Worst case we may have to carry our bikes a little way."

Dermot's response seemed reasonable. I thanked the man in the truck for his information.

Four miles down the road we came to the construction zone.

"You ladies go first," Dermot said. "The odds are better they won't tell you no."

We rode around the ROAD CLOSED barricades onto a packed dirt surface.

Mary grumbled about the unevenness, "Why do they have to go tearing up the whole road?" From what I could see following behind her, she worked her way through it easily.

We pedaled more than a mile, and then I took the lead as we approached people and machinery.

Two men looked at me and asked, "How's that on your bike?"

"Oh, it's fine," I said with nonchalance. "It's rearranging my innards."

They laughed.

I smiled, glad to have humored them, glad to continue.

After we passed the men, Dermot took the lead, and I followed behind Mary. She came to a sudden stop and fell.

"Are you stuck to your bike?" I asked. I wasn't sure what I should do, if anything. When she moved, the bike moved with her.

"Yeah," she said and struggled. Right as I figured a way to help, she freed herself, stood, and dusted herself off. "I'm okay," she said. She picked her bike up and pointed to the roadbed. "I didn't see this big clump until I was right on it."

The clod was the size of a toaster. "I'm glad you're okay," I said. "I started off this morning by falling over. I hadn't even gotten out of the motel parking lot. It's embarrassing when that happens. But funny, too. I mean, funny, once you realize nothing other than your pride got scratched."

Mary straddled her bike. "When I first started," she said, "I fell over all the time. I had two skinned knees for weeks."

"Looks like they survived the dirt clod."

Mary inspected her knees. "You go ahead. I'll be right there."

I caught up to Dermot. We waited for Mary.

"Dermot, I fell over," Mary said when she reached us.

"I did, too," he said, "when I turned around to look for you."

I hadn't seen Dermot fall although it made sense that he might have. What would the exchange have been like between them if I hadn't been there? Would she have given him a piece of her mind for taking her down the crappy road? Would he have spit back that he was always waiting for her and she was doing just fine? Would it have been the same—both of them sharing they had fallen and were okay?

"Do you ever check the Adventure Cycling updates?" Dermot asked me.

"I did once." Mike, my riding companion on Togwotee Pass in Wyoming, had told me about the closure and Adventure Cycling's updates. That evening in Dubois, I did check Adventure Cycling's website for route updates. There wasn't anything ahead of note, and I forgot the resource existed.

"Tell me, Heidi, if someone said you could take a ten-mile detour or go the road-closed route, what would you pick?"

In this heat, I would want to know if I had to go ten miles out of my way. Without Dermot, I would have heeded the warning offered by the man in the truck rather than go into unknown territory and find myself needing to backtrack. Backtracking would be torture. "Well, you convinced me to ride this route."

"It's more adventurous." Dermot grinned.

I liked adventure, but I felt burdened by my schedule and activities, especially blogging. In the evenings after riding all day, I would cajole myself to prep photos for the work I would do in the morning. I might sleep four hours, get up, and write. Every morning, the coolest part of the day and best time to make up miles, I was bent over my computer going nowhere. If all I was doing was riding, I might feel less pressure. But that wasn't my reality. Without the conference where I would be presenting results from this trip, I probably wouldn't still be pedaling across the country.

A mile farther, the earth was so bumpy we couldn't ride anymore. A machine with knobby wheels had rolled over it, leaving six-inch divots spaced eight inches apart in every direction. With the uneven terrain and the stiffness of my bike shoes, my footing went weird a few times. My left hip zapped me. I planned to check the route updates that night for other detours.

After a mile of walking, we remounted our bikes on pavement and rode into Walnut and went inside the convenience store. Dermot had coffee. I went for juice, bottled water, and an ice cream bar.

Mary got lemonade ice when she saw I had ice cream. "You know in the grocery stores you can get a big thing of ice cream for a dollar fifty," she said.

"You eat some of it, then throw the rest away?" I asked.

Dermot smiled and reddened a bit. "I eat all of it. Chocolate chip ice cream is really good."

Such a surprise that this physician would eat a half gallon of ice cream in one go. That must have been how he fueled or refueled his ride from Cadaver back to the tree where Mary had left her gloves.

We looked at our maps, enjoying the cool indoors. If I rode past Pittsburg, the last town in Kansas on the route, it was a long way to the next air-conditioned lodging. Mary and Dermot planned to stop in Pittsburg.

It was clear to me after we left Walnut that I was moving faster. I enjoyed their company, but I wanted to get out of the heat. "I'm going to ride ahead to Pittsburg," I said, "but I'd love to go out for a beer with you when you get in."

"Yes. That would be lovely," Mary said.

Mary told me her e-mail address, and I handed her a manila tag that served as my business card.

"I don't know where to put this."

"What about in your sock?" I sometimes stashed keys or scraps of paper with route directions in my socks when I was riding and didn't have pockets.

Mary leaned forward and tucked the tag into her sock. She sat upright and started pedaling again. "Yes. That will work."

"Great. See you later." I pedaled ahead.

"Stay lucky," Dermot called out to me.

I looked back and smiled.

I pedaled, sweated, and spaced out among the cornfields, soybean, and hayfields.

East of the fields were stretches of bucolic tree-lined road. I stopped for a water break in the shade of a tree. It wasn't windy like the previous day, and I had more energy. Still, the heat stifled.

I cranked through Girard and continued the remaining fifteen miles to Pittsburg, population 19,243.

I entered Pittsburg on a road with no bike lane. I stayed to the right but gave myself room so my panniers cleared the curb. A car passed me and then immediately turned right. I squeezed my brakes hard.

"Gee, that was nice," I said involuntarily. Two feet less of space, and we would have collided. The driver must have seen me.

Suddenly, I was hotter and wanted to yell. But I didn't. I hated how dehumanizing it felt not to be seen or to be seen as a target.

Maybe it was the flag. I had it stowed in a pannier because I couldn't find a good way to display it. Had it been visible, would I have been cut off?

I checked in at the EconoLodge, drew the curtains in my room, and cranked the air-conditioning. Mary and Dermot had made other arrangements before my e-mails to them arrived. Their motel was six miles from mine, an insurmountable distance in the heat for socializing, so I went alone to a nearby diner for ice cream.

Outside the diner, one of the staff was on a break. "That's healthy, riding your bike," she said. "I walk, but I smoke. That's not healthy. I'm trying to quit."

"Biking does keep you healthy."

"I keep telling myself how disgusting smoking is. I say, 'You smell bad. Your hair smells, your breath smells.'"

I quit fiddling with the stuff on my bike and went over to her. "You might try a kinder approach and see if that works."

"I'm really mean to myself," the woman said.

"I am, too." It had taken a while for me to understand that I wouldn't tolerate meanness from other people, yet I never questioned it from myself. Biking across the country seemed to be self-inflicted punishment for being fat and unemployable and for having an inflated sense of my abilities and talents. Accomplishing this trial would make me worthy in my own eyes. But could I actually do it? It was demoralizing to consider my inner critic was right. I'd pedaled all this way, and nothing had changed. As I talked to this woman, I was aware of the illogic of my inner life. "I'm still learning how to be nice to myself."

"That's really hard."

I nodded. "It is." I wanted to say something supportive. I wasn't someone who'd gotten things right. I persevered and endured because that's what I understood was required of me. I was drawn to pain because I conflated it with love. In her, I saw my inner self asking for help, wanting to experience self-compassion, longing to let love flow. I felt for her. "There has to be something you like about yourself," I said. "Concentrate on that."

She looked at me. "I like that," she said. "I'll try it."

We talked more, and then I pedaled back to the EconoLodge. When I touched the doorknob to my motel room, I thought of something I liked about myself. My capacity to love.

I entered the room. Yes, I had a lot of love to give—to others and the world—but I struggled to accept self-love. Even in rare moments when I felt generous toward myself, I didn't trust the feeling. I didn't believe the softness of my own love was strong.

29.

American Pie

The morning's sun blinded. Heat and humidity slapped my cheeks. The day was already unpleasantly hot for 7:00 AM. The American flag fluttered on the front of my bike, where I'd secured it with tape.

Today was day forty-four. I'd pedaled 2,466 miles. The conference began in thirty-six days.

I had a new map in my jersey pocket. It had an elevation profile, which meant the tedious flatness was behind me. Varied topography. A gift.

Missouri was fewer than five miles from Pittsburg. A smirk rose on my face. I looked over my shoulder. Fuck Kansas.

When I turned my attention to the road ahead, I was at the state line. I hit the brakes. I got my camera out to take a picture of the welcome sign.

"Want me to take your picture?" A man's voice surprised me. A pickup had pulled out from the gas station across the street and stopped on the road. The driver looked at me.

"That would be wonderful. Thank you." Crossing into Missouri seemed as momentous as reaching Hoosier Pass—measured by the amplitude of my suffering in Kansas.

The man pulled to the side of the road.

He didn't seem like someone who would run off with my camera. He was maybe in his forties, smooth skinned, thin brown hair, black T-shirt tucked into clean jeans finished with a belt. I handed him my camera and wheeled my bike to the sign. The grass squished with wetness.

He snapped a couple of pictures. "Got it!"

I wheeled my bike back and took the camera, thanking him.

He waited while I stowed the camera. Was he going to ask me where I was headed or where I'd come from? Did he think, like the Man with the Slit Neck Tattoo, that biking made me look good?

"All men are friendly in Missouri." He pronounced Missouri, Muh-zzrr-uh.

I smiled, unsure how to interpret his comment.

"When you get down the road in Golden City, you have to stop at Cooky's Café. They have amazing pie. Everyone who's anyone has pie at Cooky's."

Was Cooky's the place that John, whom I met while climbing Lolo Pass in Idaho, told me about? I thanked him for the recommendation.

He wished me a good ride, got back in his truck, and headed into Kansas where I knew not all the men were friendly.

I faced the rising sun and pedaled into the Show Me state. I sweated in the muggy atmosphere and puzzled over the state slogan. I watched the flag flutter. When I pedaled harder, the flag caught more air.

There were not many services in the first sixty miles. Golden City was twenty-nine miles east of the state line. In the next twenty-seven miles there were no services until Everton, a town of 322. Everton had lodging at a hunting inn, and my map indicated I needed to call for directions—it was a mile and a half off route.

Past Everton, there were some small towns and a lone gas station but no air-conditioned lodging until Marshfield, fifty-three miles beyond. The suck-up-your-misery-and-get-on-with-it me had an eye on Marshfield. The two-days-ago me that crawled into Cadaver wanted to stay in Everton.

Cooky's Café was on the main road through town, identifiable by its red sign with white block letters. If I hadn't heard Missouri State Line Man call the place "cookie's," I probably would have pronounced the place "cooky," similar to "spooky."

I hadn't expected to stop long in Golden City, but here was pie.

It was 9:00 AM. I leaned my bike against a porch post and went in. I surveyed the pie flavors displayed in a glass case by the entry and then slid into a booth. The waitress handed me a menu. She also placed a spiral-bound notebook with wrinkly pages on the table and said, "Here's our bike log, if you're interested in signing in."

I ordered eggs and a piece of peach pie.

"Regular or Dutch?" the waitress asked.

"Dutch please."

The crumble topping lit up my pleasure sensors with the sweet, bright peaches.

My ecstasy ballooned. I juiced into the chamois of my bike shorts.

"Would you like some more pie?" the waitress asked.

Could she tell how on I was in that moment? Had my scent changed? Cherry pie tempted. "No, thanks. If I have any more, I don't think I'll be able to pedal down the road." I didn't say that I might need to relieve myself of an orgasm in the bathroom if she brought me another wedge.

"Most cyclists have at least two pieces," she said and looked at me as if to say, "Treat yourself."

"You are pie pushers here," I said with good-natured accusation. "I'll give it some thought." I wanted her to go away because I wanted another piece of pie and didn't want to hear myself ask for it.

I opened the cycling log. There were the people I'd passed. John from Portland, whom I encountered on the trail in the Colorado Rockies. Matt, a photographer I talked to in eastern Colorado going from Chicago to Mesa.

The waitress returned. Pie was a distant thought with the gold mine of data about bike tourists. "What do you do with the old bike logs?" I asked.

"We keep them here in these binders." She pointed to three binders on the bottom shelf of the bus tub cart.

"May I look at them?"

She handed me the most recent one. "Be careful turning the pages, they're kind of fragile."

I could imagine the sweaty cyclist arms and hands that pressed against the paper. An entry from a 2009 Portland rider caught my attention because he'd illustrated his entry with a self-portrait, a tired look on his face and the words, "Kansas was the most challenging so far." I thought so, too. Someone else in the logbook had written: "And here I thought I was the only one who'd ever ridden across the country." Looking at the thousands of entries, I was surprised how much bike touring traffic the TransAmerica Trail got. The one binder I looked at went back to 2001. My rough estimate was 750 riders per year, but that was just based on the people who signed in at Cooky's. Likely the same number passed without any idea what they were missing.

I had one TransAm window decal left, and I decided Cooky's, while it wasn't on the list of businesses I was targeting, was one of the most appropriate places I could leave one.

The waitress filled my water bottles with ice and water, and I stopped in the restroom before leaving. My lascivious thoughts had moderated.

The TransAmerica Trail decal, which depicted a silhouetted bike rider on an American flag background, was posted on the door as I left.

Outside, a pot of red and white petunias overflowed against the building's white façade. The red and white café sign stood out against the blue sky. An American flag flapped in the breeze on a flagpole. A blue post office box stood on the sidewalk. And my bike sported its own flag. Here was America.

I pedaled away from Cooky's into a golden shimmer of heat and humidity. Gnats and airborne fluff caught light. Maybe that's why the town was called Golden City—it had a yellow, effervescent atmosphere.

While the light intrigued me, the heat concerned me. It was 10:00 AM, and I was sweating from every pore. It didn't seem possible. Maybe I wasn't sweating. Maybe it was hot moisture clinging to me. And if it was, sweating wouldn't cool me. There was too much moisture in the air to allow for evaporation. I swallowed hard. The day would get hotter.

I pedaled fast, hoping to make up for the hour I spent at Cooky's.

To distract myself from the heat, I focused on the flag fluttering on the front of my bike. Was the flag a symbol of friendliness? Missouri State Line Man told me all men in Missouri were friendly. Was that what it meant to be an American? Friendly? To anyone and everyone? Person to person? Could I hold America and Americanness in my mind and heart as all these individuals—Jeff at the Boone Store in eastern Colorado, the man who gave me tortillas in Scott City, Kansas, the road crew in White Bird, Montana?

All the various landscapes I'd traveled through, all the towns, all the people I talked to—all this was my home country, all of it was America. I was American. Strange. I tried on the idea like a new outfit. In my mental dressing room, I looked at my reflection in the mirrors. There were things I didn't like. But I appreciated America, having climbed its mountains, slept in its woods and motel beds, drunk its water, suffered in its heat, eaten at its diners, talked with its locals, and been hosted by its small-town residents.

I arrived in Everton at noon a hot wet mess. The town seemed decrepit and empty of people. My map indicated a post office, gas station, lodging, and camping. I found the post office. Where could a town of 322 people hide a gas station? I pulled to the side of the road and looked at my map. I turned my phone on and called the inn. No one answered.

Marshfield was fifty-three miles farther and had motels. The sun was overhead. Five hours to reach Marshfield in a cauldron of heat.

My head had heat itch. I was hot, but I had energy to keep going. Before departing for Marshfield, I needed to find the gas station so I could get water. It was a time before Google knew everything, so I decided to ask someone for directions. As if appearing on cue, a man got out of his truck and went into the post office. I swallowed my fear that he would dismiss me and went to the post office to intercept him when he came out. Missouri State Line Man said all men in the state were friendly. I would see if that were true.

"Excuse me," I said when he came out. "Where can I find water or ice in this town?"

Without missing a beat, he said, "There's a convenience store just down the way a bit." He pointed in the direction I needed to go and gave specific directions.

Relief. Friendly.

I would not have found the gas station without his help. I purchased a Klondike bar and Vitamin Water. When I finished my cooling treats, I filled my water bottles with ice.

A woman with short, dyed blond hair and a gray-haired man sat next to each other on a lumpy sofa under the gas station porch. I said hi, and they asked what I was doing.

"I'd do it some other way," the man said, "take a plane or something. Are you married?"

His question struck me as abrupt. "No," I said. "I'm not married. Never was."

"Look what you're missing out on."

He and the woman were smoking cigarettes. It was unpleasantly hot, even in the shade. "I'm a free bird. Gives me a chance to do this." I bent my arms and flapped my hands. What I was doing probably looked as unpleasant to them as what they were doing looked to me.

The woman chimed in, "How old are you?"

"Thirty-five."

"Oh, you have plenty of time."

Why were we talking about marriage? I was hot again and not even pedaling. The ice in my water bottles was probably melted. "I need to get moving. Thanks so much for the conversation."

"Do you have anyone knows where you are?" the woman asked. "You know it's over one hundred degrees?"

"I'm in daily communication with people, yes." I was surprised it was over one hundred degrees. I never checked the weather. Whatever I knew about the temperature was a best guess, chance, or informed by something somebody, like this woman, told me. Knowing the temperature wouldn't change the weather or what I asked of myself, because my goal was to bike to Washington, DC, I was better off not knowing the forecast. I didn't need weather anxiety to cripple my already stressful daily departures.

She looked at me half side-eye but didn't say anything.

"Would you feel better if I let you know I was okay?"

"Yes." Her body language eased.

"You have a cell phone? I can text you or something?"

"I do. Here's the number." She produced a scrap of paper and pen from her apron pocket and wrote the number. She handed me the paper and said, "My name is Nita. I have friends in Fair Grove, too. If there's an emergency, I could call them."

"Thank you, Nita. I'm Heidi. I'll be in touch." I threw my leg over my bike and pedaled off. The pavement was new and black. It radiated heat. I melted.

I cranked the pedals hard through scenic agricultural land. I stopped to photograph a triangular barn with rectangular doors, round hay bales, and cylindrical storage silos with cone-shaped lids. The place seemed built from children's blocks.

I turned onto a road that went straight up. I pedaled fast on the approach and then downshifted when the steep grade slowed me.

These roads were my new reality. There was no traversing hill contours for gentler grades. I pedaled downhill as fast as I could, hoping my momentum would carry me up the other side before I bottomed out in my easiest gear, the granny gear. I was determined not to walk up the hills, although standing and pedaling in the granny gear was like walking, and I did this several times. I wheezed at the top of the hills. My legs were wooden. I slicked the slime in the back of my throat with hot water. On a few hills, I stopped to rest at the top, thinking I might puke.

In Walnut Grove, I arrived exhausted and overheated. Neither pedaling on the flats of Kansas nor up the sustained climbs in the Rockies had prepared me for sprints in Missouri. I steered to a convenience store concerned about electrolyte loss, heat stroke, and how I was going to make it to Marshfield. I got a V-8. Potassium. And more cold water. I refilled my bottles with ice. Rested in the cool. I e-mailed my parents and Daniel.

I just wanted to be done with the day and cool down, but there was nowhere to be done.

From Walnut Grove, it was twenty-three miles to Fair Grove. There was a gas station seven miles from Walnut Grove. I had only gone fourteen miles from Everton to Walnut Grove, and that felt like a dangerous distance in the heat.

It was 4:00 PM. Marshfield lay another fifteen miles beyond Fair Grove. Even if I made good time, I would arrive at dusk.

Danger.

If I passed out, I wouldn't be able to call for help. And even if I didn't pass out but needed help, I might not have cell service between the towns.

I texted Nita: *Hi Nita. It's Heidi. I'm cooling in Walnut Grove. 23 miles to Fair Grove should not take more than 3 hours. If you haven't heard from me by 7, help!*

Three hours seemed a long time to be out in that heat. I took off in a rush.

Hills.

When I reached the gas station, I ran in for ice—my water was already hot again. I had a brief conversation with the man inside.

"You're not going to make Marshfield," he said.

I didn't need to hear that. "I don't have much choice. There isn't anywhere to stop between here and there." I left without waiting for a response.

It was impossible to outrun the heat, and hurrying intensified it. The heat ballooned inside my body, enveloped the outside of my body, blasted me from above, and roasted me from below. Hot wetness trickled down the sides of my face. My body cried.

A monstrous valley-hill came into view. I pedaled hard going down and up. Halfway up, I lost momentum. I downshifted and pedaled hard. Lost more momentum. Downshifted into my granny gear. My chain popped off. My feet spun.

I dismounted quickly. Beaten by the hill, I pushed my bike to an intersection where there was room on the road to reseat my chain.

Defeated, I crossed the intersection and tried hitching. I was eight miles from Fair Grove and twenty-three miles from Marshfield. One truck passed. Then two cars. Then a van. I roasted.

After fifteen minutes, I gave up. No one was going to stop.

I pedaled on. Twice when I heard a vehicle behind me, I stuck my thumb out. They didn't even slow as they passed.

I climbed another hill. At the top was a driveway. Two barking dogs ran toward me as I caught my breath.

While this normal dog behavior made me uneasy, I could understand why dogs chased or ran along beside bike riders—it was fun and felt good to run. I could see why dogs barked, too. They were communicating.

These dogs snarled. My skin prickled, and my body tensed. I called out to them with a friendly voice, "Hi, dogs. Hi. Are you runners?" My HALT! dog repellent was stowed in a pannier. I hoped their bluster was meant only to scare me away. I'd soon pass the house. I picked up momentum on the downhill.

The dogs flanked me. My ankles prickled. I hoped I wouldn't get bitten. "Hi, dogs."

The mad dog on my right hocked a snarl, bit into the pannier, and pulled.

"Whoa!" I yelled and tottered. My heart pounded. The same dog came around to the left side, bit into the pannier, and pulled.

I fell in the middle of the road below the crest of the hill.

A driver could come fast over the hill, and I would be roadkill. I freaked out. I didn't know where the dogs were. I scrambled to get my bike and spilled gear off the road. Ahead of me, a car slowed up the hill, passed around me, and pulled into the driveway. I focused on getting out of the road.

Just as I gathered myself on the roadside, a truck came over the hill.

I stuck my thumb out, tears streaming down my face. Words bubbled out of me, "Stop. Please stop and help."

The truck pulled over.

From above and below, men intercepted me.

"Damn dogs," the man from the car said.

"Are you okay?" the man from the truck asked.

"I don't know," I cried.

"You're all shook up," the man from the truck said.

I shivered. "The dogs didn't bite me," I said. "Can you give me a ride down the road?" I asked the man with the truck. "I'm headed to Marshfield or Fair Grove, anything would be good."

"I could take you as far as Fair Grove."

The three of us loaded my bike and gear into the truck. I thanked both men profusely for stopping and climbed into the truck.

"Hi. I'm Daryl," the man said as he fastened his seatbelt.

"D-A-R-Y-L. Most people don't spell it that way. I just voted, and now I'm headed home. My wife should be there by now, too."

Daryl was about my height, slim, with dark brown hair and a thick moustache. He wore a tan T-shirt with cutoff sleeves and jean shorts.

"I'm Heidi," I got out between hitching breaths and the crying slime in my mouth. *All men in Missouri are friendly,* Missouri State Line Man had said. So far, it proved true.

"I can take you to my house," Daryl chattered as he drove. "You can get cleaned up. We can make you dinner. Take a breather and figure out what to do next. I'll bet you can even stay with us. That's scary. Damn dogs."

My tears slowed. He seemed friendly. "Why is it called the 'Show Me' state? What does that mean?"

"You ever see *Jerry Maguire?*"

I nodded.

"It's like that," he said. "You know, like 'Show me the money!'" He thumped the dashboard. "Like 'prove it.' Show me."

Like he was doing now, showing me the men in Missouri were friendly. My tears stopped. We talked. He told me about his wife and kids.

We pulled into the multi-car garage at his house.

"We have a dog here," Daryl said, getting out of the truck. "A big nice friendly dog. He'll probably jump up on you, but all he wants to do is lick ya."

When I opened the door, the dog was right there, a fluffy Husky-looking dog. I slid into the little space it gave me. Its soft wet tongue lapped my fingers, and its rough paws pressed on my body.

Daryl pushed the dog away and put a cold Gatorade in my hands.

"Here, drink this. I'll get your bags."

The dog jumped on me again. Somehow, the dog, Daryl, and I reached the door. When Daryl opened it, his family was queued up.

Daryl introduced me. Taylor, Daryl's nine-year-old daughter, bounced in the hallway talking. Behind Taylor was Sheila, Daryl's wife, and Jessie came around Sheila to see what was going on. Jessie was seventeen and just got her braces off the day before. "Smile, Jessie," Daryl said, and Jessie obliged. We ascended the two steps into the hallway, the family backing up as we went. I couldn't see well with my sunglasses.

"I'm sorry," I said. "I can't see. Daryl, if you could, I need that red bag from the front of my bike."

I stood in the hallway and opened the drink while Daryl went for the red bag. Taylor and Jessie peppered me with questions, talking over each other. I took a few swallows of the Gatorade—it was cold and sweet.

The red bag appeared in my hands, and I put my glasses on. The dark tunnel of the hallway transformed into an open space with doors to my right.

"Here." Sheila guided me into the bathroom, one of the rooms on my right. It was the first time she said something. "Here's a wash-cloth and a towel. And a fresh bar of soap." She placed the items on the sink counter. "Wash up, take a shower, whatever you need to do."

I put the Gatorade on the counter, took my gloves off, and turned the water on.

Sheila closed the door when she left. As abruptly as the noise of greeting started, it stopped.

I washed my hands first to remove the chain grime.

Then I took my glasses off and washed my face of crusted tears, sunscreen, and salt rime. I considered taking a shower, but I didn't want to clean my body and put my cycling clothes back on. Daryl had brought my panniers in the house, but they weren't in the bathroom.

I came out of the bathroom in slow motion and turned my phone on. The kitchen was on one side of the house's main open space, and I followed the quiet female voices. Daryl and Taylor were gone. My phone didn't have reception.

"Do you need to call anyone?" Sheila asked. She had straight, shoulder-length light brown hair that curled at the ends, a quiet, thoughtful manner. No makeup. Scooped-neck shirt with flower petal print, dark pants. Jessie stood in the kitchen next to her. She was slim with long, straight dark brown hair, dark eyeliner-rimmed eyes, and wore a bright purple camisole over tight jeans.

I looked at my watch. 6:15 PM. I was dazed. What was I doing? Incrementally it came back. I was biking. It was hot. I was trying to get somewhere. It was hot. Concerning. Dogs pulled me down. Who needs to know where I am? Daniel? My parents? Friends on Facebook? Later for Facebook. Anyone else? Blank. Blank. I looked at my watch again. 6:15 PM. Something about that. Nita! "Yes. I do." I looked at my phone again. "But I don't have reception."

"Where would you be calling?"

"I don't know. I need to call someone I met in Everton. The area code is four one seven. Is that local?"

"Yeah. Here, you can use this phone." Sheila stepped out of the kitchen and pointed to a phone on a desk.

I called Nita and left a message, thanking her for being my emergency standby and telling her some people helped me and I was safe. I also wanted to let Daniel and my parents know I was okay since I'd messaged them in Walnut Grove. "Do you have Internet connection here?"

"No, we just have a dial up. But Jessie has Internet on her phone."

"I need to send a message, if I may."

Jessie got me to the Gmail sign-in page on her flip phone. I sat on a stool at the breakfast bar composing a message that would not cause alarm but explain the situation in as few words as possible. I had to press the numbers on Jessie's phone two and three times each for one letter. To Mom I wrote:

✉ I am in fagr grove. Safe. Dog attack. Me ok. No reception.

To Daniel I wrote:

✉ Dog attack. Me ok. No reception. Kiss

After the fifteen minutes it took to send those two messages, I handed the phone back to Jessie. "Thanks. You got a text."

I drank more of the Gatorade, which was still cold and tasted like orange soda. Sheila said, "You're welcome to stay here, have dinner . . . whatever. I could also drive you to Marshfield if you want."

I was done pedaling for the day, but I wasn't sure about staying the night. It was getting late for small-town America's restaurants, too, and I hadn't had a meal since Cooky's. What did I want? "I'd like to have dinner with you and then go to Marshfield if that's okay and not too late."

"Yeah. That's fine."

Sheila and Jessie were like sisters or best friends the way they conferred and then worked on dinner. I sat at the breakfast bar watching. Jessie made excited turns between the stove, cabinets, and fridge, catching my eye as she did so, delighted to make a special dinner and have such an unusual guest.

They made mashed potatoes from scratch, gravy, French cut green beans, and meat loaf cupcakes that Jessie frosted with ketchup before they went in the oven.

While Jessie frosted the meat loaf, Daryl reappeared. He'd taken Taylor to a friend's house.

"Heidi, have you ever driven a tractor?" he asked.

"No."

"Come on. You're gonna."

I brought my camera and followed Daryl to a Clydesdale-sized tractor parked in the shade at the far end of the driveway. He motioned for me to sit in the driver's seat.

It was a simple machine: clutch, gas and brake pedals, gear shifter, throttle.

"Would you take a picture of me?" I extended my camera.

Daryl took it and backed up. I smiled and put one hand on the wheel and another on the gear shifter.

I got off the tractor.

"Get back on up there," Daryl said good-naturedly. "We're not done yet."

"You're not serious."

He gestured to the tractor. "This'll be fun."

I climbed into the driver's seat.

"Push the clutch all the way in with your foot. That's here on your left." Daryl pointed. "Gas is on the right."

I pressed the pedal, and he turned the ignition key. The tractor rumbled to life. Daryl adjusted the gears and throttle and guided me through releasing the brake.

"Now, all you have to do is let up on the clutch," Daryl said, raising his voice over the engine noise.

I looked behind me. A large mower trailer was attached. I looked at Daryl, thinking, *No way in hell.*

"Don't worry about the brush hawg on the back there," he said. "It's disengaged."

My mind saw a monstrous, toothy boar-beast.

"Slowly let up on the clutch," he said and stepped back from the tractor.

I started to let up on the clutch. The tractor lurched and died. I gripped the steering wheel and hoped the lesson was over. "I let up slowly," I said.

"It's short, mostly down near the base." Daryl pointed and returned to the engine. "Try again," he said.

I didn't want to drive the tractor, but if this was a way to say thank you for being rescued from the dog attack and hot day, I would do it.

Daryl stepped away, and I released the clutch again, slower. The tractor jerked but didn't stall. It inched forward.

Daryl walked up to me. The tractor was hardly moving. "Take it down the driveway," he instructed. "At the road, make a left and drive it up to the turnaround. Turn it there and bring it back up the driveway."

I drove the tractor down the steep driveway, turned left, and inched up the road at the same speed I'd come down the hill. It was a strange experience—I didn't have to make a decision, respond to anyone, or even be polite and engaged. I just sat. My head started to fill with heaviness. A person could probably fall asleep at the wheel of a tractor.

Gravity pulled at me as I made the turn. I urged myself to pay attention, to keep the tractor on the pavement, to not fall asleep, to not tip the machine over. It would defeat the effort of my day if I died here.

I turned right, up the driveway. The tractor putted. I held the steering wheel with both hands and sat up straight, imitating attentiveness.

As I approached the crest of the driveway, Daryl stopped me. I was relieved he was going to take over and park the tractor.

"Now you're gonna do a wheelie."

I was instantly awake.

Daryl gestured over his shoulder toward the house, "Jessie has your camera."

I looked in the direction he indicated. Jessie stood gleaming a braces-free smile. "No. No. I'm not doing a wheelie."

"Yes, you are. It's easy."

In my mind's eye, I saw the tractor fall backward and squash me. I knew the brush hawg was there, and even though it was disengaged, I would be tangled in mower parts, the engine screeching. It wasn't enough to have pedaled what I thought was a hundred miles in a hundred-degree heat only to get pulled down by dogs, survive falling asleep at the wheel, and now, horror of horrors, a tractor wheelie.

Daryl guided me through the steps.

I shook my head. "I'm not doing a tractor wheelie."

"Yes, you are."

"No. I'm not."

"Yes, you are."

I looked over at Jessie. She lifted my camera, ready to document the magic.

"And then that's it. I'm done on the tractor."

"Yeah."

"Okay." I took a deep breath and let it out slowly. "For the photo."

Daryl stepped out of the way.

I concentrated and lifted both of my feet off the tractor's pedals at the same time, imagining that if I pushed down on the steering wheel and then pulled back and lifted my feet high off the pedals, the machine would rise. The tractor lurched. I stepped back on the clutch and the brake.

Daryl came over. "Yeah! Do it again."

"You said I was done."

"Do it again. Just a little different." He gestured with his hands, "Give it some gas, then pop the clutch."

Daryl stepped out of the way. I checked Jessie, who had my camera poised for the shot. "Okay!" I yelled at them. I took a deep breath, and all in one motion took my foot off the brake, pressed the gas, and popped the clutch. The tractor lurched again.

"I got it!" Jessie called.

I stepped on the brake and clutch again. Had I really done a tractor wheelie? Was I finally done with the tractor? "Daryl," I said, "show me how it's done."

Daryl took control of the tractor, and I stepped to the ground. Jessie brought my camera over to show me the image of me on the tractor with air beneath its tires.

"That's awesome," I said to her. "Thank you!"

She smiled her big, straight-toothed smile and put the camera in my hand.

I turned around and pointed the camera in Daryl's direction. "All right," I called out to him.

Almost on cue, Daryl popped the clutch, and up went the front of the tractor.

I hooted.

"C'mon in," Jessie said lit up with excitement. "Dinner's ready."

Jessie and Sheila laid out the spread in the kitchen and set place mats on the breakfast bar. Everyone served themselves. I went last. I took a little of everything even though I wouldn't have chosen to eat any components of the meal on my own. I avoided potatoes. I hadn't grown up eating canned vegetables. The cooked ketchup on the meat loaf creeped me out.

I sat at the breakfast bar with my plate, grateful for this family who had gone out of their way to generously care for me.

I stuck my fork in the potatoes first, and they melted in my mouth, buttery, salty, velvety, a hint of bitter and beef from the gravy. The lumps had the right amount of tooth and were reminders that the mash started as whole spuds. Second, I tried the green beans, which surprised me by being palatable, even tasty—wet, salty, a touch of acid, varied texture. Then the meat loaf. Chewy, savory, salty, a little acid, a little sweet, a little juicy. I dug in with enthusiasm, my appetite unleashed. I finished everything on my plate and wished that I had given myself larger helpings. I eyed the serving dishes. There was still plenty.

"May I have some more?"

"Help yourself," Sheila said.

I tried to take my time with seconds but found myself looking at a clean plate. I could have eaten more but didn't.

Daryl, who sat to my right, had been slowly eating while I devoured both servings, and now his plate, too, was clean. He sat back in his chair, looking at me as if I had an elephant trunk for a mouth. "You put away that whole second plate?"

I shrugged in response. I wasn't sure how to take the comment. Having seconds seemed complimentary of the cooking.

Sheila and Jessie cleaned up. Daryl talked in loud spurts and then disappeared.

When the kitchen was back in order, Sheila offered to take me to Marshfield.

"Should I say goodbye to Daryl? I'd like to thank him again for picking me up."

"Oh, you're very welcome," she said and gestured for me to head toward the garage. "I'll let him know you said thank you."

Jessie came along. Night had fallen. Lights from the dashboard created a purple glow in the truck's cab.

Jessie shared about babysitting, working the concession stand at the ball field, her homecoming dress, her girlfriends, and Facebook. "I'll never forget this day as long as I live," she said. She was filled with awe, which touched me.

In the truck's headlights, I watched the hills—down and up and down and up. I was relieved I didn't have to bike this section of the route—ever.

When we arrived in Marshfield, I had Sheila stop at a cheap-looking motel. The one-story whitewashed structure was snug on I-44. The fluorescent lights outside bathed the walkway around the building in ashen light.

"Do you have a reservation here?" Sheila asked.

"No, but it's rare that a room isn't available when I show up somewhere."

"If you don't want to stay here, I'm happy to take you somewhere else."

I could feel her concern rise, but I wanted the day to be over. I wanted to finally get out of my biking clothes and take a shower. I wanted to talk to Daniel. I didn't care if the motel was ratty. I wasn't going to do much more than sleep and didn't need to pay for extras.

Before we left the house, Sheila had given me her e-mail address. I wanted to be sure I had a way to get in touch, to say thank you. Knowing this moment wouldn't be our last communication, I thanked her and Jessie again and stepped down from the truck. Across the highway was a Holiday Inn Express. Concrete jersey barriers separated the lanes of travel. It didn't look easy to inquire about a room there from where we were.

I turned back to Sheila. "This one looks like it will be fine. Do you mind waiting until I check in?"

"Sure."

"Thanks." I closed the door and went in the motel office.

A mousy woman with long, graying hair and round glasses came to the check-in counter, which had a dictionary-sized opening at counter height in the plexiglass that extended across the room to the ceiling. The room smelled timeworn but not dirty.

"Do you have a nonsmoking room for one?"

"We do." She slid a paper check-in sheet with a short, eraser-less pencil across the counter. "Any pets?"

"No," I said taking the paper and pencil. "I'm on bike. Is it okay that I bring it in the room?"

"I suppose," she said. "But you need to put it on something. I don't want it on the carpet."

"Okay. Do you have Wi-Fi?" I asked gently.

"No." She sighed. "We only do so much for this rate."

"That's fine. I just wondered."

We finished the transaction in near silence, and I went to the truck for my bike and panniers. Sheila helped me unload my gear. The woman from the office opened my room and entered with flattened boxes.

"You're sure this will be okay?" Sheila asked.

"Yeah. It's not perfect, but I don't need much tonight. I really appreciate you bringing me here."

She seemed reluctant to leave.

"I'll e-mail you in the morning and let you know what my plan is. Thank you again so much to you and Daryl and Jessie."

"Okay. Take care." She climbed into the truck.

I carried my panniers inside the room. It was passable. Wood-paneled walls. Clean. Basic. It had a light chemical smell that I interpreted as this-room-has-been-disinfected or this-room-has-been-touched-with-chemicals-to-make-you-think-it-is-clean. The innkeeper laid the cardboard on the floor near the door. "You can put your bike here," she said, pointing. "Only here."

"Okay." I retrieved my bike and carried it from the door to the cardboard and leaned it against the wall.

The innkeeper handed me the room key and left. I closed and locked the door behind her. Sheila and Jessie were already gone.

The carpet, mashed from use, was a blotch pattern with two tones of brown and a mustard color that could hide spills and stains.

I suspected the innkeeper regularly dealt with dirty needles, puke, shit, violence, drunkenness, semen, blood, and/or dead bodies. Was a bike in the same category?

My phone had reception, and I stood between my bike and the bed and checked my e-mail. Daniel had written.

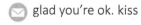 glad you're ok. kiss

I was comforted to see his message, brief as it was. Mom had not sent any messages. She was probably on pins and needles wondering what had happened. I needed to call. I wanted to tell Daniel about my crazy day, too. And I was still in my sweat-crusted bike clothes. I triaged the needs. I was first. My parents and Daniel could wait. It was just after 8:00 PM their time.

I showered off the epic day that began in Pittsburg. I called my parents. They were relieved I was okay and equally relieved that I planned to take a rest day the next day.

When I ended the call with them, I saw that Daniel had sent me another e-mail.

 Baby, I really hope you are doing well. Sorry about the
dog and the no connectivity. Kiss

My heart smiled. He was worried about me. I called him. I recounted the dog attack and the tractor wheelie. We imagined what it would be like to touch each other if there was a way to rendezvous.

After we hung up, I was amped. It was after midnight. I rinsed my biking clothes. They would still be wet in the morning, but I wouldn't need to wear them for a trip across the street.

Eventually, I lay on the bed. The dog attack seemed like a deus ex machina moment, as if I tapped into cosmic energies and brought it on myself.

Hell of a way to get a ride.

30.

Was She Hot?

I walked outside at 6:15 AM to orient myself and scout for breakfast. The air gripped me in its sweaty palm.

A barbecue place sat at the end of the parking lot. As I neared, I saw a FOR SALE sign in the window. I turned back to the motel. The innkeeper who checked me in eight hours earlier emerged from a room. She motioned to me, and I went to talk to her.

"What are you looking for?"

"Where can I get breakfast?"

"There's a place over there. Ziggie's." She waggled her hand indicating the area across the highway by the Holiday Inn. "It's behind the gray building."

"How do I get there?"

She motioned to the overpass. "You have to go up there."

I would have to merge onto the Interstate, cross two lanes of traffic to a left-turn area, and cross another two lanes of traffic to the shoulder on the far side of the Interstate to access the exit ramp. Once on the ramp, I would have to recross two lanes of traffic to a left-turn lane with a stoplight.

"It's not very safe," she said. "I don't know how you all do it. Ziggie's is the fourth light. Where are you headed today?"

"Not far."

"You need to leave earlier. It's going to be hot."

After all her pissiness about my bike in the room, I was surprised by her concern. I obviously wasn't the first cyclist who stayed at her motel.

I packed. I hadn't planned on leaving so soon, but because I had to get on my bike to go to breakfast, it made sense to take all my stuff with me.

At 8:50 AM, I checked into a clean and spacious ground-floor room at the Holiday Inn.

When I opened my computer, I had a Facebook friend request from Jessie. I accepted and checked out her page.

JESSIE: tonight was so interesting. Very brief overall. Cross Country bike rider, Heidi crashed her bike because dogs attacked her, dad found her laying in the road. He picked her up brought her home, she got relaxed, rode my dad's tractor (she'd never ridden one before) we all ate supper together shared stories, and me and mom took her to marshfield to a motel to spend the night.

JESSIE: Oh, and, she started her journey in Oregon and is on her way to Washington DC :) Tonight was great.

CORY: Haha! Oh my gosh that is insane! I can't beleive that happened. . . . That's gotta be a one in a billion chance wow lol

JESSIE: Oh my gosh. I know. Tell me about it. Lol. And she was such an amazing lady. Its not like she does it for fun either. She is doing it for two reason, 1) she's in college for Rural Economic Development so it was partially for her schooling 2) she's doing a big meeting or presentation in washington dc about cycling tourism and stuff. Like its awesome dude. Forreal

ELLIE: So is she like famouse or what ? And did she get hurt by the dogs ?

CORY: Oh my goodness Wow. . . . That will be a story to tell your children and grand children someday, I guess :) Its just so unbelieveable!! Did you get a picture with her? Lol

JESSIE: No Ellie, she isn't famous but someone i'll remember forever. And the dogs pretty much just grabbed the bags on her bike and pulled her bike down to the ground the bit her back and stuff but she's okay. My dad came just in time . . . and got them away from her :) and yes Cory, i'll def tell everyone about her. I took pictures of her :) my family is just a bunch of rednecks. She'd never rode a tractor before and my dad showed her how

to pop a wheelie and i took a picture of
it. I'll have her send it to me :) she is
an awesome person.

CORY: Haha Okay sweet :) She sounds
awesome! Was she hot? I've never ridden a
tractor before either.

JESSIE: Lol. Um. She was i'm guessing
35-40 sooo Cory your just a freak.

CORY: Lol! Hey shut up Jessie you said she
was in college so I was thinking she was
like 19 or 20... That seems normal right??
Soo You da freak

JESSIE: True. Well... Thats just wierd :)
haha

CORY: Well... I don't know. If you were a
man you'd understand haha :)

HEIDI: Cory, very hot. 100 miles in 100
degree heat. I look cooler now that I've
had a shower. What an awesome rescue by
the Turners! Thank you!

JESSIE: :) you're so very welcome! have a
safe trip (the rest of the way)

Once I wrenched myself away from Jessie's page, I wrote to Sheila
and told her where I was and thanked her again for her kindness. I
also asked for an address. My mom wanted to thank her.

The morning at my computer melted into afternoon. The Holiday
Inn's Internet went out at the same time as the alarm system was

being tested. I walked through the afternoon's hot sweat to McDonald's, where I could get Wi-Fi.

The restaurant was empty, cool, and smelled of ketchup and soft serve. I sat out of view of the staff at the checkout counter to lessen my guilt about not buying anything. While I was there, I received an e-mail from my transportation and preservation instructor reminding me that a grant I wanted to apply for had a deadline in two days. My heart raced and my breath shortened. How was I going to write a grant proposal in two days?

After perusing the guidelines, I was more confident about meeting the deadline—it was a letter of intent. I sent a few e-mails to make sure the people at work were aware of its requirements. I returned to my room and started drafting the letter.

Later in the evening when I had a preliminary draft of the project, I reread an e-mail from Sheila I hadn't been able to digest when I received it that afternoon.

 Heidi,

Thank you so much for the update, we were wondering how you might be feeling today. I will tell Daryl, Jessie & Taylor. I am so glad you decided to take a break. The fact that Daryl found you is a blessing for you and for him. Ironically, he has topped a hill and found a girl in the road before, she did not survive. She had fallen from the back of a pickup truck and the driver (her mother) had no idea she lost her. He has been really bothered about her death for a long time. Finding you and being able to help is going to be good for him and it sounds like you will be fine. We will pray for you and follow you.

You're welcome, the pleasure was ours,
Sheila

The keep-it-together bubble of my struggles over the past week ruptured. I cried for myself, for this family who helped me, and for the girl in the road who died. I welcomed the family's prayers. They would keep me safe.

When I woke at the Holiday Inn, it was before light, as usual. I heard a low rumbling I thought was early morning truck traffic on the Interstate. Despite being a rest day, yesterday hadn't been restful. Tiredness weighted my head. Through the windows in the motel dining room, I saw an electrical storm dumping rain. The rumble wasn't traffic.

I asked a man who was arranging muffins on a plate, "Do storms here blow over quickly?"

He shrugged.

The TV in the breakfast room had current weather information but fuzzed with each flash of lightning. Based on the fractured broadcast, it appeared the storm cells were moving south. I could shoot between two cells and miss the storm.

I departed at 7:30 AM. The rain was soft splats. Inside a pannier was my flag. Its dowel had broken during the dog attack, and I would deal with repairing it on a drier day. No longer in a pannier, HALT! was clipped within easy reach on my rack should an angry dog approach. The day's high temperature would be in the eighties. I looked forward to an easeful day.

Beyond Marshfield, the rain lightened, and I entered Amish countryside. The road and its surrounds purred with gentleness. Nothing was urgent. The grass wasn't in a hurry to grow. The people weren't in a hurry to do. The roof of a red barn wasn't in a hurry to collapse. The sky wasn't in a hurry to rain. The sun wasn't in a hurry to shine. The long-horned cow behind a bar gate wasn't in a hurry to low. And the horse-drawn buggies depicted on road signs weren't in a hurry to appear. Even I was not in a hurry to get anywhere.

The sky remained overcast and the rain intermittent. I wanted to sleep. Several cups of tea hadn't changed the heavy feeling in my head.

I checked in to a motel in Summersville and used motel bar soap on my riding clothes. I hoped the rose-scented soap would rid my clothes of their acrid mulch smell. I arranged them to dry on chairs outside.

After showering, I went to the Trail's End with my laptop. I e-mailed Daniel first. He was traveling to New Jersey for a family gathering and his mom's seventy-fifth birthday. Daniel had the trip planned, time requested off work, and plane ticket bought before I left Eugene. We were hungry to see and touch each other, but there wasn't a reasonable way for him to modify his plans so we could intersect.

Tired as I was, I sent e-mails for the grant letter due the next day. This small effort moved the grant project forward and added to my sense of the day's eighty-seven-mile accomplishment.

31.

Welcome to the Ozarks

The nineteen miles between Summersville and Eminence introduced me to the Ozarks. The Ozark Mountains are among the oldest mountain ranges on the planet, more ancient than the Appalachian Mountains, and cover southern Missouri, northern Arkansas, and small, eastern portions of Kansas and Oklahoma. Federal protections for parts of the Ozarks began with the establishment of the Ozark National Forest in 1908 and include the Ozark National Riverways, which was the first National Park based on a river system and established in 1964. The presence of springs and other water features with limestone lends to the formation of caves, sinkholes, and waterways that disappear underground. The numerous caves provide habitat for bats, many of which are threatened or endangered. Aboveground, cliffs interrupt rolling hills.

The dense deciduous forest enclosed most of the road, which went straight up and straight down. The shady route vibrated with cicada ratcheting, and a haze proved I wasn't imagining the air's soupiness. The narrow road had an abrupt edge.

Undulations in the long, steep climbs hid oncoming vehicles, and road shoulders were nonexistent. Trucks traveled fast and hauled horse trailers, canoe trailers, RV trailers, log trailers, and junk trailers. I hadn't seen this trailer traffic anywhere the previous day.

I was the only bicycle. The climbs were formidable, and I stood to pedal, turning the cranks at walking speed.

The ambient air temperature was hot. I sweated up the climbs. The exertion was like advanced cardio in a steam room while fully clothed with a periodic horn blast from behind.

I'd been honked at twice since leaving Summersville, and it was terrifying. Automotive horns are designed to be heard from inside other motor vehicles; they're piercingly loud without the dampening bubble of metal and glass and the noise-canceling rumble of an engine. I assumed the honking was drivers' frustration about getting stuck behind me, but I couldn't get out of the travel lane and had zero room for error if I crashed. If I stopped to let a vehicle go by, I'd have to walk the rest of the hill. If I was being honked at because people were concerned about my safety, I wished they understood how startling the noise was and how it compromised my safety.

At the top of a lengthy climb, I entered the Ozark National Scenic Riverways. The plunging hillsides were soft with deciduous forest. I descended to Jack's Fork, which teemed with canoe and raft flotillas.

I climbed another steep hill to reach Eminence. The place swarmed with people, surprising for a town of 548 residents on a Friday morning. I rolled through the hubbub to the post office.

The woman behind the counter brought out a pile of mail for me.

"Are you staying in town?" she asked.

"That's my plan."

"Do you have a place already?"

"I don't. I thought I'd see what caught my interest."

"You might have a hard time. The Trail Rides are in town, and most places are full up." Later, I learned the Trail Rides were a week-long event in Eminence with horseback riding, river recreation, and music and dancing every evening. "Are you staying tomorrow?"

"I hadn't planned on it. Should I?" How would I write the grant letter?

She looked over the top of her glasses at me. "People are starting to leave from the Trail Rides today, but they'll also be leaving tomorrow. The road will be busy with all those horse trailers and canoe trailers. The traffic should be better Sunday. Let me call a couple of places for you."

Everywhere was full.

"There's a new bed and breakfast just down the road," she said. "They might have room. If they don't, then try this other place." She handed me a scrap of paper with a street address on it.

"Is this someone's house?"

"Sometimes they take people in, but not regularly."

"Thank you. Do you have a bag I could put this mail in?" The woman gave me a bag, and I tied up my box, mailer envelopes, and postcards, perched the load on top of my rack, and secured it with a bungee. I went to the B&B, where a man and woman were sitting on the porch swing.

"May I help you?" the woman asked.

"Do you have any room for this evening?"

"No. We have a room tomorrow but not tonight."

I wasn't sure what to do. I was scared to go up to someone's house and ask to stay.

"Do you have a tent?" the woman asked. "You're welcome to stay in the yard."

"Yes!" Problem solved. "I'm also interested in the room for tomorrow."

"That's good, yeah. The Trail Rides have everything pretty busy," she said. "You're welcome to hang out in the living room here."

"Do you have Internet?"

"We do."

I did a mental dance. "I have something I need to get done. Is it really okay if I spend all day in the living room?"

"It is. You can use the bathroom on the main floor, and if you want to take a shower, I'll let you use mine downstairs. The backyard is safe, and you can find a place wherever you like. Make yourself comfortable." She gestured behind her and then introduced herself as Susan and the man next to her as Tim.

I parked my bike next to a tree and opened my mail. I received chocolate, postcards, a letter, and a packet from Daniel that included a long letter and *Archy and Mehitabel*. I didn't even open the box of food I sent myself. After tidying my gear, I took my laptop inside. By late afternoon, I finished the grant letter. Afterward, I returned to the yard, set up my tarp, crawled inside, and changed out of my cycling clothes.

At the grocery store, I bought a couple cards and asked the clerk, "Where can I go for a drink and dinner?"

The man in line behind me asked, "How much do you want to spend?"

"It doesn't matter."

"Well, if it doesn't matter, would you like to buy me a drink?"

I didn't reply but moved to the end of the cashier stand to put away my change. I slid the cards into my journal.

Meanwhile, the cashier rang up the man's purchases. As he passed me, he stopped and said, "Excuse me. Can I buy you a drink?"

He was tall and trim with a thick moustache and goatee and short graying hair. His jeans and short-sleeved collared shirt were clean. In my head, I heard, *All men in Missouri are friendly.* "Okay."

I followed him to his truck.

"Where is it? Walking distance?" I didn't want to be taken far, although I did want to celebrate finishing the grant letter.

He opened the passenger side door. "Two blocks. My name's Wayne. Hop in."

I peered in the tidy interior of the truck. It was ridiculous to drive two blocks to wherever we were going, but maybe this was Missouri chivalry. I climbed in, feeling a touch princessy.

As soon as we got a table, he lit a cigarette. "Oh," he said. "I should have told you. I smoke."

I ordered a drink and a burger. We talked.

Wayne had been in Eminence since he left the military, four years prior.

"I love canoeing," he said. "I'd been here before, and when I was ready to move, I thought this would be a nice place to spend some time. I do commercial mowing. I have two and a half acres with a three-bedroom house and three sheds. I got it all for $40,000."

The idea of having an adult life with less of the competition that came with city living appealed to me.

When Wayne asked about my journey, I told him about the conference in Washington, DC, how I went back to school to hide out from the Recession and hopefully gain a "relevant" degree that would give me access to a career, but mostly I wanted to ride my bike.

When I finished my drink and dinner, I was ready for fresh air and me time.

"Do you want to go for a ride tomorrow since you're not leaving town?"

Wayne's offer seemed similar to the airplane ride with Bill and driving Daryl's tractor. One thing my ride taught me was being open to other people and the local experience. And receiving. I agreed.

"ATV or Harley?" he offered.

"Harley. How do we do this?"

"Tell me when."

"How about noon?" I wanted the morning to write and talk to Daniel. I also didn't want to be out late. "Let's meet somewhere between here and where I'm staying. It's a small town, we'll find each other."

"Sounds good. See you then." He left me in the bar parking lot and drove off.

I woke to a cool morning with a gentle sun and the scent of moist outdoors. I entered the B&B. Coffee and sweet bread tickled my nose.

"Good morning," Tim said. He was making breakfast. "How did you sleep?"

"Pretty well." Half-truth. Crawly things under my sleeping pad kept me awake until midnight. "It smells good in here."

"You're welcome to have breakfast with the other guests."

"Yes, please."

"Can I get you anything now?"

"I'd love a cup of black tea."

He brought me a big mug.

I thanked him and promised to return for breakfast.

I iChatted with Daniel from underneath my tarp. I longed to kiss his lopsided smile. He was excited to be in New Jersey. It sounded like a nonstop party weekend. We enjoyed I-show-you-mine-and-you-show-me-yours until Daniel needed to get back to family.

When I opened the B&B door, peach French toast and bacon pulled me in.

Not long after breakfast, my room was ready.

I dismantled my tarp and checked in.

At noon, I walked across the street to wait for Wayne. He rode by, and I waved. He came back around, handed me a helmet, and I got on.

"How about we ride the road ahead, and you can check out where you'll be riding tomorrow?"

"Sounds good." I'd been hearing stories about Powder Mill Hill. On my map, the elevation profile went straight up.

We hardly went over fifty miles per hour. I sat upright and hooked my index fingers into his belt loops. There wasn't a stop on the back of the Harley, just a wedge to keep my ass from sliding off. I would have felt more secure putting my arms around his waist and leaning into his back, but I didn't want to get that close. I slid back on the seat on two steep hills. I gripped tighter on Wayne's belt loops and hoped I wouldn't slide off.

He took me to the Eagles Lodge in Ellington.

"What's the deal with this place?" I asked, curious that Wayne used a card to enter.

"They don't allow fighting here, so if you're with someone who you're not sure would appreciate the rough and tumble of the other bar, it's good to come here. I don't come here much. I'm sure they were surprised I had a card."

Wayne had a beer and smoked. I sipped unsweetened iced tea, apprehensive that I would be riding on a motorcycle with someone who'd been drinking.

"What was your job in the military?" I asked.

"That's a good story." He told me about an incident that hampered the rest of his military career that involved the fiancée of a major. The story had nothing to do with Wayne's job in the military. He finally told me he played trombone, which wasn't the infantryman job I expected.

We motored away from the Eagles Lodge on the sunny and humid afternoon. Wayne turned down a dirt road. In my mind, I heard suspenseful music, and I wanted it to stop. I yelled to be heard over the engine noise, "Where are we going? I'm really ready to head back to Eminence." In addition to feeling uncomfortable about being alone with him in the woods, I had cramps.

He didn't respond immediately and drove farther down the road before stopping. "You ever sit in the driver's seat of a Harley?"

"Nope." I hoped he wouldn't put a move on me.

"You'd look good on one. Give it a try." He got off, and I slid to the seat. "For sure," he said.

"Will you get a picture of me for my blog?" I held my camera out to him.

He took a photo and handed the camera back. I looked at the image and smiled. "That's excellent."

"Ready to head back?" he asked.

Back out on the pavement, I relaxed some. There were more eyes on this road than the dirt one.

In Eminence, we stopped at the bar where he'd taken me the previous evening. He lit a cigarette immediately. I didn't want to hang out, but I didn't know how to end the visit. It seemed impolite to say "Thanks. I'm done."

"I'll give you a ride to Ellington tomorrow in my truck if you want."

"It's such a pretty ride. The three big hills seem tough but doable. Thank you for the offer, but I'll pedal."

Wayne chain-smoked. All the while, I was trying to figure out how to leave. Somewhere around the seventh or tenth cigarette, I really needed fresh air.

"Thanks so much for the ride, Wayne. I need to get on to the next thing now."

"I sure hope you come back this way some day."

I thanked him for treating me while I'd been in Eminence and then walked outside and breathed deeply.

32.

Wet Heat, Dead Bat, Shut-Ins

Day forty-nine. I woke early in the comfort of the B&B bed, swallowed two ibuprofen, and wrote. After an unsuccessful attempt to repair the American flag, I rolled it up and stowed it inside a pannier.

When the gate at the B&B closed behind me, the bank clock across the street read 8:40 AM. So much for an early departure. It was already humid and hot. I guessed the temperature was more than eighty-five degrees. I couldn't afford to feel defeated. I focused on pedaling. All I had to do was turn the cranks.

Before tackling Powder Mill Hill—about five hundred feet of climbing over one mile—I would encounter a similarly proportioned warm-up hill a few miles out of Eminence. After Powder Mill Hill was a third monster hill.

As I climbed the warm-up hill in dappled shadow, I sweated, inching upward. When I reached the hillcrest, I sucked wind while struggling to keep my bike upright.

A few short, steep hills challenged me. Then, I flew down a precipitous descent with gentle curves. There were hardly any vehicles on the road and not a single trailer. I crossed the Current River at top speed and glided up a short wall of a hill on the other side. The road briefly canted down before Powder Mill Hill came into view, the road's higher reaches hidden in trees.

I pedaled as hard as I could until the steepness sapped my momentum. I downshifted to my granny gear. All I needed to do was keep pedaling for one mile. My lower back whimpered. I gave myself permission to stop if I needed to. I groaned and sweated. My muscles pinched. My breath shortened. I stopped at a little plateau and did trunk twists to release the grip in my lower back while I caught my breath. I appreciated Wayne's offer to drive me and the other ways he rolled out the red carpet for me while I was in Eminence. And even though what I was doing was difficult, it was what I wanted—my thing, my way, and I didn't have to worry about being hormonal around anyone.

From the side of the road, I pushed into the travel lane to get enough momentum to direct myself back up the hill. I angled back to the right and kept cranking. Tight lower back. Chuffing breath. Wet heat.

Beads of sweat made snail tracks down my scalp. They tickled and itched. I dared not take a hand off the handlebars.

The hillcrest inched into view. The front of my bike waggled. I stood and pedaled. I sat and pedaled. I couldn't get to the top any faster. Five more pedal strokes. Five more.

At the top, I unclipped and stood straddling my bike, chest heaving. I leaned forward and rested my forehead on my crossed wrists. Breathed. Sweated. Rotated my pelvis to release the tension in my lower back.

The two longest climbs of the day were behind me.

I stood and did trunk twists and then kept going.

Some short ups and downs. A long, speedy descent.

The third climb rose up and up and around and up. At the steepest part below the hillcrest, I stood to pedal in my granny gear, a slow, controlled movement. In the travel lane ahead was a massive pot-hole. As I passed between the hole and the side of the road, I looked into the hole's bottomlessness.

With the shift of my body as I looked, my handlebars twisted to the side. I couldn't recover. My feet unclipped from the pedals, and I landed standing astride my collapsed bike.

"Poor bike. You're exhausted," I said, looking down at it. I took a couple breaths before picking it up. The hillcrest wasn't far from where I fell. I pushed my bike to the top and stood a moment to ac-knowledge my completion of the three climbs. I did it with a bad hip, a tired menstrual body, and without a shred of fun.

I clipped back in and rolled down the road. The hills moderated but were a regular pattern of up, plateau, up, down, plateau, down, and up. Repeat. The heat and humidity intensified.

In Ellington, I drank juice and filled my water bottles with ice.

From there, the route followed a wider road with gentler climbs and fewer trees. Despite being a wider road, the shoulders weren't paved, so I pedaled at the edge of the travel lane. In the blazing sun.

After a few miles, I was so hot I would have traded the gentler road grade for the long, steep, but shady climbs.

My thoughts kept looping on the heat, how I couldn't get out of it, that I didn't think I'd make it to wherever I was going.

I withered. My water bottles were full of hot water. I loathed the idea of swallowing any. My clothes were saturated. I needed to rehy-drate. I made myself drink.

My feet were heavy as cinderblocks. I couldn't move my legs. My body was full of liquid lead.

Having stopped, I leaned my head on the handlebars the way I'd done at the top of Powder Mill Hill. My uterus crimped. My pores vomited. I couldn't keep going. There wasn't a thread of cool air to breathe.

I had to keep moving. But I couldn't pedal.

My body shuffled. I pushed my bike.

A dead bat lay on the roadside—small, brown, flat—one wing tucked under its body, the other out to the side with the long fingers bent down. It looked as if it had been hitchhiking and fell face-first in the empty road.

If I didn't keep moving, I would end up dead like the bat. I urged myself to get back on my bike, but my body didn't move. I was in the middle of Missouri with no cell service. My chest twinged. I needed to cry.

I closed my eyes and gave myself a moment. A few tears came. Pathetic. I couldn't even muster a proper bawl. The bat was a sign. Keep moving.

Conveyed by a primal sense of self-preservation, I remounted my bike and turned the pedals.

I rode into the Johnson's Shut-Ins State Park visitor center area dripping sweat. The place teemed with cars, minivans, trucks, and people. A man drank at a water fountain.

"Is that cold?" I asked when he finished.

"No. I wouldn't say cold. But I'm so thirsty, I'll drink it. It's more like cool."

I refilled my bottles at the fountain and drank deeply. Like the man said, the water wasn't cold, but it was less hot than my body.

In the bathroom, I washed my face with warm water from the automatic sink. Back out on the plaza, I lay on a bench in the shade. I tried to cry again but couldn't make one tear.

After many minutes, I got up, leaving a perfect sweat shape of my body on the bench. I went to my bike and squished an energy gel into my mouth.

I looked at my map. Farmington was thirty-eight miles from the state park with an eighteen-mile hill. It sounded daunting to attempt in the sun and heat. Pilot Knob, a town of 697 people with a motel, was two miles off route and only fifteen miles from the state park. If I went to Pilot Knob, I would be in air-conditioning. The universe was offering me a break. I took it.

The road narrowed. The shoulder disappeared, and the roadside trees stood closer. I pedaled from shade puddle to shade puddle. The humidity continued to suffocate. The road climbed. My focus locked on air-conditioning.

When I checked in at the motel, I learned that I rode through Pilot Knob to the adjacent town of Ironton. The woman at the front desk handed me tourist brochures of area attractions, including Johnson's Shut-Ins State Park, along with the room key.

I took the brochures but didn't look at them. "What's a shut-in?" I hadn't found information at the visitor center plaza explaining it. I guessed it referred to people who holed up in a house with guns, but I didn't understand why that would be a state park.

"A shut-in is a rocky area along the river where the water gets trapped. The shut-ins are a series of pools."

It made sense why the park was busy. "I see. Good place to cool down. As long as you don't have to bike home."

"It's gonna get hotter, honey. You be careful out there." The temperature was in the low nineties with 58 percent humidity and a heat index between 99°F and 106°F.

I couldn't do a damn thing about the weather. Being careful meant staying put, but that wouldn't get me to Washington. I pushed my bike to my room.

Mom was concerned about the lack of cell service in Missouri. She e-mailed, "The phone is more than a communication link, it's your security system. And I'm your Mommy." She also wrote, "When you are tucked in for this evening at a place with air-conditioning, Wi-Fi, and an in-room phone, give us an e-mail with the motel # where we can talk to you. When we see the message, we will call you back."

I sent her my information and added:

✉ Tough day, but now it's done, and as much as I can tell,
I blazed Missouri. I think it's pretty much downhill from
here with not too many short steep hills left. Did em
almost all today.

I also forwarded a picture of Daniel. I told my parents about Daniel only a few days prior. We felt solid enough as a couple that it seemed time. I wanted my parents to know who else was helping me through the distance. They'd been quiet at first, and then Dad said, "I wondered." Now they had a face to put with the name.

33.

Meltdown

I departed Ironton at 6:30 AM in damp riding clothes and an atmosphere of muggy stew. I had tricky navigation ahead that involved a series of turns and railroad track crossings that would connect me to a bike path. Those navigation details didn't need to be top of mind because I would pedal more than an hour before the first turn.

The climb out of Pilot Knob was gradual. The wide shoulder was a mess of potholes, rough edges, loose rock, and huge, flaring cracks. I swerved in and out of the travel lane to avoid these hazards.

Railroad tracks rattled me to attention. I was in a town. The track crossings were supposed to be in the country. I stopped to look at my map. I hadn't registered my surroundings since I'd been too focused on the crappy road. I backtracked to the cycling route.

I needed to be more attentive.

A sign for Old Bismarck, the first turn, caught my attention. I turned and crossed the railroad. The next turn was at a major intersection. I would know I was on the cycling route when I crossed the tracks again.

The major intersection brought five roads together and spidered before me with the railroad arcing through three legs of it. None of the legs of the intersection was signed as Pimville Road, the one that connected to the bike path. My anxiety rose. I didn't want to make a wrong turn. I took a deep breath of atmospheric steam, let it out slowly, and turned onto the road my gut chose.

A few pedal strokes into my decision, a man mowing on the side of the road looked at me and slowed his mower.

I rolled up to him. "Is this Pimville Road?"

"Yeah. Where're you headed?"

"Farmington."

"You don't want to go that way. You'll be walking your bike. The road is really steep. You're better off taking the highway."

I trusted Adventure Cycling to have a good cycling route. If it were preferable to take the highway, the route would have gone that way. "Isn't there a bike path?" People who primarily drove didn't necessarily understand the difference between a bike route and a driving route. "The map says when I get into the park there's a bike path."

"Oh, yeah. That's a lot more level than the road. That'll be okay. Yeah. You go up the road, and on your right is a trailhead."

I couldn't blame him for not thinking about the bike path, and I was glad he knew it was there.

"It's hot out," he said.

"Indeed."

"It's supposed to be one hundred and sixteen tomorrow with the humidity and not cool down any until the weekend, not even at night."

"Really? Not until the weekend?" I almost cried. Sweating would not help me in this heat. My body would get hotter and hotter. Even if I could replenish my water bottles regularly with ice, the ice would melt and turn into hot water in a few miles. Hydration alone wouldn't protect me. Eventually my brain would cook.

It was one thing to suffer through a day of this heat, but knowing I would face this torture for a whole week killed. Sleeping outside as I did at the B&B in Eminence would not be an option. What would that mean for how far I could go each day? And what if I couldn't reach air-conditioning? I wouldn't arrive in Washington in time for the conference if I averaged fewer than fifty miles per day. I still had more than a thousand miles to go. My stomach sank.

I was already frustrated about following the route. Now the heat was going to suffocate for days. I would have to constantly monitor myself for signs of hyperthermia. And if I noticed myself sliding into the danger zone, what would I do, try to use my cell phone, which didn't work between towns, and call whom? And if I passed out or couldn't call for help, what then?

Pimville Road pitched upward. I labored, fretted, sweated. A sign with a bike on it appeared, and I turned right at a TRAILHEAD sign. I followed the path a short way and then stopped. I checked my map and read the directions again, rereading a critical bit four times, "At the trailhead, turn left."

It didn't appear that there was a left option at the trailhead. I looked behind me at a fence across the path.

"Left, huh?" I said aloud to reinforce the lunacy of what I saw. In addition, left didn't correlate with where I thought I was headed. Was I already too hot? Ride into the fence? Was it going to dissolve when I approached?

I turned around expecting to prove the directions wrong. I was in Missouri, the Show Me state. Show me the way through, damn it. Remarkably, Missouri lived up to its motto. The fence across the path was offset so people and bicycles could get through, something I couldn't see from the trailhead.

As I rolled through, I piled irritation about this missed turn onto the morning's other miscues.

The path climbed steeply. I sucked in hot air and powered up the rises, although I barely managed. It would be defeat to walk my bike up a hill on a bike path. With all the steep roads in Missouri, why couldn't the engineer of this path use a gentler grade? I was a fit cyclist, albeit hauling gear, but I almost couldn't make it. What about a little kid? Or adults out for a leisurely ride? Who used this path?

A highway was near, which didn't jive with the route cutting through the state park. I stopped and looked at my map again. There was a direction on the path to bear right. Did I miss it? The mower said this was a gradual way through the park. I didn't think I was in the right place, but I kept going.

At a fork in the path that I wouldn't have described as offering a "bear to the right" option, I stopped again and looked at my map. I turned the map around hoping it would spin an arrow to point me in the proper direction. It didn't.

I was done with the path and aimed for the highway.

Ahead was a woman and two young kids. She collected the children to her when she saw me.

"Hi," I said, slowing. I stopped in front of them, not too close. "How do I get to the road?"

"Which road?"

"I don't know. Any road. How do I get out of here? To the highway?"

"Just get on that road and go that way." She pointed to the right.

"That way?" I pointed to the right, incredulous.

She nodded.

The path went toward the highway but then curved away from it. At the point where the path curved, I dismounted and shoved my bike under the path barricade. It wasn't my bike's fault, but I was pissy about how my day was turning out. Anger was transforming to rage. Perhaps that was why the mother was protective of her kids. She could tell I was enflamed.

I entered town, looking for Maple Street. At a major intersection I followed a bike route sign. I passed a few business signs and learned I was in Leadington, which wasn't on my map. Where the hell was I?

At a gas station where I stopped for water, juice, and ice, I asked the woman at the cash register for directions.

She pulled a local map from a box on top of the display case of energy shots.

I looked at the map and found Maple. "How do I get here?" I pointed.

"You take Highway 32 to 67, and you'll get there."

I didn't want to go the same way as the cars. Was there an alternate route? "Where's this road, Woodleaf?"

"I don't know."

"Well, where are we on this map? Are we even on it?"

"We're kind of off the edge. Up here." She pointed. "Woodleaf is down in front of the Kentucky Fried Chicken there." She identified a spot on the map.

I sat down at a table with my drinks and the map. It was nearly noon. I compared the gas station map with my cycling map.

Farmington was about seven miles away. If I didn't get lost, I'd be back on route in thirty-five minutes. I returned the map to the box on the display case.

Back in the heat, the road in front of the KFC was not called Woodleaf. I turned onto the west side frontage road, but it was the U.S. 67 on-ramp.

Despite not being the road I thought, I continued because the Interstate-like highway was on my map. The highway was noisy with fast-moving traffic and big vehicles, but the shoulder was wide. I had space to navigate around the glass, rocks, and tire debris while staying within the rumble strips, which were to the right of the fog line. Someone pulled over onto the shoulder ahead of me but didn't leave room for me to go around. I anxiously checked for a gap in traffic and rode in the travel lane to pass the car. I cut back into the shoulder over the rumble strips. My heart pounded.

I approached Farmington and discovered, to my horror, that the Highway 32 exit was in the left lane. Before long, a sizeable gap in traffic opened. I raced across three lanes to the left-side shoulder.

Highway 32 through Farmington was a business highway and not hospitable for biking. I rode with singular focus to get through town alive. I'd been turned around so many times that morning, all I wanted to do was get back on a quiet country road.

Finally, I reached my turn onto Route F.

I looked at my map while I pedaled. Farmington was the end of one panel, and I flipped the map to see what was ahead.

There were no services on route for twenty-seven miles.

No ice. No air-conditioning. No water refresh. No visitor center bench to lie on.

It wasn't quite 1:00 PM and intolerably hot.

The day of the dog attack, twenty-three miles was a concerning distance, and I began my race that day against overheating at 1:00 PM in ten- and fourteen-mile increments. Pedaling twenty-seven miles without respite from the heat was all-caps DANGER.

I put the map away and wiped the sweat on my upper lip with a damp glove. My cycling gloves were slimy inside. I sipped warm water.

The heat intensified. A winery sign directed passersby to a steep downhill road that bent around a green hill and disappeared. Maybe there was ice at the winery, but it seemed a time and energy gamble to find out. Plus, my sweaty, stinky condition didn't lend to being welcome at such a place. I passed the road without slowing.

Like the day I had pedaled into Cadaver, Kansas, I thought of Sisyphus and Prometheus. In my cursed state, I would always have five miles more to pedal before reaching the relief of ice and air-conditioning.

A whine whistled in the back of my throat and threatened tears. Heat gripped my neck. I sipped hot water. The skin over my cheekbones prickled.

I approached a construction area where a flagger stood on the side of the road in the shade.

"Do I need to stop?"

"Yeah. You picked a bad way to come."

Every minute I waited in the heat extinguished a minute of my life. "Can anyone give me a ride?"

"No. Maybe on the other side."

"How far is it to Ozora?"

"Fifteen miles, but it's mostly downhill. There's just one big hill between here and there."

Fifteen miles? I started crying. Surely I had covered more ground than that, and now I had the pleasure of being baked alive like all those children in "Hansel and Gretel." Either the flagger didn't notice my tears or pretended not to. He stood in the shade looking away from me. I burned in agony. The landscape was rolling green hills, stands of healthy deciduous trees, and humidity haze.

After several minutes, the flagger spun his sign to SLOW. I waited for the cars queued with me to go ahead. My legs felt made of sandbags. A MoDOT truck passed, and the driver waved. It pained me that he didn't offer a ride, but I hadn't indicated I wanted one. How could some people I'd encountered be genuinely concerned for me and others, especially those who worked on the road, approached me as if I were immune to the elements? Did the road workers admire my chutzpah for getting out there and pedaling anyway? Did they think if I was insane enough to try it that I deserved to deal with the consequences? Their purview of road safety had to do with engineering, maintenance, and vehicular interactions. Heat exposure was a different department. Not their problem.

I pedaled two or three miles and arrived at a turn for Route P. From there, five miles separated me from Ozora. The flagger had lied! But probably he didn't know how far Ozora was. With five miles to go, I could make it. Even if I staggered the last miles into Ozora the way marathoner Gabriela Andersen-Schiess did during the 1984 Olympic Games in Los Angeles, I would be okay. Either I would be able to help myself or there would be others there who could help me. I would stay in Ozora.

Highway P had a steep but short hill. I tried to pedal, but my sandbag legs would not lift. I got off and walked. At the top of the hill, I got back on the bike. A monster hill came into view.

I rode as far up the hill as I could and then walked. At the top of the hill, a woman in a utility locating truck waved as I tottered. I didn't wave back, but maybe I nodded her direction. Instinct had taken over my body, and my thoughts were disconnected from the machinery that kept me moving.

I kept on. Like I was riding through molasses. One hill. Another. Pure. Torture.

Inching along in a steam oven day after day wasn't fun.

Why was I punishing myself? Because I was an unemployable worm of a human being and deserved to be tortured for having grandiose thoughts about the contribution I could make to the world? Who was I kidding about sustainable transportation? I was wrong. Idealistic. I wasn't creative. I was foolish.

The people out here didn't care about the glaciers. They were too far away. Ice in nature didn't exist. Glaciers were a conspiracy. Bees weren't dying. Who cared that glaciers were cold and the care for them could remedy everything that was wrong with this moment? Rural communities were absolutely part of the solution to this heat, but they were seen as too many degrees of separation away. The economics didn't make sense.

But I could see it. Rural America held authentic experiences people craved. The experiences were difficult to reach, but that made them more desirable. America wasn't just a flag and Pledge of Allegiance. It was a container for everything I'd been experiencing—the landscape, the people, the solitude, the food, the weather, me. Was I out of my mind?

All these days and weeks I'd been fighting by steeling myself, enduring. It's what I knew how to do, how I had survived growing up in Wyoming and being a little sister, and how I faced other trials I asked of myself. No one was there to protect me from the hurt. I learned to take the punches. Take the pain. Dissociate. Recalibrate my tolerance for hurt. Be my own source of comfort or deny that I needed any.

What was the point of continuing? This torture of heat would persist, and I couldn't pedal out of it, not if I wanted to live. If I quit, the pain would stop.

Up ahead, a collection of boxy buildings and houses appeared. Ozora. I went straight to the gas station, where I purchased juice and water and sat at a table in the adjoining restaurant under some fans to cool down.

"Are you dining?" a woman wearing a short waist apron asked.

"The man at the gas station told me I could sit in here. Is that okay? I'm too hot right now. I can't think."

"That's fine," she said and left me alone.

I swallowed my drinks in big gulps. Sweat ran down my body, through my shorts and chamois, and pooled on the vinyl chair seat. It seemed impolite if not grossly unsanitary to sweat on the restaurant chair. I was probably still bleeding from my period, too. Despite my heat-addled state, I got up and wiped the seat with my hankie. I reentered the sweltering heat and walked my bike across the parking lot to the motel.

"Do you have a nonsmoking room for one for this evening?" I asked a gray man at the reservation desk.

"We do."

"If I stay a second day, when do you need to know?"

"As soon as you know, but eleven o' clock at the latest."

Unsure what to do, I disappeared into my room.

I texted Daniel, "I'm done. I can't do this anymore."

He responded quickly, briefly, and with appropriate concern. We arranged a time to talk in forty-five minutes.

I called my parents. "I can't do this anymore. It's too hot."

They had me on speakerphone. Mom asked, "Where are you now? Are you near air-conditioning?"

"I'm at a truck stop called Ozora off I-55. I'm in a room. Cooling down from the day. It's such a fight to keep going."

The other end of the line was quiet for a moment. Then Mom again, "What are you thinking?"

"I'm thinking I'm too hot. Maybe I can catch a train somewhere cooler and bike there until it's time to get to the conference. I don't even know where in the country it's cooler. Maine?"

Dad asked, "Is it just the heat that's the problem?"

"It's so hard to stay with it. No one is with me tracking when I might be too hot. I have to do that myself." Tears welled up in my eyes. "It's exhausting and scary. I never imagined it could be too hot to ride, but it is."

Mom chimed in, "You're probably too hot right now to think about this clearly."

I wiped the tears from my cheeks. "Undoubtedly."

"Get yourself situated and cool down. We'll look at what might be nearby to get you a break from the heat."

"Okay." I wiped my cheeks again. I was a wreck and would likely change my mind after I cooled down.

34.

Escape Plan

In the cool shower, I soaped salts off my body.

My thoughts locked on seeing Daniel. He would be in New Jersey for a few more days. It was probably cooler in New Jersey than Missouri even if it was hot and humid. Much of my extended family on Mom's side was in New Jersey, too. Instead of seeing family at the end of my trip, perhaps I should see them sooner, then return to the cycling route, and arrive in Washington a few days before the conference.

The thought of seeing Daniel brought a smile to my face and a tingle between my legs. Toweling off, my despondency from the trials of the day lightened. I dressed and paused to enjoy the comfort of dry cotton on my skin.

I rinsed my cycling clothes in the bathroom sink. The water turned a foul, cloudy gray. I drained and refilled the sink four times until the water didn't cloud anymore and then washed each item individually. I hung the clothes on furniture in front of the air conditioner.

"What if I came to see you in New Jersey?" I asked Daniel.

"That would be wonderful! I'd love to see you and show you Margate."

"After all that wishing we could touch, I can't believe we're going to see each other!"

"I know." His voice was chirpy. "Doris and Arthur would be happy to have you here. I've been telling them about your trip. What you're doing is so impressive. How do you think you'll get here?"

"Train. But I haven't looked at details yet."

"Come to Philly. I can pick you up there."

After our call, I checked Amtrak routes online. St. Louis was a major stop.

Planning to see Daniel and my urge to touch him and be touched by him masked my defeat about departing the route. Sex at the end of the week was a powerful motivator.

I called my parents.

"I have a plan. I'm going to New Jersey."

The phone was quiet on their end.

"Daniel is in Margate, near Atlantic City, visiting his parents. I'm going to see him. He said it's eighty-seven degrees there. That's not exactly cool, but it's cooler than one sixteen with one hundred percent humidity or whatever insanity is happening here."

Mom asked, "Are you sure?"

"Yes. Daniel says you would like Margate. It's where Monopoly is set, and they have Lucy, an elephant-shaped historic house."

"I've heard of Lucy." Mom's tone changed from concern to you're-speaking-my-language.

I still needed her help planning this break. "Could you find out what your family's plans are? I don't know where Margate is in relation to them. Daniel returns to Eugene on Saturday, so I won't have long with him."

"How are you getting to New Jersey?"

"The train. It boards in St. Louis."

"Okay. I'll make some calls."

I thanked her, and we ended our conversation.

I consulted Google Maps. The results showed travel on minor roads adjacent to the Interstate, which sounded promising. I returned to the truck stop convenience store for a map. There was a faint, dashed line of "Trail" that followed the east side of I-55 into St. Louis, the same line Google Maps produced. I could have kissed the map for confirming this way to St. Louis that didn't require me to ride I-55. Along this route, St. Louis was seventy miles from Ozora.

I returned to my room and opened my laptop. Mom had e-mailed. There was an excessive heat warning for St. Louis that remained in effect until 8:00 PM Thursday.

> * PEAK HEAT INDEX VALUES DURING THE AFTERNOON AND EARLY EVENING HOURS ARE EXPECTED TO BE 105 TO 115 DEGREES OR GREATER THROUGH THURSDAY. ACTUAL HIGH TEMPERATURES WILL BE IN THE UPPER 90s WITH HIGH HUMIDITY. OVERNIGHT LOWS IN THE UPPER 70s AND LOWER 80s WILL PROVIDE LITTLE RELIEF FROM THE HEAT.

> * THE LIKELIHOOD OF HEAT RELATED ILLNESSES WILL INCREASE EACH DAY BECAUSE OF THE ACCUMULATED HEAT.

I nearly snorted as I read the preventions and precautions that warned against "prolonged work in the sun" and that encouraged people to "spend some time in an air-conditioned environment to give your body a break from the heat." My circumstances weren't funny, but I had probably already won a medal in the intentional heat-related illness competition. Maybe not gold. That would be death.

I was doing everything wrong to prevent heat illness.

Mom had sent a synopsis of heat illness. The first-degree symptoms were cramps.

> **Symptoms:** Muscle pains and spasms—usually in the abdomen, arms, or legs—usually caused by strenuous activity, which triggers heavy perspiration.
>
> **Treatment:** Stop all activity and rest in a cool place. Drink cool, clear water, juice, or a sports beverage. Avoid strenuous activity for a few hours after cramps to prevent heat exhaustion or heat stroke.

I had some abdominal cramps during the day, but I attributed those to physical exertion and menstruation.

Second was heat exhaustion. I fit the description for someone exercising in a hot environment for several days of exposure to high temperatures, but I wasn't sure I had the symptoms. Heavy sweating and weakness applied to my experience, but was that heat-induced weakness or fatigue? I chalked it up to bicycle-unfriendly road engineering.

None of the symptoms related to mood or the ability to think clearly, but these were the signs that told me I was in trouble. Like my inability to follow the route that day. Being rough with my bike. My irritation with the woman at the gas station in Leadington who was actually being helpful. Crying when the construction worker told me it was fifteen miles to Ozora. My defeat at not being able to pedal up hills. My inability to answer the café waitress when she asked if I was dining.

The third degree of heat illness was heat stroke—the body in crisis and no longer able to sweat. That was not my experience, but

I had no way of knowing how close I'd come. I could potentially go from sweating profusely to not sweating and miss the subtle changes during heat exhaustion of becoming faint and my skin getting cool and clammy. If I experienced cramps, nausea, and vomiting, that would be an indicator, but those symptoms did not always manifest, especially, I reasoned, if I stayed hydrated and replaced electrolytes.

But if I stayed hydrated with hot water, I couldn't bring my body temperature down. Drinking hot water actually helped prolong my ability to exert myself in the heat, which was good and bad. Good because I could get myself to the next cool place. Bad that I kept going. What if I had been between Farmington and Ozora and suddenly stopped sweating or passed out? I didn't even know if it was possible for me to continue pedaling my bike if I had heat stroke. I could be dead within ten to fifteen minutes.

The important outcome was that I had already decided to escape the heat.

I dug into the logistics of getting to New Jersey. The ride to St. Louis from Ozora looked straightforward. Since the route followed the Interstate, there would be regular opportunities to stop. I hoped to be rolling at 6:00 AM, if not earlier, which would have me in St. Louis around 1:00 PM.

On the train from St. Louis, I would transfer in Chicago and again in Pittsburgh. I could take my bike in a box to Pittsburgh, but there wasn't an option for it between Pittsburgh and Philadelphia. I would need to ship my bike from St. Louis or Chicago. If I opted for St. Louis, I'd have to complete my ride from Ozora before bike shops closed for the day.

I booked the train ticket and forwarded the details to Daniel and Mom.

By the time I finished, it was 10:30 PM. I lay in bed, my thoughts tumbling. I was ecstatic to see Daniel and held onto being in physical space with him like a life preserver. But my defeat about quitting was louder. Leaving the route felt like failure. What would I say on my blog? How would I convey the joylessness and danger of forcing myself through the heat? How could I claim to be a bicycle tourist if I couldn't keep going? What about the credibility of my research? No one would hire me—I was a quitter.

Part 3
ARRIVAL

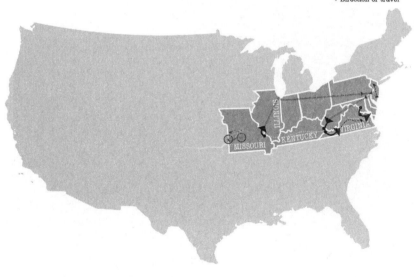

TransAmerica
Bicycle Trail
By bicycle
By train
By bus
By vehicle
▶ Direction of travel

35.

Break

Day fifty-two. At 7:55 AM, the train in St. Louis started moving toward Chicago. In thirty-one hours, I would see Daniel.

I clutched my excitement as I settled into my seat and watched the arch and city buildings disappear from view. I read a *National Geographic* story that I'd carried from Saratoga, Wyoming, about Robyn Davidson's solo trek across Australia.

Somewhere in the vastness of rural Illinois, the train stopped moving.

A woman across the aisle from me harrumphed. I looked at my watch. We'd been stopped for ten minutes with no explanation. The woman rummaged in her purse, mirroring my agita.

Twenty minutes after we stopped, the conductor announced there was an issue with the track. Under an exterior of calm, my mind ran multiple calculations. I hated going nowhere, but if the train wasn't delayed more than five hours, I would still make my connection in Chicago.

The woman across the aisle huffed and got up. I returned to my magazine.

An hour passed.

The conductor's voice scratched in the loudspeaker, "Crews are working on the track. As we have more information, we'll let you know."

While I was lost in the Australian outback, the train lurched. The landscape moved. I checked my watch. Two hours.

The train departed Chicago on time at 6:40 PM. I chatted with the man sitting next to me, glad to be moving again and free of the press of people and diesel exhaust in the station. I read the other *National Geographic* story I'd carried from Saratoga about Peter Jenkins's walk across the United States.

Two hours after leaving Chicago, the train stopped.

Thirty minutes into the delay, a conductor shared there was something wrong with the train's electrical system. We wouldn't be moving again until the problem was fixed.

How was I so unlucky? Did Amtrak ever run on time? If I could have pushed the train, I would have. Adding to my feeling of entrapment, there was no Wi-Fi, and my phone had no bars. I couldn't even vent my frustrations via text or e-mail.

Inside, I screamed.

The train darkened when the sun went down. I fretted. I had a two-hour layover in Pittsburgh, and we'd been stopped more than two hours.

The man next to me wheeze-snored against the window. I rustled in my seat. My hip squealed. I may have slept. I thought we moved, but it was another train passing nearby. My thoughts alternated between despondent and shrill.

I looked for a place to lie down away from my noisy seatmate. Everyone on the train appeared asleep. Some snored. Most leaned against one another with mouths hanging open or stretched into empty adjacent seats. Even the observation car was fully occupied by sleepers. Why was I the only one awake? I returned to my seat.

I was overtired and had to pee. With the electricity out, I was scared the restrooms were dark and disgusting.

In the car's lower level, the restroom alcove was illuminated by an overhead light and smelled of urine. I opened a door. The floor was wet—I told myself it was water—as was the seat, the area around the sink, and up the mirror wall. I closed the door and a faint light came on. Dim civility. The flush button worked. The bowl filled with blue liquid and whooshed down the drain. I hovered over the seat and then flushed again. I washed my hands in warm water and brushed my teeth, looking in the warped mirror at my stretched face.

Upon exiting the restroom, I noticed an area with baggage on the other side of the stairs. And a seating area. With unoccupied seats. I almost hooted.

I lay across two seats and fell asleep.

When I woke, the train hadn't moved. How would I get to Philly? Even if I had wanted to, I couldn't pedal. My bike was in St. Louis or in transit to New Jersey. Maybe I could get out at the next stop or Pittsburgh and rent a car and drive? Driving was my choice of last resort, but I'd do it if it meant I saw Daniel. Damn this delay. I couldn't even research alternate travel options.

In the hour before sunrise, I returned to the observation car. People were awake, and I spoke with several of them as the sun rose and the car flooded with light. One man told me he hated flying, and while the delays on the train were bothersome, he would choose rail over planes any day. Another man commented on the social aspect of train travel. A couple considered the train civilized. Other people in the observation car chose not to engage. Perhaps they were quietly passing the time. Perhaps they were fuming, trapped, late, needing a smoke, wanting fresh air. Even I was not having a tantrum, although it stirred under my skin.

When the train moved again, the cars had become muggy, sun-warmed tubes of humans who smelled of burger and onion. With the power on, the air system cooled the train and cycled in fresh air.

My phone had intermittent reception. I texted Daniel and then e-mailed Mom asking her to do some alternative travel research for me.

The conductor announced that everyone who was making a connection would be taken care of. I canceled my request with Mom and texted Daniel again.

Daniel texted about his own delay—he departed Washington, DC, where he'd been to a Green Day concert, and was stuck in an epic traffic snarl. Neither of us was happy about having less time together, but my panic subsided, knowing he was also delayed. We promised to do what we could to ensure we arrived in Philly alive no matter the time.

Instead of stopping in Pittsburgh, the train terminated in Harrisburg, Pennsylvania, where the station was empty and apology pizzas arrived for dinner. There, I boarded a nighttime commuter train.

The train arrived in Philadelphia at 11:27 PM, eight and a half hours late.

I smelled. While I was out on the road, I didn't care much about my body odor. But now that I was returning to civilization and what I knew was Daniel's sensitive nose, I was self-conscious. I should have bought deodorant during my layover in Chicago.

With panniers slung across my body and rack in hand, I stepped onto the escalator. My heart pounded as I rose. As I neared the top, the grand, high ceilings and Daniel's head came into view. My stomach somersaulted, and the skin over my cheekbones tingled with a face-stretching smile. He smiled past his ears, his brown eyes sparkling, his hands behind his back. At the top of the escalator, I stepped into Daniel's open arms and set the rack at my feet.

"Baby," he said and kissed me and wrapped his arms around me.

"Oh, my god. I made it." I wrapped my arms around him. He trembled. "I can't believe I'm actually touching you."

"Oh, baby." His voice was all delight. He kissed me again and handed me a rosebud made of cloth and decorated with a tiny green ribbon.

"Aw. Thank you," I said and took it, kissing him, my nipples rising.

We loaded my gear in the trunk, and Daniel piloted us into Philadelphia at midnight.

"Do you need anything?" he asked. "Food? Drink?"

"I'm dying to take a shower, but I can wait until we get to Margate."

"I wanted to get you fresh flowers," he said. "I told the station guy that you'd been out on your bike for weeks. He thought it was such a cool story and agreed that you should have some. It was too late to buy flowers nearby, so he walked me over to an arrangement in the station and invited me to take something out of it for you."

I looked at the rosebud in my hand. "Nice improv."

We crossed the Delaware River into New Jersey and left the city behind.

I reached over the hand brake and found Daniel's thigh. He looked at me and then back at the road.

"How long to Margate?" I looked at him as if he were melting ice cream.

"About an hour."

"I still can't believe this is actually you. Am I dreaming?"

"How could we be having the same dream?" His eyes twinkled.

"How do I know you're having the same dream I am? I could be dreaming that you said you were dreaming the same dream."

He reached for my hand and moved it to his crotch. "This is how," he said. The zipper of his Carhartts was firm.

"Isn't that uncomfortable?" I worked his belt free, then unbuttoned and unzipped his pants.

He kept one hand on the wheel and adjusted himself without taking his eyes off the road.

He still looked bound up by his boxers. I explored with my hand and admired the firmness I found inside. My parts tingled. "An hour, huh?"

Daniel exited the highway into a large parking lot. He steered toward a dark corner and turned the car off.

He unbuckled his seatbelt and turned to me, his mouth on my mouth. I kissed him while trying to free myself from the seatbelt. The shifter and hand brake poked between us.

"Let's get in the back," Daniel said as my seatbelt *ziffed* into its holder.

I scooted across the leather of the bench seat and angled my hips out of my yoga pants. Daniel stood over me on the right side of the car, one foot in the well, the other leg bent on the seat. His pants and boxers fell in one motion. The smooth tip of his hard-on caught light. I kicked off my shoes and got my pants off one leg. Daniel clunked the car, and we shuffled our legs making room for each other. I slid farther toward the left side of the car and wedged the right side of my head against the door.

"Hold on a sec," I said as Daniel found the room he needed to get close. "My hip." I pulled my left knee close and supported it with my left hand. It was an odd angle with no support for my arm. "Okay."

"You're sure? I don't want to hurt you."

"I'm sure."

I loved the feeling of Daniel inside me—the return of my long-absent friend. Daniel came quickly and sacrificed one of his socks to my crotch when he pulled out. "It's clean," he said. It would not do to leak sex juice in his dad's car.

His excitement excited me, and I hoped to get mine, too.

Daniel opened the door behind him and backed out. I lay on the seat holding the sock with one hand and my left leg with the other. I lifted my left knee, and the joint ground. I sucked in my breath. When the discomfort dissipated, I hooked my right foot over the end of the seat and pulled my body toward the open door, unkinking my neck.

"Are you okay?" Daniel asked through the door.

"Yeah. Maybe we can try that again when we get to Margate and have a little more room?"

I looked past my knees out the door and saw his eyes glint.

After a few breaths, I sat up and wiggled back into my pants with the sock between my legs. "May I keep your sock for the ride?"

"Certainly."

My left leg refused weight when I stood up, and I hoped I could walk come morning. I resituated myself in the front passenger seat.

"Ready?" Daniel asked.

"Kiss me."

He leaned over, and we kissed a few times.

I sat back and fastened my seatbelt. "Ready."

I stretched and opened my eyes. Daniel was sleeping on his back next to me. I smiled.

Sheer curtains muted the outside light. I looked at my watch. 8:12 AM.

Last night when we arrived, we'd hardly stepped into the room when Daniel offered, "Shower?" He got in with me, which surprised me since he'd showered before departing for Philly. I wasn't sure I could fully relax around him until I washed my stink off and had a chance to brush my teeth. He stood behind me and soaped my pits into slippery froth and then smeared the bubbles all over my body. Ivory, the soap of my childhood.

It was a relief to wash off days of nerves, heat, and pain. I closed my eyes in the pelting hot water and followed the motion of his hands and hard-on.

After all the riding, I felt more confident in my body and appreciated Daniel's interest in a sensual shower, but I couldn't get comfortable with the setup. His parents' room shared a wall with the bathroom. We were standing in a bathtub. My hip had limited strength and range of motion. What if one of us slipped?

I turned around and kissed him. "You feel so good," I whispered, "but I'm not quite ready for that." He kissed me back, and we hugged. We rubbed our bodies against each other, but the mood deflated along with his erection. He rinsed off and got out.

Hot water pelted me. It was difficult to ask for what I wanted and disappointing that I killed the mood.

Daniel's room shared a wall with another room where his sister slept. I climbed under the sheet and blanket Daniel held up next to him on the futon. He let the covers fall, and we snuggled our naked bodies close. He fell asleep moments later.

Looking at him in the soft light of morning, I couldn't believe we were naked in the same bed. How did I know I hadn't died on the road? I moved my hand under the sheet and rested it on Daniel's arm. He felt real. Was that enough proof? He turned his head and looked at me, his golden-brown eyes alive. "Good morning," he said.

"Good morning."

"Welcome to Margate."

"Am I really here?"

"Yeah." He rolled on his side to face me.

"I still feel like I'm dreaming."

He looked at me and rested his hand on my waist. "Baby. There's so much I want to show you. Would you like to go get breakfast?"

"Sure, but I really need to do laundry." I was self-conscious again. I ran a catalogue of my clothes. My dress probably didn't smell too bad. I could get away with wearing my yoga pants and socks. The T-shirt I wore on the train was a no, but the red long-sleeved shirt that I'd worn on top of it during the night-long delay was probably okay.

"Do you need to do laundry before breakfast?"

"No. But I need my panniers."

He hopped out of bed. "Good. Let's get breakfast, and then we can come back and start laundry."

"Okay." It appeared that was it for the morning cuddle.

"I'll go get your bags." He pulled on a T-shirt and shorts. "Be right back." He kissed me.

When I stood, my body creaked. I stretched my arms overhead, and my left hip zapped me. I picked up my pants and socks from the floor and pulled my bra from my T-shirt. I sniffed the pits of my red shirt. It was okay. There was a mirror behind the door, and I checked my hair, running my fingers through it a few times.

I had my bra, pants, and socks on by the time Daniel returned with the panniers. I slipped into my dress and then pulled on the red shirt. "Ready."

Daniel led me downstairs, through the front room, and poked his head into the kitchen. "We're going out for breakfast," he said to his parents, who were at the breakfast bar eating cereal with blueberries, the newspaper spread between them.

I'd met Daniel's parents briefly in Eugene in the spring. I'd been surprised that in the five minutes we were together they talked nonchalantly about Daniel smoking pot. I didn't know how Daniel introduced me then or if he'd shared an update on our status. Regardless, it was clear they were comfortable with us.

Daniel's dad, Arthur, wore shorts with a collared short-sleeved shirt tucked in. He had a full head of white hair that was combed back in tidy ripples. He was trim, tan, heavily freckled, and the skin on his head showed signs of sun damage. Daniel's mom, Doris, was a slip of a woman who held herself close. She wore makeup but was in a T-shirt and black sweatpants, her short, gray hair still rumpled from sleeping.

"Good morning," Doris chirped.

"Have fun," said Arthur.

"Good morning," I said to them. "And happy birthday, Doris."

"Oh, thank you," she cooed.

Everything seemed normal, and I felt accepted.

We passed back through the front room. Family portraits and photos hung on the walls and stood in picture frames on every table and shelf.

Outside was warm and humid. With the air-conditioning inside, I forgot it might be muggy.

My hip hurt. "Breakfast is close?" I asked.

"Only a few blocks."

Daniel was several paces ahead of me on the sidewalk, bubbly.

"Cool. Could you go a little slower? Apparently my hip isn't used to sex, and it's cranky this morning." My next step zapped me. I flinched and stopped and almost cried. It wasn't fair that in choosing sex I invited pain into my body. I was concerned. Fair or not, was this pain something I would have to live with? Was there a remedy?

"Oh, baby." Daniel came over, took my hand, and kissed me. "Would you rather drive?"

"No. Let's just take it slow." When I returned to Eugene, I would have diagnostic imaging of my hip done that revealed I had worn away the cartilage in my joint to bone against bone. The fix was full hip replacement.

By the time we finished breakfast and had walked to the beach to check the waves, much of the sun-blocking moisture in the air had burned off, the light sharp. Sweat ran down the small of my back and soaked my underarms. I stunk.

Daniel washed my laundry and hung it to dry before we headed out again. The house was empty. Doris was working at her sister Penny's shop, and Arthur was taking Daniel's sister, whom I'd met as they were leaving, to the bus station. I looked at the family photos.

Daniel explained who was in the snapshots. I lost track right away.

We went on a driving tour of the area but first stopped at the post office so I could mail the Allen wrench key for the theft-resistant bolt on my bike's seat post clamp to St. Louis. They couldn't ship my bike until they adjusted the seat.

Hardly anyone in Margate walked or rode a bike. When I mentioned this to Daniel, he confirmed that Margate was the kind of place where people got in the car to go two blocks.

After the post office, we dropped by Penny's shop. Doris looked put together in khaki slacks and a leopard-print blouse. We found Penny in the office, a cramped storage room. She wore the same dark eyeliner as Doris and glasses, but her hair was shoulder length, straight, brown. She was short and slender in her skinny jeans and blousy top. She seemed troubled, which gave me the impression she was showing her real self. I liked her for it.

Daniel drove past Ventnor Avenue and Marvin Gardens in Margate, Baltic Avenue in Atlantic City. Every street, even the ones that weren't part of Monopoly, had a story from his growing up. When we passed the boardwalk, he told me about seeing an older man in a red track suit on the boardwalk one morning when he'd been up all night partying with friends, and the man in the track suit was Arthur, who thought he was coming on a bunch of hoodlums. Arthur would tell me this story, too. No matter how Daniel strayed, the love between him and his parents was strong.

He glowed.

We ditched the car at the house and walked. I needed some activity even though my hip hurt. We held hands. Daniel matched my pace. Our palms sweated against each other, and we let them, only unlatching twice to wipe them dry. I pushed thoughts of him leaving in the morning out of my mind and focused on the time we had together, to soak up his tenderness and affection. I felt sunshiny.

We returned to the house around 4:00 PM. Doris was home, sitting in the den with a week-old Sunday *New York Times* puzzle. Arthur was in the kitchen.

"Arthur was just making martinis," Doris said. "Would you kids like to join?"

"Yeah, thanks," Daniel said. "Is Alice coming by?"

"I'm going to get her in a minute," Arthur said, delivering a martini to Doris.

"The Steinbergs are having their annual party across the street later tonight," Doris said.

"Are you going?" Daniel asked.

"Oh, no. But you kids should go."

Arthur brought me and Daniel each a martini and left to get Alice.

I wanted Daniel to myself. This was the only evening I had with him before he returned to Eugene. I knew he didn't see his family often, but so far, our rendezvous was light on the private, tender connection and gentle, deliberate skin-on-skin that I craved.

I nursed my martini for four hours as family members came and went. I would have excused myself, but I would be staying on with Arthur and Doris after everyone left—I wanted to be a good guest.

By the time the family had gathered, drunk, and eaten, I had a buzz and was exhausted.

Daniel and I stood on the sidewalk waving to the last departing family member. We could finally go up to his room and fool around.

Across the street, the Steinbergs' party was underway. A man waved to us from the front porch.

"Come on, let's go," Daniel said.

Before I could ask for a pause, he took my hand and led me across the street.

"Come in, come in, my friend," the man said to Daniel when we reached him. "Long time no see."

We entered the crowded living room. I swore we were on a boat. The whole room tipped to the side. Daniel introduced me to many people, put a drink in my hands, and left me in the hallway with a young couple. I sipped my drink. There were speeches and group singing. I talked to the couple for a while. They didn't know anyone either.

Eventually Daniel caught back up with me. My head was floaty and fuzzy.

"Are you having fun?" he asked.

I liked the feeling of not being in my body, although I could have done without all the people. "Like a dream is fun and weird." I looked around the room as if I were inside a fishbowl.

"Are you ready to go back to the house?"

"Yeah. You're leaving when tomorrow?"

"Five-thirty in the morning."

"Gosh, that's early."

"Yeah." He took my hand. "Let's go."

Daniel steered me across the street. The sky was black.

Inside, the house was quiet, the lights off. The steps were like climbing a mountain. I brushed my teeth and crawled under the covers of the futon. Daniel disappeared.

"Baby?" Daniel asked.

"Hi." I opened my eyes. I felt like I was bobbing in water. "You were gone a long time."

"Just brushing my teeth. Did you fall asleep?"

"Maybe." My eyes closed.

"Scoot over so I can get in bed," he said.

I wriggled toward the wall and stopped when I felt its coolness on my arm. "That enough room?"

Cool air puffed under the covers. The warm touch of his lips kissed my cheek. "Good night," he said. "I love you."

His words slid into my sleep, and I didn't know whether I said, "I love you," before everything turned into nothing.

Daniel sprang out of bed when the alarm went off. I opened my eyes and registered there was no light through the window.

"What time is it?" I asked, watching him dress.

"It's a little after five." He went downstairs.

I lay in bed a few minutes reviewing the evening. I liked being intoxicated, but I hadn't even kissed Daniel before falling onto the futon. I wanted more physical connection with him beyond the contortions in Arthur's car and the awkward moment in the shower. All my effort to get here, hardly any sex, and no orgasm.

It was work for me to meet so many people and try to fit in. I wriggled off the futon and dressed. It also wasn't fair to expect Daniel to have refocused his attention on me. Still, I felt cheated.

Daniel was finishing a bowl of cereal when I entered the kitchen. He looked up from the paper and smiled.

"Good morning," I said, smiling back, and I helped myself to a glass for water. There were no glasses larger than eight ounces. "Sorry I wasn't with it last night." I filled the glass at the tap and chugged it. "How are you feeling?" I refilled the glass and drank.

"I'm good." He finished the last spoonful of cereal and put his dish in the sink. "Did I tell you that Arthur is particular about the dishes?"

"You did. It feels strange to not clean up after myself."

Daniel opened the fridge and collected items for his sandwich. "I know," he said. He set a big jar of mayonnaise on the counter. "But it's really better to leave the dishes for Arthur."

"Got it." I set my water glass in the sink and then patted Daniel's butt and sat down at the breakfast bar with a cup of tea.

I swiveled the chair and watched him.

I wasn't a mayo fan. Never bought the stuff. Considered it a good way to ruin a sandwich.

The size of the jar told me mayo was an everyday condiment in his parents' house. Most things in the kitchen were small, like the glasses, cereal bowls and, thinking back to the previous morning, Doris herself—everything except the jumbo container of mayonnaise.

Daniel wrapped the sandwich in waxed paper.

"All set?" I asked. I hoped in the spare minutes before 5:30, we might go upstairs and make out.

Daniel sat down next to me, "Yep," and looked at the newspaper, which was open to the funnies.

I looked at him with longing in my heart and between my legs. He looked at the paper. With a gulp of hot tea, I swallowed my disappointment that there would be no last-minute cuddling. "I'm really glad it worked out that we got to see each other," I said. "I wish we could have had more time together."

He looked at me. "Yeah. I loved having you here and introducing you to my family and Margate."

"It was a lot to take in." I reached over and rested a hand on his thigh.

He looked back at the paper. "It seemed like you had a good time."

"I did. I just would have liked more time for the two of us."

He looked up from the paper and kissed me. I kissed him back and gave him a little slip of tongue. He pulled away, his eyebrows raised, face smiling.

Arthur appeared in the kitchen doorway, looking tidy as ever. "Ready?" he asked Daniel.

"Yeah. I'll say bye to Mom and get my bag." He stood and took my hand. I went to his room at the back of the house while he stopped in his parents' room. I sat on the futon and looked at his packed suitcase.

Daniel entered the room, and I stood to hug him. He wrapped me in a tight, two-armed embrace. "I love you," he said.

"I love you, too."

We kissed, and I reached for his crotch.

"Can't wait to read the next blog post," he said.

"Looking forward to reports from your console." I gave his parts a gentle squeeze.

In 2012, we would marry in Hood River, Oregon. Our rehearsal dinner was a private sightseeing tour on the Mt. Hood Railroad. The day before we exchanged vows in a park overlooking the Columbia River, we went biking with friends and family on the Historic Columbia River Highway.

We kissed again, and he took his suitcase and left. I listened to his footsteps on the stairs. The front door opened and closed. A car started and drove off.

After Margate, I stayed with my cousin Sherry and then Auntie Cookie. Both lived in northern New Jersey.

In Auntie Cookie's kitchen, I wrote a birthday blog post for my mom. Then I started assembling the grant proposal I'd been invited to submit based on the letter of intent I had written in Eminence. The proposal was to fund development of an all-ages all-abilities scenic bikeway based in Cottage Grove, Oregon, that included seventeen miles of rail trail along the northern shore of Dorena Lake. The proposed bikeway traveled by several covered bridges, including a rare, covered railroad bridge. I was hopeful. If the proposal was successful, I would have a paid project during the last year of my master's program and an opportunity to apply what I'd learned during this research trip. I completed and submitted the proposal before the annual Gone Fishin' weekend at the family cabin in Pennsylvania.

Once a two-story hay barn, the "cabin" was cold and musty and had rooms aplenty, indoor plumbing, and hot water, but no Internet or cell reception. Outdoors was the draw. There was more mud, sweat, and campfire with my family than could be had in Margate, but I felt trapped without my bike. I was also still bummed that my visit with Daniel hadn't been more of what I wanted, and the technology break gave me time to sit with my feelings. There was something besides finding a mate compelling me onward. I didn't know what it was, but I could grasp that it had to do with my relationship to me.

To deal with my disappointment and stuckness, I chopped wood. It was green and full of knots, and all I could find to split it was an axe with a three-pound head. Still, it soothed me to use my body. My arms were weak. The wood was heavy. I reduced what I could of the rounds to burnable wedges and slivers of kindling and then made a fire for lunchtime s'mores.

Later that afternoon, I sat in the front passenger seat of cousin Aimée's Element as she piloted us along wiggly roller-coaster roads in the Pennsylvania woods. I loved Aimée's idea that we go somewhere. I didn't care where. Sherry was in the back seat, monitoring her phone for reception.

Aimée stopped in a gravel area at an intersection. We had long views of rolling hills and fields.

"Here we are," Aimée said. "It's the closest place with reliable connection."

Aimée got out, opened the back of the Element, and sat with her phone. I turned a few circles in the gravel while I texted Daniel to see if he was available to talk. He wasn't.

At this time in our lives, this is what it looked like to hang out with my cousins, sitting in a car on the side of the road sending texts and e-mails and checking Facebook. It was a small thing, having a getaway from the getaway, and just what I needed. As Aimée drove us back to the cabin, the day seemed brighter.

TransAmerica
Bicycle Trail
By bicycle
By train
By bus
By vehicle
▶ Direction of travel

36.

On Bike

I sat on the train to Charleston, West Virginia, watching the sun-filled and leafy greenness blur past the windows. In two weeks, I would be in Washington, DC. With twelve hours on the train, I finished *Archy and Mehitabel*, the book Daniel sent me in Eminence, and dug into Haruki Murakami's *What I Talk About When I Talk About Running*, which I purchased at the Philly train station. I was glad to be by myself again, returning to my journey.

I planned to stay the night in Charleston and take a day or two to return to the TransAm Trail in Elkhorn City, the easternmost town in Kentucky on the bike route. I had taken two weeks off from riding, and I couldn't return to the route where I departed and still arrive in Washington, DC, in time for the conference. I was sorry to miss the Kentucky landscape, which I'd never seen, but glad to avoid potential dog attacks.

I felt ashamed about skipping the 630 miles between Ozora and Elkhorn City. But I hadn't set out intending to pedal every inch of the country. My plan was to ride my bike to the conference in Washington, DC, and study bicycle tourism along the way, which was what I was doing. There were many unexpected things a bicycle tourist could encounter, especially as a solo rider and lone female, and part of the experience was dealing with those surprises.

At a station stop, I turned my phone on and checked my e-mail. I had a message from one of my contacts at Adventure Cycling Association. Someone at *National Geographic Traveler* reached out to them because of a blog post I'd written for Adventure Cycling about Cooky's Café. *National Geographic Traveler* wanted to do a blog post about my journey, too. I was four-exclamation-points and emoticon-smiley ecstatic. I helped other people see the connections I saw. I created interest where there hadn't been much or any.

By the time I arrived in Charleston, I had finished reading Murakami's book and given some thought to how I might answer *National Geographic*'s questions, which were included in the forwarded e-mail. I took a cab to a B&B downtown and wrestled the bike box onto their porch. Inside, lace doilies decorated the furniture, and the dining table was set with china. My hosts greeted me and showed me a place in the entry to get my bike out of the way until I was ready to unpack it.

After breakfast at 9:00 AM, I dressed in my sun-faded cycling clothes. The fabric of my knee warmers was no longer black but medium brown between knee and mid-thigh. I congratulated myself for my choice to cover up. Much better to destroy clothes than my skin.

I opened the bike box and found two bubble-wrapped packages— one with the saddle and seat post, the other with pedals. The new tire I bought in St. Louis was also in the box but hadn't been installed. My heart swelled when I looked at my bike's yellow-orange frame.

Both of my bike's tires were shredded. Weird, since I'd only noticed issues with the front tire in St. Louis. I replaced the rear tire, which looked in worse condition, and planned to get a tire for the front at the bike shop in town, which opened at 11:00 AM.

I pedaled through Charleston along tree-lined streets, soaking up the joy and comfort of being reunited with a beloved. I felt relief and freedom in being able to take myself where I wanted when I wanted. The day was sunny and moderately humid. Warm but not hot. Perfect riding weather to begin the 915-mile trek to the conference, which began in two weeks.

At the bike shop, the guys gave my bike a quick tune-up and installed a new tire on the front. Given the heat, one of the guys said it made sense that my tires were shredded.

It was nearly 2:00 PM as I began my journey out of town. U.S. 119 cut through a steep cliff. It had four lanes with a center turn lane and a wide shoulder. Traffic noise ping-ponged against the cliff walls. My legs were heavy. Had fifteen days of rest undone the fitness I achieved from seven weeks of continuous pedaling?

My lower back strained.

Something wasn't right. I hadn't been bedridden for two weeks, but my body felt ill prepared to ride five miles. I stopped at the edge of the shoulder to check my saddle height. The saddle was loose enough that I was able to readjust the height without loosening the seat post bolt. I retightened the bolt and gently chided myself for not having tightened it sufficiently when I reassembled my bike on the porch. I gave the bolt a couple extra cranks for good measure and continued uphill.

With my saddle adjusted, my body responded better to the climb. But less than a minute later I was struggling again. I pulled over, repositioned the saddle, and wrenched the bolt. The bolt turned when it shouldn't have. I wrenched it again, and again it turned. I unscrewed the bolt and screwed it back in. Same result. Something was stripped.

I remounted and pedaled. The saddle sank. I was in a suburban area about seven miles from downtown Charleston. I didn't want to turn back to the bike shop.

On a bluff to my left were big-box stores. An orange sign caught my attention. I did a double take. Home Depot? I rode toward what seemed a mirage. The road to the top of the bluff pitched up at a ridiculous angle. While I had no concept of how steep a 25 percent grade was, I guessed this road was close to that. In reality, the grade was probably between 11 and 14 percent. I sat on the saddle and pedaled hard. I arrived at Home Depot—not a mirage—at almost 3:00 PM stunned by the lucky coincidence.

I wheeled my bike into the fasteners aisle and found a likely replacement bolt. I checked it in the seat post clamp. The threads engaged. Once the bolt was tight, I pounded on my saddle. It didn't budge. Success.

I rolled back down the bluff to U.S. 119 and started back up the long climb. My lower back tensed. My neck tired of holding my head up. My hands tingled. My girl parts and sitting bones rubbed against the chamois in my shorts despite the smear of Butt'r I applied that morning.

My legs were okay. With the saddle at the right height, my body fit the bike's geometry, and it felt like an extension of me. While pedaling required effort, and I breathed harder than I might have in Missouri, my legs welcomed this return to work.

After a few miles, I crested the hill. To mark the accomplishment, I stood in the shoulder drinking water, doing trunk twists, and rolling my chin across my chest to loosen my neck.

As I started down the hill, my gut offered a pinched, watery rumble. I hoped the sensation was in response to the water and trunk twists. I picked up speed, coasting the highway's gentle turns, and appreciated the landscape opening to tree-lined fields. My gut gurgled again with a low abdominal cramp. I took note. After a few minutes, a gas station came into view.

I dismounted my bike in the parking lot, and my gut surprised me with a twisting cramp. My hands shook. I hoped no one was in the restroom, wherever it was. I pushed the gas station door open with cold sweat moistening my upper lip. The restroom was to the right of the entry, unoccupied. I darted in, locked the door, and barely got my shorts down in time.

I wanted to take a shower after the forceful emptying of my intestines, but I settled for a thorough wash of my hands with antibacterial soap. I exited the restroom with pretend nonchalance and bought a V-8. I wanted to be farther along and feeling better, but maybe it didn't matter. Maybe this is what returning to my journey looked like.

My gut was probably upset because I was stressed about my late start, the issue with my saddle, and what I intuited was the unrealistic distance I expected myself to pedal each day to arrive at the conference on time.

Unsure what my gut might do, I planned to stop at the first place that had lodging and a restaurant. I pedaled along wooded hills. I didn't pass any gas stations and was grateful for stopping when I did. I could have handled an emergency stop, but just because I would survive one didn't mean I wanted to. I passed two churches, but otherwise the countryside was empty of structures.

After almost two hours of pedaling from the gas station, I descended a hill and saw a town pressed between the highway and a river. As if on cue, my guts gurgled.

A sign on the motel's office door indicated check-in was at the restaurant. I stood at the restaurant counter with my grumbling belly while the waitress-innkeeper took a food order, delivered a table of four's food, and then checked me in.

Cold air spilled on me when I opened the room door. Inside, it looked like someone had sprayed foaming carpet cleaner all over the floor and forgotten to vacuum it. Before I could inspect further, my abdomen winced, and I ran to the bathroom. After the gas station, it didn't seem possible there was anything left in my body to shit out, but I was wrong. I appreciated the hot shower afterward.

Warm and clean and wrapped in the motel towel, I tiptoed across the carpet back to my bike. I unhooked the pannier that held my clothes and opened it on the bed. I stood on my Mary Janes and dressed. I slipped my shoes on and stepped around the filamented mounds on the floor to the air conditioner and turned it to heat. I picked my way back to the bed, left my shoes on the ground, and peered over the edge of the mattress as if the carpet were a lake of toxic waste. It wasn't foaming carpet cleaner on the floor but mold. My gut rumbled.

Before I could even acknowledge I wanted to cry, I called Daniel.

"Hey, Kitten," he answered.

"Hi, Tom Cat." I smiled and made my voice sound cheery. "Are you home?"

"On my way. Walking. Where are you?"

"Your namesake town, Danville. I did tell them you go by Daniel, but no one in these parts could pronounce Danielville. So, sorry, I'm in Danville."

"And where is Danville?"

"West Virginia. Somewhere between Charleston and Kentucky in the heart of Appalachia. Actually, I don't think I'm that far from Charleston. Maybe twenty-five miles. Been kinda slow going today."

After I asked about his day, I said, "I'm a bit freaked out at the moment and not sure what to do."

"What's wrong?" Daniel's voice was immediately concerned.

"Among other things, my motel room floor is covered in mold." I peered over the edge of the bed and stared at the calamity that was the carpet.

"Oh, baby," he empathized.

"I paid thirty-five dollars plus tax for the pleasure, but I don't want to touch anything, especially the floor."

"You should ask for another room."

"But I already took a shower." It seemed unkind to have used the bathroom the way I had and then get another room.

"You do not have to tolerate a moldy floor. It doesn't matter how much you paid for the room."

"You're sure?" How would I explain the fact that I took a shower even though it was clear something was amiss with the floor when I entered the room?

"You didn't ask for a room with a moldy floor, did you?" Daniel prompted.

"No."

"It's reasonable to expect that if you pay for a room, the floor won't be moldy."

"Okay. I'll ask," I said.

"Good."

I sighed. "I love you."

"I love you, too."

Every table at the restaurant was full, and two more women were helping the woman with long white hair who originally checked me in. One of the women greeted me and asked me to wait. I stood there for five minutes.

"What can I help you with?" the white-haired woman asked, stepping behind the counter.

"Could I move to a different room? There's mold all over the floor in the one I'm in."

She looked at me.

"I took a shower already. I'm sorry. But I didn't get in the bed or anything."

She looked at the reservations list. "Here, I can put you in the room on the end. It should be fine. Come back and let me know if it's not. That can happen if the room is too cold."

I didn't want to know how long it took for mold to bloom in a refrigerated room or what state of cleanliness the carpet was in that it had molded. I thanked her and inspected my new room. It was cool but warmer than the other room. No mold. I returned to the moldy room, grabbed my gear and rolled to the new space.

I stretched out on the bed and looked at the ceiling. This was another gift. My belly agreed with silence.

West Virginia was lush. The temperature at 6:30 AM felt more moderate than what I experienced on the Great Plains and the Ozarks at that hour.

Because I didn't have a bike map that covered the day's route, I planned to ride U.S. 119, the principal highway in the area, along the river for nearly a hundred miles to Pikeville, Kentucky.

Pikeville was a town of nearly seven thousand people, and the downtown was in a strip of flatland between Levisa Fork and cliffs. In mid-April, Pikeville hosted Hillbilly Days, and any time of the year people could follow the Hatfield and McCoy River Trails and take in other inspirations from the Hatfield-McCoy Feud. Somewhere in town was also the University of Pikeville.

My motel room was mold free and my body tired but not exhausted after the ninety-five-mile day. The day's mileage accomplishment restored my confidence in my physical condition. Even after the two-week break, and after what felt like months since I'd logged more than sixty miles in one day, I could still pull off a long ride.

The day I'd pedaled from Riverside, Wyoming, to Granby, Colorado, had been the first time I rode more than a hundred miles in one day. There had been several days I'd come close—within five miles or fewer of one hundred—such as this one. Each time felt notable to cover that distance on my own power. And when I added each day's pedaling together, I'd covered nearly three thousand miles to reach Pikeville. It didn't seem possible. Yet, I pedaled all those miles. Here I was in Kentucky. Proof. I let it sink in.

In the morning, I departed for Elkhorn City, situated twenty squiggly miles from Pikeville along the Levisa and Russell Forks. In Elkhorn City, I would reconnect with the TransAmerica Trail.

When I arrived, I scanned town for a breakfast spot. I saw a lone male bike tourist push off from the side of the road and pedal toward Virginia. I smiled, delighted that the exact moment I reconnected with the TransAm I saw a bike tourist. More than any sign, this man's presence announced that I was back on track.

During breakfast, I looked over my Adventure Cycling map to see what lay ahead. Elkhorn City was at a low spot on the route with an elevation under a thousand feet. Seventy-five miles from Elkhorn City was the highest point of elevation for this map—not quite four thousand feet. Between the high point and the low point in Elkhorn City were two steep climbs, about a thousand feet each, followed by steep descents. A few miles out of Elkhorn City were three short, steep climbs.

I folded the map. I would aim for seventy-five miles, but I would be okay wherever my day ended.

A mile out of Elkhorn City, I descended to the river and crossed into Virginia at Breaks Interstate Park. Breaks received its name from Daniel Boone, who is credited with discovering the gorge as the water passage through this part of the Appalachians.

Steep didn't even describe the lunacy of climbing out of Breaks. Unlike the roads in Missouri that took the hills straight, these roads made short switchbacks. The grade on the inside edge of the switchbacks was too steep to pedal even standing up, so I took them wide into the other lane. Vines encroached on the road edges—mile-a-minute weed and kudzu were similar invasive species in the area.

Once through the three climbs, I rested briefly in Haysi. Then, I climbed roller-coaster hills for seventeen miles to the base of the first of the two thousand-foot climbs, a mountain called Big A. Partway up Big A, I encountered the touring cyclist I saw when I first arrived in Elkhorn City. My confidence puffed up. I'd caught up to him even after stopping for breakfast. He wore a state of California jersey—red and white with a grizzly bear. I said hi and pedaled past.

After the next few curves, I stopped to catch my breath at an intersection. The man caught up to me as I stood there. Devin was about my age and on sabbatical from a tech company. He was slim and tan and had short brown hair and a hairless face. He was a daily bike commuter in California, and this trip was his first bike tour. He was headed to Virginia Beach to meet friends.

"What route are you taking?" I asked.

"I'm making it up as I go." He pulled a driving map from his handlebar bag and pointed to some hand-drawn lines. "I have the Adventure Cycling route marked with this dashed line, but I like the surprise of exploring the country without knowing much about it. My route is the solid line."

"Where do you stay?" This was in the days before Google knew everything about everywhere and when it was still easy to be in areas of the country without cell service. Hearing him describe going off route spiked my anxiety. I needed to know what was ahead. Distance to services, such as a gas station, cell connection, or motel with air-conditioning, were essential.

"Just about every town has a bar. When I'm done riding for the day, I go to the bar, get a beer, and see how conversation evolves. Most of the time if I'm talking to one person, they'll invite me to their place or connect me with someone who can host me. Lots of times I camp in people's yards."

I cringed. It sounded like a dangerous way for a woman to find lodging. It didn't sound like a safe way for a man to find lodging either, but here he was almost to the East Coast. "Wow. Have you ever found yourself in a sketchy situation?"

He chuckled. "One time in Colorado. A guy with a Charles Manson beard invited me to stay at his place. It was far from town, down this little dirt road that had a suspense-thriller vibe. His house was run-down, and the yard was full of junk and bones. I thought I'd made the biggest mistake of my life. He was actually really nice, and I wound up staying there for two nights."

I shuddered. I was reassured that a man in his late twenties or early thirties found that situation unnerving. "I'm glad it worked out for you. It's remarkable that was the only time you were uncomfortable."

"Yeah. There are the people on the road who shout and honk, but I almost always encounter people who are curious about what I'm doing or who go out of their way to be nice."

"I've been surprised how concerned people are that I'm okay," I said. "And helpful. There will always be people who take issue with something. That's as American as apple pie. But there are far more warm and neighborly people in America than the ones who feel a need to holler. I imagine you get a good flavor of that talking to folks in bars."

"I do. Generous people are everywhere. It doesn't matter what their politics or religion are or how much money or education they have. That stuff doesn't even come up. We're all just people relating around our common humanity. Going on a ride like this surfaces the ways we all suffer, struggle, and long to connect. Makes it easy to engage with people where it really matters. In the heart."

I liked his perspective. I hadn't considered how my journey enabled people I encountered to recognize their own need for love—whether they knew that's what it was or not. The woman in Pittsburg, Kansas, who talked to me outside the ice cream shop longed for some love from herself. Sure, riding a bike was a healthy choice and fun and liberating, and I understood how she and others could find the easy relationship I had to cycling attractive. I had also learned on this ride that even something as healthy as cycling could tip into unloving activity. It wasn't cycling itself that could be unhealthy but rigidity. Dominating thought. Making myself ride and should-ing myself into pedaling didn't have the flexibility of love. Flexibility wasn't lassitude; it wasn't limp or wilted, but it gave. A flexible building could withstand an earthquake. A rigid one crumbled.

Devin and I decided to ride together to Rosedale, where he planned to depart the Adventure Cycling route.

We didn't talk on the climb. It was tough and slow going. Devin pedaled ahead of me but not so far that I couldn't see him. He waited for me at the top of the Big A climb, and we congratulated each other on the effort. I sped ahead on the downhill.

The road down had short climbs, and at the base of one of them a coal truck rumbled behind me. I looked over my shoulder to size it up and gauge my options. The right side of the shoulder-less road dropped off, and there was a right-turning switchback ahead followed shortly by a left-turning switchback. There wasn't room for the truck to pass me on the steep grade before the curves nor anywhere I could pull over to give it room to pass. I would have to reach the left-turning switchback before I could get out of the way. I pedaled hard in my granny gear. The truck came up close behind me, the engine groaning with its load and the slow pace. I hoped I was moving faster than its idling speed.

I cut the right-turning switchback close and stood on my pedals and pulled up on them with each stroke to power my turn. When I made it through the curve, I pedaled fast and shifted up. I stood and run-pedaled up the brief straight toward the left-turning curve. I tired before reaching the turn, lowered to my saddle, and downshifted. After giving myself a few pedal strokes break, I stood again and upshifted. I huffed to the wide part of the curve and pulled as far to the edge of the road as I could. I unclipped and stood until the coal truck passed.

The truck snorted through the turn, working to gain momentum on the steep road. Devin followed a distance behind, and I waited for him.

"How about coal trucks?" he asked.

I pushed off from the side of the road, and we pedaled together. "There isn't an inch of space on these roads. It's hard to believe those trucks can make it through the turns without getting high-centered."

"What's worse," Devin asked, "having one behind you on the downhill or the uphill?"

I thought about the weight of one barreling down on me. What if I slipped on the road? "Both. But probably downhill is worse. Where did it pass you?"

"Right at the transition from downhill to uphill."

"Freaky?" I looked at the dark mirror of Devin's sunglasses, wishing I could see his eyes.

"Some."

"I felt badly I couldn't go faster," I said. "I hope the drivers aren't paid by loads per day like the log trucks in Idaho."

I looked around at the leafy landscape. It seemed like a fantasy place with the steep curving road and the dense canopy that shaded us. The road had a nuanced lay on the land. I hadn't passed any sign that indicated how steep the road was, but we had to be pedaling grades greater than 10 percent. The inside of the curves seemed more than 30 percent.

Devin rode ahead of me on the downhill. On the left side of the road was a gas station, and he turned into it.

We were outside the gas station by the bikes when two men in gray coveralls each carrying a large Styrofoam cup stopped to talk. One of them was tall and slim with wavy blond hair; the other was shorter with a full moustache and straight dark brown hair. Both had thick fingers that looked rough and stained like car mechanic hands, and they wore stiff, scuffed leather boots.

"That's impressive what you're all doing," Moustache Man said. "Where you all riding from?"

"The Bay area in California," Devin said.

"Oregon," I said.

"How long does that take?"

"About three months," I said.

"I can't imagine. What do you all miss?" While the other man seemed interested in the conversation, he didn't say anything.

Sex was top of my mind, but I wasn't going to say it.

"This is an amazing adventure," Devin said. "Every day I get up and love what I'm doing."

Devin's ability to touch the complexity of the experience fascinated me. A ride like this contained freedom, awe, challenge, risk, and joy. "Yes," I said. "I totally agree, and I do miss salad."

Moustache Man raised his eyebrows. "I talked to one woman out biking like you two. She said she missed shaving her legs. Only time I ever saw a hairy-legged woman."

I smiled, bent forward, and pulled down my left sock. I stood up and pointed my foot in the direction of the men. "I don't shave my legs, so I don't miss it. Now you've seen two hairy-legged women."

Moustache Man's eyebrows went up. "Well, I'll be."

I pulled my sock up.

The men were running coal loads. Moustache Man pointed with his thumb toward the road. "We see you bicyclists out here sometimes and wonder how you do it."

"It's fun and a challenge," Devin said. "I also really enjoy meeting people and hearing their stories."

"When I saw you there on the road, I had to wonder," Moustache Man said.

"You were the truck that passed us?" I asked.

"Yep."

"I really appreciated you waiting for me to get out of the way," I said. "I tried to go as fast as I could, but I know it was slow."

"There's nowhere to go on those roads. That's why I say I don't know how you do it."

"I hope the other drivers are as understanding as you," I said. "I'm not out on the road to slow people down."

"It's a tough spot to get through. You did the right thing."

Rosedale was six miles and two effortful climbs from the gas station. Devin and I passed and repassed each other. I pedaled harder to keep him in my sights than I would have were I alone.

It was near 7:00 PM when we stopped at a lone gas station at a T-intersection that was supposed to be a full-service town. I asked the station attendant about the town and services.

"The restaurant and motel closed," he said. "There's a church down the road where you can stay, but there's nowhere to eat or get a drink nearby beyond what's available here."

I turned to Devin. "Want to find dinner here and take it to the church?"

"Yeah."

We walked up and down the aisles. I stopped in front of the Chef Boyardee ravioli, remembering my gas station dinner in Muddy Gap, Wyoming. The two cans here were dusty but had pull tops. I took one. In another aisle, I selected a small can of cashews and another of smoked almonds. I grabbed a small bag of salt and pepper chips and a sleeve of Starburst. From the juice cooler, I pulled out a bottle of orange juice.

I stowed my purchases in a pannier and looked at my map. A hostel was identified. "We're in luck," I said to Devin who was fitting a large bag of Fritos into a pannier. When he was ready, we pedaled down the road.

My body twinged uncomfortably, and I recognized my exhaustion. My lower back ached, my legs were heavy, my neck crinked, and my sitting parts were sore with needlelike pricks. I hoped rest and sleep would remedy the saddle soreness for the next day's climbs, which looked torturous.

We found the church nestled in trees off the main road. It was landscaped with flowerbeds, rock paths, and a bench swing. A tan, blond woman was in the swing, lit by the warm colors of the sun low in the sky. I assumed she was the church lady who tended the garden. I loved that she got to enjoy the space on such a beautiful evening. Devin and I angled toward her. She waved.

"Is this the hostel?" I asked as I pulled up near the swing.

"Yes. Heidi?"

How could the church lady know my name? I did a double take. "Oh my goodness! Mary?"

"How wonderful to see you," she exclaimed. "I thought that bike looked familiar."

"This is Devin. We met today and were going to stop in Rosedale, but—"

"The restaurant and motel are closed," Mary interrupted. "Yes, us, too. Dermot's inside. Come in, come in."

I turned to Devin. "This is Mary. I met her and Dermot in Kansas, and we rode together to Missouri. They're from Wales."

"Nice to meet you," Devin said.

Mary and I had kept in touch via e-mail since I last parted ways with them outside Pittsburg. I shared news of the terrain ahead, construction, lodging options, and the like. I told her about the dog attack outside Fair Grove and to be cautious. I exchanged messages with her from Ozora and St. Louis when I decided to leave the route. I'd been two or three days ahead of them when I took my two-week break in New Jersey. I couldn't believe that with all my various travels, the day I returned to the bike route I ended up in the same accommodations with them. I expected they would have been ahead of me.

"There aren't any beds," Mary said as she led me and Devin on a tour.

"What are you sleeping on?" I asked, knowing they weren't equipped for this kind of surprise.

"We put all our clothes out on the floor, and we have these light sheet sacks. You know how hostels sometimes require you to have some kind of sheet?"

"Yeah."

"Well, that's it." Mary was upbeat. This facet of their adventure seemed to amuse her.

"Do you want any more clothes for padding? I don't have much extra that would help, but you're welcome to it if you'd like."

"Oh, thanks. We'll be okay."

When Mary finished with the tour, Devin and I fetched our gear and took our time settling in. Mary and Dermot joined us in the dining room. There were several plastic banquet tables, and I studied them as I ate my dinner.

"I'm going to sleep on one of these tables," I announced.

"You're serious?" Mary asked.

"Yeah. When I was at Elaine's place in Bazine, I couldn't fall asleep with all the noise under my sleeping pad from the bugs."

"Aren't you afraid of falling off?" Mary asked.

"Sort of, but it's not any different than sleeping on a bed. Somehow your body knows."

After Devin and I cleaned up from our respective dinners, Devin pulled out his laptop and map. Mary and Dermot disappeared to their nest. I inflated my sleeping pad, arranged it on one of the tables, and then threw my sleeping bag on top.

"Are you blogging?" I asked.

"No, but I'm keeping a journal." He pointed to the notebook. "I'll want something to go back to after this trip is over."

"Do you ever get lonely?"

"Not really. Pretty much every day I make a solid connection with someone."

"You sound really positive about your journey. I like how you're making it up as you go, and I loved what you said to the guys at the gas station."

"Yeah. If your dream was to spend the summer riding your bike and seeing the world and it was granted to you, how could you not love every day of it?"

"How do you deal with the challenges?"

"I don't know. I guess when I'm having a hard time, I stop and remind myself why I'm doing this. I look out at the scenery. I take pictures. I talk to people. I try to be present with my experience."

Devin seemed like the Buddha. "I never had any ambitions to ride across the country until I thought I could spend the summer biking my way to this conference. It seemed like the perfect answer to what

I wanted, but I have all this pressure and stress. To write every day. To make it to the conference on time. To stay alive." I climbed on the table and draped my sleeping bag over me.

"That's a lot to do. I'm meeting friends in Virginia Beach, which is a deadline of sorts, but not like what you're doing."

"Yours sounds like a real vacation. Mary and Dermot are on vacation, too, and also seem to be enjoying the experience a lot. I'm working, and even though it's dreamy work, I can't miss the conference. It's weird though. I've learned so much about myself and America that has nothing to do with work. Like, if I want to enjoy the experience and follow my curiosity, I need to build the space for improvisation and flexibility into whatever I'm doing."

I thought back to our conversation on the Big A climb, where I first met him. "And as you said, there are more commonalities among us than differences. America is a vast, beautiful place, like a fractal. On some level, I was looking for home, and I think I found that as I connected with America at the scale of my body and its senses. I came home to me."

We were both quiet. Devin hadn't made his bed yet. He would ride back to Rosedale the next day to pick up the road he planned to travel. He was in no hurry. Mary and Dermot planned to leave early, and I wanted to ride with them.

I broke the silence. "I really appreciated riding with you today. It's nice to have company."

He nodded. "I enjoyed riding with you, too."

I wiggled into my sleeping bag. "The light won't bother me. Sleep well when you get there, and may you stay on top of the table."

"Thanks. You too."

I rolled onto my belly, pulled my left knee up, and fell fast asleep.

In the morning, Mary, Dermot, and I pedaled in the cool, moist air. Grassy fields and forest patches bordered the road.

"Did dogs chase you in eastern Kentucky?" I asked.

"Yes," Mary said. "When we saw them, Dermot would ride ahead and stop to distract them. Then I would ride by. It worked pretty well."

"Sometimes the dogs weren't too keen on me," Dermot added.

"And one time I did get chased," Mary said in a way that made it sound scary in the moment but funny now. "Dermot called after me to go faster while he got on his bike. I used my pepper spray but missed."

"There didn't seem to be anything I could do in that situation except for us to get out of its territory." Dermot's tone was similar to Mary's.

"Nice that you could help each other," I said.

"Why do Americans let their dogs run after whatever passes on the road?" Dermot asked.

I shrugged. "I wish they wouldn't, but it might be dog nature more than Americans. Some people put up electric fences that you can't see, but if a dog is intent on chasing something, a shock won't deter it."

"Why would anyone bother putting up an electric fence, then?" Dermot asked.

"Maybe it's cheaper than other fence options. It doesn't ruin their view? I don't know. Because they can?"

"In some places it seems like people train the dogs to run after bikes," Mary said.

Dermot nodded.

"Probably," I said. "And unfortunate."

"And you really didn't get hurt when the dogs attacked you in Missouri?" Mary asked.

"No. They bit the panniers. Once I hit the road, they lost interest."

"That must have been scary," Mary said.

"It was. I still can't laugh about it, although there's a part of me that thinks I conjured the attack so I could get a ride." I looked at Mary. "You told me about hitching, and I thought I would try it that day. But I didn't seem in trouble or need. After the dog attack, I instantly got a ride."

"Weird coincidence?" Dermot asked.

I shrugged. "Hard to know."

"I hitch a lot," Mary said. "There were a few times when it was really hot, I hitched a ride into town. That day we arrived in Pittsburg, Dermot and I both hitched into town. The next day, Dermot rode out to where we got picked up and pedaled back. I stayed in the air-conditioning at the motel."

I looked at Dermot. "You're out to pedal every inch of the country, aren't you?"

Dermot didn't say anything but gave a slight nod. His eyes twinkled.

A hill rose before us, and the road disappeared into the trees. Dermot pedaled ahead, and I matched my speed with Mary's. We didn't talk much but breathed hard in our effort.

My sitting parts hadn't recovered overnight, and I worried over the pinpricks I felt. I wasn't sure this critical part of my physique would tolerate a long day of climbing. If I ripped the skin open, I would have to take time off from biking to heal.

On paper, it seemed the easiest thing to pedal sixty to seventy-five miles a day, but on a hill with sore sitting parts, it seemed impossible.

Mary and I crested the hill.

I realized with a painful stab in my ass that if I paid attention to and accepted what my body needed, I wouldn't make it to Washington on time. I considered how I might reduce the climbing and shorten the distance I had to pedal.

Mary and I rode the ups and downs with Dermot ahead of us following his dream. Before long, we began the ascent of the thousand-foot climb. I stayed with Mary. She downshifted to her lowest gear, strained at the pedals, and then stopped and walked.

"Are you okay?" I asked.

"Yeah." Her tone was even, but it was the first time I hadn't heard her voice sparkle. "I'm not pedaling any faster than walking," she said, "so I might as well walk. It's easier."

I had stopped when she stopped, but I didn't want to walk. I looked over at her.

"You don't have to wait for me," Mary said.

"I don't mind. Is it okay if I pedal along with you?"

She didn't say anything.

I pedaled in a low gear, keeping pace with her, and alternated between standing and pedaling and sitting and pedaling. "During my first bike tour down the Oregon and California coast," I said, "I was struggling to get over the coast range in far northern California. It was misting, and I couldn't see through my glasses. My sitting parts were rubbed raw. A lone cyclist pulling a trailer rode up next to me. I was embarrassed to be caught at a low moment. He was kind and without judgment. Matched my pace. We talked to the top of the climb. On the downhill, he disappeared ahead of me. He never asked my name. I never asked his." I chuckled a little. "I couldn't see any better on the downhill, but at least I didn't have to pedal. One less thing to cry about."

"Did you ever see him again?"

"Nope."

We were quiet a moment.

"It was kind of like that with Devin yesterday, too," I said. "I saw him when I first arrived in Elkhorn City, but we didn't start riding together until we were on the climb out of Council."

"That was a tough climb. I walked a lot of it."

"How do you manage climbs like that? Does Dermot ride up to the top and then ride back down to meet you?"

"Sometimes he does, but I get rides, too."

"Just up the hill or to your end destination?"

"Oh, it depends."

"How do you let Dermot know if you catch a ride?"

"A lot of the time he'll wait with me until I get a ride, or we'll decide once we meet up on the road again. Or he'll catch a ride with me and then go back like we did in Pittsburg. We bought cheap cell phones when we arrived in the States, so we can call each other if there's service. But as you know, you can't count on there being cell service out here."

"Sounds like you have a system worked out. I'm impressed that you get rides so easily."

Mary asked about my trip off route. I asked about their gear.

Their panniers contained only clothes and their few other personal effects. Not being weighed down by stuff made it easier to ride, but it also meant they were dependent on lodging and restaurants for food, snacks, and shelter, which was a more expensive way to travel than camping and cooking. Whatever they were doing seemed to translate into a marital harmony that gave them space to undertake this epic journey together while still accommodating their different ambitions.

We reached the top of the climb, where Dermot waited, and I sped down ahead of them, happy to enjoy my own recklessness. The three of us regrouped at the base of the descent and rode together to the next steep climb. Dermot rode ahead, and I pedaled with Mary.

We stopped at the gas station in Meadowview, a town of nearly a thousand people situated on a railroad line and near I-81. The cool morning had warmed to a pleasant, sunny day. Mary and Dermot had coffee. I opened my Adventure Cycling map.

Interstate 81 east of Meadowview was cut off on this panel of my biking map, but it reappeared again on the next panel. I could save my sitting parts and stay close to the Interstate instead of following the TransAm up the mountain.

"Are you ready to go?" Mary asked. She and Dermot had finished their coffee and stood.

"Sure," I said, not certain I was ready to go or where I would be going. Out at the bikes, I said, "I don't think I can do this."

"Sure you can," Dermot said.

"You're strong on the hills," Mary said.

"It's my sitting parts," I said. "I'm saddle sore."

"You can do it," Dermot said.

No amount of strength could toughen my thin, raw skin.

Dermot and Mary mounted their bikes. I followed them and their confidence in my ability down the road and under the Interstate. I slowed. A lesser highway intersected the road ahead and paralleled the Interstate. My instinct was clear: turn. "I'm turning here," I called out. Neither Mary nor Dermot looked back.

My body quivered with adrenaline. It seemed wrong to leave them like that.

I rode the south service road for a couple miles wondering what I would do. Given the functionality of Google Maps for Android in 2010, I couldn't pull over and recalculate biking directions. I stopped at the top of an overpass and pulled out my bike map. I wanted to be on the north side of the Interstate, but I didn't know if a road paralleled it on that side. I called Daniel.

"Could you look up Meadowview, Virginia? I'm riding east along I-81, and there's a gap in my map between Meadowview and Marion."

"I'm looking now."

"Thanks. Something tells me I would be better off staying close to the Interstate."

"Are you okay? What's wrong?"

"I'd rather not rip holes in my behind, if you know what I mean."

"Oh, baby." His voice was concerned and tender.

"The terrain is brutal. The climbs are short but ridiculously steep. I hadn't considered how out of condition my sitting parts could get in two weeks. My legs can handle it, but, man, my ass is taking a beating. Well, it's not my ass. You know where I'm talking about."

"I do," he hummed with interest. "There are a couple towns between Meadowview and Marion."

"So if I cross to the north side of the Interstate, I can ride a service road that parallels it?"

"Yes. Looks like twenty miles to Marion."

"That's manageable. I might try some other travel options if they're available. Would you look up Amtrak routes in Virginia?"

"Okay, just a sec."

I could imagine him gingerly pecking at the keys. I still had adrenaline in my system, and I wished he could type faster. I took a breath and waited.

"I'm not sure Amtrak will be all that useful. It looks like there's a stop in Roanoke and farther east in Lynchburg."

"What about Greyhound?"

"Hold on." He clicked the mouse.

I knew little geography of Virginia or the East Coast.

"There's a station in Marion." His excitement bubbled through the phone.

"Excellent." My brain gyrated. Was Greyhound like Amtrak when it came to bikes and would only take them on at larger stations? If I had to box my bike, would they have a box? "What about schedule? Are there any more departures today?" I didn't want to dawdle if there was only one stop per day that departed in the afternoon or evening.

"Where are you going?"

"I don't know. Try Richmond. Friends of the family live near there."

"There's a ten-twenty AM bus and one at almost midnight."

I exhaled, and tension in my body eased. "Sounds like I'm going to Marion."

Later that evening when I was situated in my Marion motel, I had an e-mail from Mary:

Where did you disappear to???? One minute you were there and the next you'd gone. I know you said something but didn't hear what!! Are you ok?

We cycled to Troutdale and are staying in church hostel.
. . . Bunks but no mattresses!! Good though! No one
else here. I got a ride up the big hill on a vehicle carrying
mountain bikes and people up to a trail. Cost me $10,
money well spent.

Let us know what you're doing!

I appreciated their concern and loved how they encouraged me when we rode together. I replied with an outline of my Greyhound plan. We kept in touch throughout the remainder of the ride and congratulated one another when we finished our respective journeys. The day after my conference presentation, they would surprise me by showing up in Washington, DC. We met near a metro stop for lunch and giggled together over their attire—Crocs for footwear and plastic takeout sacks for day bags. From Washington, they would return to the West Coast and visit friends in California. Daniel and I hosted them in Eugene for a night before they drove to Seattle for their flight back to the UK. Mary would return in 2012 when Daniel and I married.

The Greyhound ride from Marion to Richmond came with hiccups. The rules were to box a bike for bus travel, but there were no bike boxes in Marion. The station staff said it was driver's discretion whether I could put my bike on without the box. The bus was an hour late arriving, but the driver did let me board and stowed my bike in an empty baggage compartment. In Roanoke, the station staff improvised a box-ish envelope with packing tape and cardboard. It was good enough for them and good enough for me.

I stayed two nights with Art and Ellen, friends of the family who lived outside Richmond. The day I planned to bike from Richmond to the Atlantic coast and Yorktown, the end of the TransAm Trail, Hurricane Earl was expected to make landfall. Rather than pedal into the hurricane, I accepted a ride from Ellen.

Grassy fields and leafy trees whizzed by as we headed to Yorktown.

When we arrived, we poked around the Colonial National Historical Park Visitor Center. Yorktown was one of eight original shires established by colonists in 1682. It blew my mind that any European settlement existed in America before the 1800s, even though I knew the Declaration of Independence was signed in 1776, Plymouth Colony was established in 1620, and explorers were in and around Florida and the Gulf of Mexico in the late 1400s and early 1500s.

The visitor center gift shop glimmered with stars and bars. Yorktown was the finish line for cyclists traveling west to east—the culmination of a patriotic bike ride and end point for a more than four-thousand-mile trek that people pedaled every year since the route's establishment in 1976. There weren't any people waiting on the road, in the park, or at the visitor center to cheer arriving bicyclists, so it didn't matter that I arrived with my bike, not on my bike.

I stood before the flags. A spark of guilt burned me for filching the flag in Kansas. I drew a four-inch by six-inch flag from a holder. Thirteen stars. I looked for a flag with fifty stars, but there were none. What message would I send flying a flag with thirteen stars from my bike? It didn't matter. I doubted I would fly a flag from my bike once I completed my trip.

My heart stirred. I wanted a flag.

For me, the American flag had come to symbolize the receptive hearts of the people—community, openness, and generosity. People across the country made space in their hearts for me through gesture, conversation, and service. Their love worked on me like magic and helped me find my way to my own radiant heart, to recognize the light of connection and support. Tears quivered in my eyes. I was proud to be an American. The feeling expanded inside my torso like a deep breath. I purchased the thirteen-star flag and said a silent thank-you to the people in Kansas for decorating their driveway with flags.

At the waterfront, Ellen took a picture of me on the beach in my dress-with-pants town outfit, the sky lightly overcast and wind blowing my hair. Documenting my arrival on the Yorktown beach seemed like something I ought to do, like so many people talked about dipping the wheel of their bikes in the ocean on either end of the TransAm. I hadn't dipped my bike wheel in the Pacific Ocean even though I'd pedaled to the Pacific coast with a friend three months before departing on my cross-country ride. I wasn't surprised at how anticlimactic my arrival in Yorktown was. When I'd finished my first bike tour down the Oregon and California coast to San Francisco, none of the many people present cheered for me at the end of the Golden Gate Bridge, although I wanted them to.

We lunched at a waterfront café. At one table, there were three people wearing cycling clothes. Seeing them made my shame rise. I imagined talking to them and being asked where my bike was. How could I claim to have ridden across the country when I hadn't pedaled the whole way? It was as if I were sitting under a flashing IMPOSTER sign.

Ellen drove north to Callao, a town on Adventure Cycling's Tidewater Potomac Heritage Route. Hurricane Earl was supposed to make landfall that night or early the next morning.

I hopped out of the truck in the Northumberland Motel parking lot.

"I'll wait for you," Ellen said. "Make sure it's what you want."

"Thanks. I shouldn't be long."

The Northumberland was what I wanted—modest, mom-and-pop, tidy, roll in, cheap. The café in town was open until 6:00 PM.

I opened the passenger door of the truck. "This is perfect. I'm a little inland and going farther inland tomorrow. Thanks so much for all your hospitality and giving me a ride."

"Wonderful. It's nice to go on an adventure and such a treat to have you."

I smiled and unloaded my bike and gear. Like so many who were now symbolized by the thirteen-starred flag I carried, she was another helping hand on my journey, another person who showed me I wasn't alone. "Thanks again!" I said through the passenger door. "Travel safely."

"You too!"

I closed the door and then waved as she pulled out onto the road.

As morning broke, I stepped outside to check the weather. The precipitation was between mist and drizzle, the temperature gentle, the air still. Not what I expected for a hurricane.

I dressed as I normally would for a riding day. It wasn't wet enough to bother with rain gear.

As the stresses associated with biking were concluding, pressure over the tasks I needed to accomplish when I arrived in Washington mounted. I hadn't written responses to the *National Geographic Traveler* questions, completed my paper for the conference, or started my presentation slides. The latter two were held up because I hadn't

integrated my experience and couldn't summarize the interrelation-
ship of bicycle tourism and preserving historic roads. I could tell
stories about my research topic, but what were the takeaways? The
riders were a varied lot. Mary and Dermot's approach was different
than John's from Portland. They were taking their time, finding
lodging, and eating out, but they enjoyed inexpensive ice cream and
not paying for water. John advocated buying something at every
stop, yet he was pedaling twice as fast, which meant half as many
investments in lodging. The students and young people were on tight
budgets—they mainly camped and cooked at camp. The friends I
met in Missoula—the architect and criminal lawyer—stayed at a
hostel, which was how they met in the middle. And Devin. His approach to lodging seemed more about meeting people than needing
a free place to stay, but maybe I was wrong about that.

Bicycle tourists seemed barely interested in the historic aspects
of travel, but they preferred natural areas, scenic byways, and quiet,
low-traffic roads. They were probably historic road fans and didn't
know it. If they were traveling with Adventure Cycling maps, the
route finding had already been done. They could also read about
local history on the maps.

Towns with motels got the biggest economic benefit from bicycle
tourists, but they had to be on a bike-touring route or advertise their
accommodation in some way to reap the benefit of two-wheeled vis-
itors. Cyclists weren't going to travel far out of their way for lodging
unless there was another benefit to doing so. There had to be a connection. Maybe it was in the transportation palimpsest. Maybe there
was infrastructure from the past that served cyclists in the present.
Did it have anything to do with towns being spaced about twenty-
five miles apart?

On top of my undone writing and thinking tasks, cramps woke me at 3:00 AM. I swallowed two ibuprofen.

Twenty miles from Callao and just before 8:00 AM, I stopped in Montross for hot chocolate. The gray sky lightened, and the precipitation eased. The people there told me the weather wasn't hurricane related. Earl had approached Cape Hatteras, North Carolina, with winds of 105 miles per hour and bounced off the land and weakened to a tropical storm.

Pedaling on the neck of land between the Rappahannock and Potomac Rivers, the precipitation stopped. I followed King's Highway. I passed but did not stop at the birthplace of Robert E. Lee, a National Historic Landmark, and George Washington Birthplace National Monument. I crossed into King George County, jarred by the unfamiliarity of kings in America's history. The weather remained pleasant as I pedaled past green fields and rolling hills topped with leafy trees.

About twenty miles beyond Montross, I turned onto a quiet, two-lane road and rested at a wide spot in the shoulder to eat an energy bar. In the oncoming travel lane, a man in a pickup stopped.

"Do you need any help?" he asked.

"No, I'm fine. Thanks for asking." I held up the energy bar. "Just having a snack."

"Ah. Your partner's up ahead. Looks like he might need some help."

I didn't know what the man was talking about, but I nodded and said, "Okay. Thanks."

He waved and drove on.

I finished my snack and pedaled toward Fredericksburg. Two miles ahead, I came upon my "partner," a fit, thirty-something man in black riding clothes sitting in the grass on the side of the road looking at an iPad. (The iPad was the first tablet introduced to the public and was released in April 2010. In the summer of 2010, I saw the iPad as a luxury item.) His bike was upside down and looked as though its guts had been ripped out and strewn along the grass.

"Hi," I said, pulling up. "May I offer you a hand?"

He looked up from the iPad and scrambled to his feet. "Yes, please." He had a British accent, and his name was Dermot.

It was the only time I witnessed a man on the road puzzled over a flat tire and a woman rode up to him and offered to fix it . . . and he let her.

This Dermot was on holiday and bought an entire touring kit complete with bike. He may not have known all he bought, but he seemed to have been specific about color-coordinating everything. He had a spare tube with a Schrader valve, but his wheel had a smaller diameter opening for a Presta valve. How did he end up with the wrong valve? Had he bought prepackaged kits online without knowing to check for compatibility? Since he didn't know how to change the tube, I expected he didn't know there were two valve types.

"I take it you don't know how to patch a tube?" I asked.

He looked at me and gestured to the iPad. "I could look it up."

"Don't worry about it. I'll give you my spare tube."

"You don't have to."

"It's not a big deal. I'm almost done with my tour. Besides, that tube won't work with your wheel," I pointed to the flaccid tube on the grass. "You should have at least one spare. Two would be better."

I showed Dermot how to check the tire and wheel for puncture-causing debris, how to replace the tire without pinching the tube, and how to ensure the tire was seated securely in the wheel rim. Last, we wrestled the back wheel onto the frame and closed the brake calipers.

"Thank you," Dermot said. "Can I give you some money?"

I stood. "Do you know the expression 'pay it forward'?"

He cocked his head. "It's a generosity chain?"

"Yeah. You can pay me back by offering assistance or kindness to someone else in need."

His face lit up. "Okay."

"Enjoy your journey," I said and pushed my bike back onto the road.

"Thanks." He waved and then looked down at his gear, hands on his hips.

I arrived in Fredericksburg around 3:00 PM. I turned into the parking lot at the first motel I saw, a single-story Relax Inn. The office looked like a high-security movie theater ticket counter. The small, tiled entry was absent furniture and decoration. Its defining feature was an interior window with yellow bulletproof glass that had a mail slot–sized opening at the sill. An unsmiling man with black hair came to the window.

"How can I help you?" he asked with an Indian accent.

"How much for a single room?"

"For overnight, forty-five dollars."

"Okay." I slipped my debit card through the slot.

The innkeeper disappeared into a back office.

Given the security precautions, I was anxious that my bike might get stolen. I hoped the innkeeper would be fast. Just as I was about to check on my bike, he returned.

He slid my card, the receipt, and the room key through the slot. "Lock the deadbolt when you are inside," he said.

"Should I be concerned about people breaking in?"

"It is a good precaution."

The motel was situated on the business highway two blocks from the HISTORIC DOWNTOWN sign. Across the street were a gas station and empty lots that bordered the river. The Relax Inn was a U-shaped building with rooms oriented toward the center of the U. I wheeled my bike across the parking lot. Apart from my instant impression of heavy use, the room seemed okay. The floor wasn't moldy. I pushed my bike in and closed and locked the door.

On the wall high above the bed, a hole the diameter of an orange was patched. The bedspread had a cigarette burn, and the carpet had several burns, one of which was a melted streak. The wooden desk and chair where scratched, and the corner of the desk was broken, showing it was made of laminated particleboard.

In the bathroom, a light brown streak stood out on the shower wall at waist height. I hoped it wasn't jizz. Could jizz stain plastic? The towels were grayish white but folded neatly on a metal rack next to the sink.

I took a deep breath. What would Maggie Gyllenhaal do?

I stripped. Naked on the bath mat in front of the sink, I washed my shorts. The ibuprofen had effectively numbed my cramps, but it hadn't prevented me from bleeding. I hung my shorts on the chair and then showered, careful to touch as little of the tub, curtain, and walls as possible. I dried off and put on my yoga pants and T-shirt.

At the visitor center, I learned Fredericksburg was the kind of place a heritage tourist would visit. It was a prominent port during the colonial era and the site of Civil War battles preserved and interpreted at the Fredericksburg and Spotsylvania National Military Park.

The next morning, I packed my gear with satisfaction that it would be the last day I packed in this way, for this purpose. The trip had surprises and other modes of travel, but those elements hadn't changed the fact that I had ridden to Washington. I pedaled over the Rocky Mountains! I cranked across America's breadbasket! I nearly perished in the heat! But I didn't want to get too ahead of myself—I was nearly seventy miles from Mt. Vernon, my official arrival in Washington.

One last day.

The sun shone. The end was in sight. I was buoyant.

At a recommended coffee shop, I ordered tea and a scone and sat outside with my laptop open.

I wrote to Daniel.

 The last leg, finally!!

> Today is the day I originally thought I would turn up in DC. What are the odds?
>
> Much love, some kisses, a bit of play, and all that other good stuff,
>
> tiger

My ride to Washington was through terrain similar to what I had pedaled from Callao to Fredericksburg. It was lush, divided by fence lines and hedgerows, and buildings stood here and there.

Halfway into my ride, I stopped at a convenience store, pained by menstrual cramps. I swallowed ibuprofen and rested for thirty minutes. The pain eased as I pedaled, but the sparkle of my morning didn't return.

I rode on autopilot. This was the big day, arrival in Washington, and it was as anticlimactic as reaching Yorktown. I had cramps, and all I wanted to do was find a clean place to sleep that had Wi-Fi and wasn't too expensive. As I neared Washington, traffic increased, and the landscape disappeared in my attention to the vehicles. How would I find lodging? Where could I get food? In America's small towns, I didn't have to wonder these things. Everything was close. By contrast, the city was impersonal. At the southern edge of Mt. Vernon, I turned into the predictability of a Hampton Inn, grateful to find a vacancy during the Labor Day holiday weekend. No one knew what I had just accomplished, nor did I offer it. It was just another day.

I couldn't reorder my days to complete my journey with triumphant arrival. Yet, my epic days were part of this final day. I couldn't have gotten here if I hadn't been there. Attending the conference was the catalyst, but everything I learned about myself and America, that was why I was out here. And I didn't need to be anywhere in particular—I just had to make myself available to what the universe offered. Being on my bike seemed as good a way to encounter myself as any. The journey was the destination.

Tired as my body was, a smile crept to my mouth. I couldn't escape myself, but I could accept myself. Here I was, all the time.

The next day, I woke in my Mt. Vernon motel room after sleeping eleven hours. The sleep-in felt celebratory and indulgent.

I felt I should walk around with a flashing sign to let people know what I had done. Wasn't that what people who finished riding across the country did? How many orchestrated a cheering squad for them-selves? Rather than excitement, I was relieved. I would not have to push myself physically today or tomorrow or any day until I wanted to.

At breakfast, I celebrated with a chocolate muffin and second cup of tea.

My accomplishment seemed unreal. The country was too big to grasp the entirety of my experience as a singular event. To do so would require an astronaut's-eye view.

37.

Destination

In the days before the conference, I wrote. I caught up on my blog and responded to the questions from *National Geographic Traveler*.

With *National Geographic*, I had the opportunity to speak to a broad audience about the importance of road safety, the kindness of strangers, and supporting local businesses. I shared the experience of bike bliss—a sparkle in everything that made even dirt clods on the side of the road beautiful. I considered what history meant and whose story was told. I offered tips and encouragement for would-be bike tourers. And I landed on a personal note about America and me and coming home to both.

I felt proud and satisfied with my work on this piece, although I was unsure the story would post since I had delayed responding for two weeks.

I put on my new skirt, shirt, and clogs that I bought two days after my arrival in Washington for the conference welcome event. A link to my blog was on the conference website. I was interested in who might know I was the crazy person who had biked to the conference.

Something about the ride gave me magnetism even with people who had no idea someone had biked to Washington from Oregon. When someone asked about my research, and I started talking, more people came over to listen. I was talking with four people when a man approached, listened for a moment, and introduced himself. Nathan worked at the U.S. Fish and Wildlife Service and said he'd read parts of my blog. He was a biker himself but had never gone on such a grand tour. He was impressed I'd chosen to go alone and admired my drive. He would become a champion in my search for work.

Following the welcome event, I fretted about my slide presentation and conference paper. My presentation was part of a session on tourism along historic roads, which generally addressed scenic byways and heritage tourism. The bicycling perspective was new. I hoped to touch on the unique ways bicycling historic roads amplified the experience, understanding, and appreciation people could have of these historic resources while also offering economic reasons for communities to market these tourism experiences to bicyclists.

The presentation background was easy. I'd already written it, so it wasn't a stretch to discuss how the Good Roads Movement in the 1890s, which was launched by the League of American Wheelmen, was the impetus for the road-building craze in America. Bicyclists wanted better roads to ride on than the muddy, rutted tracks that were standard. The League even published a booklet to help people touring on bike find suitable countryside restaurants and lodging. Activism on the part of the League paved the way for further road development when automobiles became more affordable to the general population.

In the early 1900s and on the other side of the country, Oregon established a registration fee for bicycles that required a tag serving as proof of payment be displayed on the bike, the precursor to license plates. By the 1910s, automobile touring was a popular pastime, and America's first scenic driving route, Oregon's Columbia River Highway, was designed and completed in 1926.

The question I struggled to answer related the present economic value of bicycle tourism to rural communities. Bicycle tourists weren't a homogeneous group even if our perceived craziness to ride long distances made us seem the same. Young people tended to camp, ride longer daily distances, and spend as little money as possible. Older people generally stayed in motels, rode shorter daily distances, and spent at least $50 per day to stay in a room and eat at restaurants.

That pattern didn't hold across the board. John from Portland, who was adamant cyclists should spend money in every town, often rode more than a hundred miles per day. The salt-and-pepper-haired John whom I met on the road up to Lolo Pass told me camping in the national forest was free. And there were the two buddies I met at the hostel in Missoula who had different ideas about bike touring—the architect preferred to stay in hotels and the lawyer educated me about the many ways a person could economize on a bike tour. Camping topped his list.

I created a slide to describe the different types of bike tourists along a spectrum of spending with "comfort" cyclists on one end, "shoestring" cyclists on the other, and "economy" cyclists in the middle. The middle category was my catchall for what didn't fit neatly on the ends.

I added the picture of Jeff in the Boone Store and my red-white-and-blue photo of Cooky's Café to discuss the benefits of making it easy for cyclists to find places to spend money and to create a buzz, either through logbooks or word of mouth. If businesses or governments needed numbers on how many people were coming through, all they had to do was count the logbook entries. As far as I knew, no one was counting the logbook entries, but it was an opportunity for future research and to engage businesses benefiting from bicycle tourism to support local bicycle infrastructure investments.

I wasn't sure the annual numbers of bicycle tourists or their spending would be large enough to keep a restaurant or motel in rural America open, but it was clear that bicyclists would spend more time traveling through an area than someone in a car. The fact that bicycle tourists traveled slowly meant they were bound to spend more money than car drivers. As an added benefit, bicycle tourists weren't burning fossil fuels in this slow tour of the country.

The potential was also there for bicycle tourists to return to areas or communities they enjoyed and invest in more substantial ways, such as moving there, buying property, starting a business, or stewarding the land. A married couple I interviewed near the beginning of my ride in Baker City, Oregon, had done just that. The overhead was low for two artists. He painted portraits of dogs, and she made football-sized ceramic lamps that looked like travel trailers. They were both avid cyclists and organized cycling events in Baker City that they wanted to participate in.

I felt confident about my research but less sure about distilling the stories into useful content the session attendees could apply to their work. I also kept having flashbacks to a school assignment from December that required me to watch a video recording of myself giving a presentation. For that presentation before peers, friends, teachers and clients, I had been less prepared than I wanted. As I watched myself read and "um" through notes, I was mortified. I was afraid of a repeat performance in front of the audience I hoped would open doors to job opportunity.

The *National Geographic* interview posted amid this conference presentation stress. Surprised, I clicked the link my contact e-mailed, delighted to see the image of my bike in the DeVoto Cedar Grove at the top of the story. I e-mailed the link to my mom. I didn't have time to bask in the accomplishment—urgency to finish and practice my presentation spurred me on. The moment was like other significant ones during my journey, such as my summit of Hoosier Pass that was cut short by a thunder and lightning storm.

Saturday morning, I took my place at the podium in front of the room and went through my slides and notes. I did okay. I got carried away recounting some experiences, and when I looked at Christopher, the conference co-organizer who championed my presentation proposal, he was waving a red card that meant my time was up. Since I didn't have a conclusion, I wrapped up the story I was telling and took my seat.

Few people sought me out when the session was over. After the attention I received at the welcome event, I was disappointed that no one engaged me in the presentation content. A few people came up and said hi and referenced it was tough to stimulate an audience before 9:00 AM the last day of conference sessions.

I stood alone in the hallway like a deflated balloon, my journey complete. Fatigue pulled at me. The conference was like my last two days on the road, and I experienced the same anticlimax and exhaustion as I had rolling into the motel in Mt. Vernon.

Back in my room, I opened my laptop and clicked on the browser tab with the *National Geographic* post. As I reread what I had written, I was touched. I had noted the importance of setting reasonable goals that could deliver solid accomplishments but that weren't overly ambitious. It was important to make space for one's heart to sing.

And there was the bit at the end about homecoming to my country and myself.

I sat up on the bed.

Here I was.

EPILOGUE

During and before my journey, I was used to life as a soloist. I always had plenty of things I wanted to do that didn't involve other people. For this journey across the country, I hadn't imagined the difficulty of the tasks I set myself—to publish a daily blog post of my experience and pedal all day, every day. I was comfortable being alone. I didn't necessarily like not having a companion, but it didn't pain me to be on my own. I doubted I could have even done what I did with someone else; I would have been distracted by attending to his or her discomforts. Odd, how the presence of other people sidetracked me from putting myself first. Even that moment in Meadowview, Virginia, with Mary and Dermot, guilt punched me when I turned to take care of myself. And it wasn't just in-person people who drew me away from me. My audience—blog readers, Facebook friends—influenced my actions, too. I didn't want to let anyone down, didn't want to be a person who couldn't just grit her teeth through pain and get on with the plan. Yet, that act of listening to what I needed and attending to myself was one of the trip's big lessons.

Mine was a solo journey, but I was not alone. When I was in Missouri, I finally understood what it felt like to have people care, to know that I was not the only person on the planet looking out for me. I had to push myself to an extreme to feel it. I discovered others' care for me was present, and I was able to acknowledge a need for and receive help, unlike times in the past when I pushed myself to frightening edges and couldn't see the way other people supported me. The U.S. flag, for me, symbolized this caring community and reminded me that my struggles weren't invisible, even to strangers.

People helped me on my journey in myriad ways. Daryl, Sheila, and Jessie and the people who stopped after the dog attack aided me during a perfect storm of dangers. Nita in Everton who gave me her cell number and said she had friends in Fair Grove who could help. Bill from Twin Bridges who took me on the airplane ride. Linda and Tom in Halfway who treated me to garden-grown veggies and happy-hour storm watching.

The kind folks at the Eminence post office, the hosts at the Eminence B&B who let me sleep in their yard, the Prius angel who offered me blueberries at the Sweetwater interpretive sign, the man in Kansas with the slit throat tattoo who said biking made me look good, the women at the Chinese restaurant in Florence who welcomed me in from the downpour and offered me tea, and Joe who gave me a ride to the Riviera, Jeff in Boone, and Wayne from Eminence all helped me practice receiving by offering what they could.

The woman in the gas station in Leadington who pointed me down the road to Farmington. The man in Kansas who gave me corn tortillas. Elaine and Dan in Bazine, who soothed my pains with cobbler. Alfred in White Bird, who welcomed me with conversation and laundry soap. The road crew who offered to buy me beer at the Silver

Dollar. I was grateful to Bill in Guffey with his skeletal sculptures; my Warmshowers hosts Jim and Julia in Lander; Gillian in Ordway who offered me a trailer for the night; Rick and Mike, the gandy dancers in Missoula; the coal truck drivers from the Big A mountain; the broken-bodied flagger who let me ride down Hoosier Pass on fresh asphalt ahead of the cars; and so many others who offered big and small kindnesses and concern.

I'd like to thank the people I met on bike and with whom I rode including Mary and Dermot, JD, Mike, Devin, and the other cyclists I talked to on the road. My family and friends gave support, companionship, camaraderie, and buoyed me through the challenges and long days pedaling.

I liked the mild climate in the Pacific Northwest. In summers, temperatures rarely reached over a hundred degrees. In winters, temperatures rarely dropped below forty degrees. I could ride my bike year-round, even in the rain.

And I liked the rain. I liked what it did for the landscape and how it imbued the place with softness and ease. In this place, I continued learning how to listen to myself and be gentle. It gave me space to unlearn bracing for the gut punch that Wyoming taught me. Rain made green, and even in the grayest of winter days, the green glowed.

During spring, rain burst into color, scents, and textures that worked on me like a love potion, and I searched for Calypso orchids on shady slopes during March and April. In the summers, the rain rustled in platter-sized bigleaf maple leaves and bobbed near the peaty forested floors in sword fern fronds. And when the sun shone, its brightness illuminated the landscape's fecundity right down to the mushrooms, beetles, ants, and worms that made the soil.

I sank into my life the way the rain sank into earth.

I was awarded the grant in September 2010 and developed the nation's first all-ages, all-abilities scenic bikeway.

In 2011, a year after I departed on my journey, I finished my master's of community and regional planning and found the conclusion I couldn't articulate at the conference. I compiled my research results in a picture-book report that people across the country could use.

At age thirty-six, I had a full hip replacement. After surgery, it was as if I never had pain in the joint, and two and a half months later, I participated in one of Oregon's annual weeklong event rides.

My friendship with Mary and Dermot endured as did their taste for adventure. I followed along on Instagram in 2019 as Dermot rode across Australia and Mary drove a support camper van.

Daniel and I didn't last, but my relationship with my bike did. Five years after my cross-country ride, it was there for me as I worked through my breakup pain. I rode to work, the grocery store, appointments, and social events. Weekends, I participated in organized rides or did my own centuries. I pedaled to nature for the relief that comes from crying.

My relationship with America has been troubled, especially with the proliferation of technology and media, the entrenchment of identity groups, and the reduction of travel. The American culture narratives and clannishness led to assumptions about people I didn't believe were true. In revisiting my journey and reconnecting with the gifts everyone showered on me—rides, places to sleep, conversation, pie and logbooks, tractor wheelies and meat loaf cupcakes— my heart knows that America is still alive in caring individuals everywhere.

ACKNOWLEDGMENTS

My gratitude to everyone who has been part of my journey is profound. Thank you to everyone in my story, listed here, and the many, many people who have touched my life but are not named. I love you.

I recognize my bike, the orange creamsicle Trek 2.1, which made this ride possible and carried me into my life as a writer. I am humbled by your strength and willingness to journey with me. Thank you also to the land, which I love, for being habitat, ecosystem, playground, solace, interface with the Underworld, and all-around awesome.

Thank you to Darcie Abbene and HCI Books for seeing the potential in *Heidi Across America*. There is no book without you, and I am grateful for the care you have taken with me and my work. Thank you to Larissa for your expert handling of the cover, graphics, and for layout, and designing a book that I love. Deep gratitude to Lindsey Triebel for all your efforts to ensure my tour was a success and *Heidi Across America* made it across America.

Thank you, Broads: Darlene Pagán, Phyllis Brown, Pat Philips West, and Mary Kibbe (and the Hof's back table). I learned to be a writer from and with you. Special thanks to Darlene for continued weekly accountability, reading everything, and sending me that lead.

To Karen Karbo for your mentorship, thank you. Thank you for reading everything, for stretching me, for your encouragement and support, for happy hours in Portland and other celebrations during milestones, and for luring me to France in 2019 to Come to Your Senses. Thank you for Todos Santos Writers Workshop hybrid memoir Saturdays during the pandemic and prompting me to see my future. Thank you for offering a solution to my passport mishap in 2022 and creating a transformational space for Come to Your Senses 2023. My apologies again for crushing the marjoram in your garden, but I know that was the universe's way of signaling I passed through a portal. Who knew leaping through cosmic windows could be so magical and fun!

To Brian Benson, thank you for your work at Community Cycling Center and *Going Somewhere*. You influenced my journey long before our first conversation and my first workshop with you at the Attic Institute. Thank you for teaching me to be a better reader and writer, pointing me toward the Atheneum, and prioritizing community.

Thank you, Whitney Otto, for saying that fateful day in late 2017, "You gotta write about the bike ride." Joe Wilkins and Charles Finn, thank you for affirming the power the high desert has in shaping people and writers and welcoming me into a community of artists formed by this environment. David Oates, you gave me the starting point in the Fall 2013 Wild Writers cohort where I seeded this book with two shorties.

Thank you also to Erin Moline, Cami Ostman, Michelle DuBarry, Mia Birk, Judith Wilding, Ellen Michaelson, Kate Kaufmann, Rachael

Duke, Liz Rusch, Heather Brown, Tricia Peebles, Chanin Hardwick, Emma Kerss, Amy Goeke, Lisa Wells, Cathy Corlett, Trish Tallakson, Risa Phelps, Ella Barney and the crew at JOP, Sarahjoy Marsh and the 2020 cohort of Hunger, Hope and Healing and tea time regulars, Jill Clark, Carla Conforto, Cheryl Crooks and the First Friday women, the 2023 Come to Your Senses cohort, Janet Murray, Everett Aison, the Red Wheelbarrow Writers, Terry Benioff, Melissa Coffey-Rubio, and Laura Ridenour. Writing isn't just writing.

Barney, thank you for loving me as I am, your unwavering support, and sticking with me when I cry at restaurants (and home and all the places).

For my ride and what came after, I am grateful to the University of Oregon PPPM program, LiveMove, Chris Bell and the 2009 Transportation and Preservation class, Elisabeth Walton Potter and the Oregon Heritage Program, the Women in Transportation Seminar Portland Chapter, Gerardo Sandoval, Marc Schlossberg, Lane County Economic Development, Frank Wu, Kevin Belle, Paul and Monica Adkins, Lane Kagay of CETMA Cargo, Greg Lee, Paul's Bicycle Way of Life, Yizhao Yang, City of Eugene, Eugene GEARs, Richard Hughes, Bright Crosswell, David Koteen, Steve Brodsky, Becky Mares, Patrick and Mickey Blake, Barbara Hegarty, Christopher Marston, Dan Marriott, Nathan Caldwell, John, Ellen, Emily and Laura Tirpak, Margie and Stan Berk, Sam Lippman and Ellen Law, Rebecca Gleason, Dr. Shah, Travel Oregon, Oregon Parks and Recreation, Alex Phillips, Susan Howell, Gresham Area Chamber of Commerce, Metro, Dan Kaempff, Brian Monberg, Dana Lucero, Corinna Kimball-Brown, Abbot Flatt, Karen Buehrig, Clackamas County Tourism, West Columbia Gorge Chamber of Commerce, Columbia Gorge Tourism Alliance, and Friends of the Columbia Gorge.

ABOUT THE AUTHOR

Author Photo by Cheryl Crooks

Heidi Beierle is an artist, writer, and adventurer who grew up in the wind and high plains of Wyoming. Her writing about her cross-country bicycle ride has been published in *National Geographic Traveler, High Desert Journal, VoiceCatcher Journal, Journal of America's Byways,* and on the Adventure Cycling Association blog. She lives in Bellingham, Washington. Find out more at heidibeierle.com.